PICADOR COOKSTR CLASSICS

Irena Chalmers shows readers that anyone who can understand a few basic home cooking tricks can be a star in the kitchen.

The Confident Cook demonstrates that there are in fact only four or five basic cooking methods and that with these methods you can vastly expand your recipe repertoire. A simple beef stew can be transformed into a hearty Mulligan or a fancy French beouf bourguignon.

Learn how to make a stress-free soufflé for the first time or fancy up a sirloin steak by stuffing it with mushrooms sautéed with ham and garlic. Chalmers shows you how to whip up a bountiful meal with whatever supplies you have available, empowering home cooks to expand their kitchen creativity and confidence.

With two hundred practical recipes and techniques depicted in quaint and informative illustrations, *The Confident Cook* will make you the savvy cook you've always wanted to be.

publishers' note

※

Picador Cookstr Classics is a series collaboration between Cookstr and Picador. It brings to the forefront some of the most beloved cookbooks of the last decades, with recipes and techniques that today's chefs continue to draw from again and again. Presenting these enduring titles in their original form, with the recipes and headnotes just as they were written decades ago, preserves a unique piece of food history while reminding us just how relevant these masterfully crafted cookbooks are to a new generation of home cooks. New forewords champion what made each Picador Cookstr Classic such an important cookbook when first published, and why each is well worth rediscovering.

about the author

After studying at the Cordon Bleu School of Cooking in London, IRENA CHALMERS established her own cooking school in Greensboro, North Carolina. She taught professional food writing at the Culinary Institute of America for sixteen years, has appeared on numerous television programs, and has given lectures and cooking demonstrations around the country. Chalmers has written more than eighty specialty cookbooks that are sold both in the United States and abroad.

also by Irena Chalmers

Great Food Jobs 2: Ideas and Inspiration for Your Job Hunt

Food Jobs: 150 Great Jobs for Culinary Students, Career Changers, and Food Lovers

The Great Food Almanac

An Edible Christmas

The Food Professional's Guide

The Working Family's Cookbook

Irena Chalmers' All-Time Favorites

Good Old Food

The Great American Christmas Almanac

The Great American Food Almanac

American Bistro

The International Association of Cooking Professionals Cookbook

Bride's First Recipes

the
confident cook

the
confident cook

BASIC RECIPES AND
HOW TO BUILD ON THEM

IRENA CHALMERS

DRAWINGS BY ROBERT GRAHAM PENNY

PICADOR COOKSTR CLASSICS | NEW YORK

picadorusa.com • instagram.com/picador
twitter.com/picadorusa • facebook.com/picadorusa

Picador® is a U.S. registered trademark and is used by Macmillan Publishing Group, LLC, under license from Pan Books Limited.

Drawings by Robert Graham Penny

The Library of Congress has cataloged the Praeger Publishers edition as follows

Names: Chalmers, Irena.
Title: The confident cook : basic recipes and how to build on them / Irena Chalmers ; drawings by Robert Graham Penny.
Description: New York : Praeger, 1975.
Identifiers: LCCN 74000328 | ISBN 9780275521905 (hardcover)
Subjects: LCSH: Cooking.
Classification: LCC TX651 .C48 | DDC 641.5
LC record available at https://lccn.loc.gov/74000328

Picador Cookstr Classics ISBN 978-1-250-14627-4 (paper over board)
Picador Cookstr Classics ISBN 978-1-250-16286-1 (ebook)

Our books may be purchased in bulk for promotional, educational, or business use. Please contact your local bookseller or the Macmillan Corporate and Premium Sales Department at 1-800-221-7945, extension 5442, or by email at MacmillanSpecial Markets@macmillan.com.

First published by Praeger Publishers, Inc.

First Picador Cookstr Classics Edition: June 2018

10 9 8 7 6 5 4 3 2 1

Some cookbooks are to be tasted,
others to be swallowed;
some few to be chewed and digested.

—SIR FRANCIS BACON

contents

❖

acknowledgments

※

Part of the pleasure of cooking is in the joy of sharing the abundance of the good earth. I am grateful to those who have shared their knowledge, wit, and wisdom not only with me but with countless thousands of others. I am particularly indebted to Muriel Downes of the Cordon Bleu School of Cookery and to my late friend and teacher Albert Stockli. I am an ardent, though distant, admirer of the integrity of the writings of M. F. K. Fisher, Julia Child, and the late Michael Field and Dione Lucas. I will be eternally grateful to David Grimes, who consistently believes there is another way of doing things, and I also want to thank Susan Wright and Adrienne Zausner, whose help has been invaluable all along the way.

Finally, I bow to all the people who came to my cooking school, because they taught me as much as I taught them.

foreword

"I'm never afraid to take a risk," says Irena Chalmers. Her first step into the professional kitchen came long ago at a Chicken Contest on the Delmarva peninsula. The organizers wanted a motherly lady rather than the flimsy model who turned up to demonstrate fried chicken. With her two children and plump contours, Irena filled the bill and she was picked out from the crowd.

A month later, when helping at a fundraiser, she met Muriel Downes, codirector of the Cordon Bleu in London, and a spell at that pioneer cooking school followed. I myself was a very junior teacher there, and our friendship has progressed ever since, in and out of the kitchen, on and around our shelves of cookbooks.

Irena loves cookbooks and founded a publishing company centered on them. Her favorite, she declares, is *The Great Food Almanac*, in which she was able "to combine my love for the absurd and the unexpected." ("A" stands not just for Apples and Asparagus, but also Aphrodisiacs, Alligators, and Athlete's Food.) Irena's books reflect her own personality—intelligent, inquiring, quirky; she will dart off at what appears to be a tangent, only to circle around to an entirely logical conclusion.

The Confident Cook was Irena's "first real book" (her words), a collection of basic stocks, sauces, custards, and techniques such as roasting and deep frying, all enlivened with headings such as "Rescuing Mayonnaise in Distress." Her intelligence and culinary knowledge already shine through. The original manuscript, Irena laments, had been further embellished with anecdotes that were slashed out with a red pencil by the editor. "It was an early lesson on swallowing your pride to be a professional," she says.

Published by Praeger in 1975, *The Confident Cook* was an immediate success and chosen as the Book of the Month Club main selection. It remains a storehouse of indispensable recipes, all carefully described step by step and just as relevant as the year they appeared. The rock-solid foundations of everyday, simple cooking will always be the same.

Anne Willan
April 2018

introduction

Can you remember the time when you thought you couldn't boil an egg? Then one day you discovered it wasn't difficult at all. All you had to do was to put the egg into a pan of water and cook it for five minutes. The only difficulty lay in remembering where you put it and when!

Once you can boil an egg, you can make a whole range of dishes. After all, it's just as easy to poach an egg as it is to boil it. You have only to break the shell and add a pinch of salt to the water. If you substitute a fresh trout or a tender chicken breast for the egg, the only thing you need add is four more minutes of cooking, and lunch is ready. For a dinner of boiled beef, you just have to lengthen the cooking time. Boiled beef, poached chicken, and poached fish are just variations of a boiled egg.

So many dishes seem at first to be made from entirely unrelated recipes, and yet there are very few methods of cooking. All foods are eaten either raw, boiled, roasted, or fried. Poaching, braising, baking, and deep-fat frying are simply variations of these processes. It is the character of the ingredients themselves that determines the method of cooking. A tough piece of meat, for instance, becomes tender if it is stewed in a liquid for a long period of time; a filet of beef is already tender and needs only to be broiled or fried for a few minutes to make it culturally acceptable. The same techniques of broiling and frying apply equally to all tender meats and poultry, while all stews follow a similar pattern. It is only the substitution of one ingredient for another that makes a French boeuf Bourguignon appear to be an entirely different dish from a Belgian carbonnade of beef. In fact, the preparation of these two dishes is almost the same. They are related not only to each other but to all other stews. Similarly, the principles of making stews apply to the preparation of many soups, many sauces, and an infinite variety of other dishes, from beef Stroganoff to kidneys in mustard sauce.

Good cooking is not necessarily elaborate cooking, but it is important to know how to make the simplest of dishes before you can tackle more intricate preparations with confidence. The recipes that seem most complicated always turn out to be just a series of simple steps.

The purpose of this book is to describe these simple steps, which are the basic techniques of cooking, and to show how the steps are linked together to form whole families of dishes. A cheese sauce becomes a spectacular soufflé just by the addition of a few egg yolks and a huge gulp of beaten egg whites. The whole thing is then inflated further by the heat of the oven and the admiration of the assembled company. Although this basic-techniques approach may take some of the mystique out of cooking, it certainly makes everything in the kitchen a lot easier. If you think of a soufflé as merely a humble cheese sauce, it doesn't pose nearly so much of a threat!

Once you have learned how the same principles of cooking can be applied to a variety of dishes, it may be interesting to reverse these principles, in a sense—to see how similar groupings of ingredients can be cooked in a variety of ways to achieve entirely different results. Thus, if you assemble the ingredients used for making cream puffs, you can produce eclairs merely by changing the shape.

Deep-fried and sprinkled with cheese, the very same ingredients may be eaten as tiny cocktail puffs; dusted with sugar, they can be serves as miniature pastry puffs. If you poach spoonfuls of the mixture in water, they form dumplings. Add some ground fish, the potential cream puff becomes a quenelle!

The best cooking results from a sympathetic understanding of the personalities of the ingredients. When you get to know an egg really well, you are much more tolerant and understanding of its vagaries. Eggs, I have found, have much in common with small boys. If they are hurried, overheated, or overbeaten in the beginning, they tend to turn on you, and no amount of future love and concern can right the wrong. As you come to be able to predict the behavior of the ingredients, it becomes easier to complement or even substitute one for another.

Cooking often involves not so much the art of creation as the relief of retrieval. Knowing which ingredient to bring to the rescue can result in the difference between a disaster and a triumph.

This book, you'll discover, is arranged as if it were a series of lessons. You may complain bitterly that you cannot find the fish section, only to discover that there is no fish section. Instead, the fish have landed in the poaching, frying, and broiling sections, so it is necessary first to decide how you like your fish cooked and then turn to the appropriate chapter. You can track down any recipe in the index. More important, it is hoped that having made a recipe once, you will not need to find it again, for you will know all there is to know about cooking fish, or whatever. Occasional food biographies have been included, because knowing provides part of the pleasure of cooking.

the
confident cook

1. soups

BROWN BEEF STOCK • VEAL, LAMB, CHICKEN, OR FISH STOCK •
CHICKEN AND CLAM BROTH • CLARET CONSOMMÉ • TOMATO
CONSOMMÉ • JELLIED MADRILÈNE • ONION SOUP • VEGETABLE SOUP
WITH BEEF • CHICKEN SOUP WITH RICE • TOMATO SOUP • TOMATO
AND CLAM SOUP • TOMATO SOUP WITH BEER AND DILL • TOMATO-
ORANGE SOUP • ASPARAGUS SOUP • CAULIFLOWER SOUP • POTATO
SOUP • VICHYSSOISE • WATERCRESS VICHYSSOISE • PEAR AND TURNIP
SOUP • CARROT SOUP • MUSHROOM AND BARLEY SOUP

I remember a story about a soup told by a friend who was an apprentice at a formidable French restaurant. The proprietors were justly proud
that all of their ingredients were at the peak of perfection. The vegetables and herbs were grown on their own land, and the fish was
brought in daily from the rivers and lakes in the vicinity.

The fish chef was an irascible fellow who worked entirely on his own
and silently, except for snarling at anybody who came near his section
of the kitchen. He was also a creature of habit. Early each morning he
would don his white chef's hat and go out into the adjoining garden to
gather bouquets of herbs, which he then laid out in neat bunches along
the length of his chopping block.

Next he arranged one of each type of fish in military formation, heads forward, tails to the rear. Then the work began. Stooping over his fish, he confronted them, eyeball to gleaming eyeball. Hands bent on chubby knees, he smelled each fish and each herb. Then, slowly and thoughtfully, he selected one herb from this bunch and one from that and chopped them into myriads of combinations. He put a little tarragon in this group, a touch of sorrel in another, and a few curls of parsley here and there. The gentle, soothing rhythm of chopping continued until each herb was so fine it could dance an arabesque on the head of a pin. Each combination of herbs was then matched to each fish until the parade was flanked with small mounds of fragrance.

The inspection then began again. The chef picked up the first fish in line, rubbed a pinch of herbs onto its shiny skin, sniffed it delicately, smiled smugly to himself, wiped his hands on his clean white apron, and proceeded to the next. By the time he had reached the end of the line, he was supremely content. His apron was green with sweet-smelling herbs and very slightly fishy.

One memorable night, the apprentice chef stole the master's apron, which by now had become a historical record of the day's activities. He dropped the flavored apron into a broth and simmered it gently for twenty minutes. The result was a glorious fish soup.

That is the way soup is made. You take a little of this and a little of that, and, if it pleases you, you put it all together and cook it until it is done. There are no hard-and-fast rules for making soup, but if you look at the following recipes it is extraordinary how similar they all are. Keeping the proportions of the ingredients the same, you can substitute one vegetable or meat for another and one herb for another. The basic liquid may be chicken broth, beef broth, beer, wine, milk, fruit juice, or even water. By rearranging your palette, you can make an infinite variety of soups.

CLEAR SOUPS

A clear soup is simply a flavored liquid, made by simmering one or many ingredients in a broth. Chicken broth, beef consommé, and jellied madrilène are all clear soups, which are sometimes used as the basis for other soups. Sometimes two flavored liquids are combined; if you add red wine to beef broth, for example, you will have made a claret consommé. Having produced a marvelous-tasting base, you can add one, two, or many more ingredients to give the soup a greater variety of taste and texture. If you add some vermicelli to the claret consommé, for example, the soup will gain another dimension. A touch of lemon juice will heighten the flavor, and a garnish of finely chopped chives completes a simple masterpiece.

Chicken broth can be built into a more substantial soup in a similar way, perhaps, by adding pieces of chicken and a little rice. If you think you might still be hungry, you could add a handful of carrots, peas, tomatoes, green peppers, chopped spinach, and/or herbs. When the soup is ready, each ingredient should retain its own form and be clearly identifiable.

The ultimate flavor of clear soups, as of all other soups, rests on the quality of the basic broth. Very few people have the time or the inclination to prepare homemade stock to be used as a soup base. Some of the commercially canned chicken and beef broths are both excellent and inexpensive, and though, undeniably, they are not so good as the homemade variety, they are satisfactory alternatives. In case you decide to prepare your own stock, this is how to go about it.

BASIC BROTH (STOCK)

Stock is derived from the long, slow simmering of meat bones, aromatic vegetables, and a group of herbs known as a bouquet garni. Stock is the foundation on which almost all soups, sauces, and stews are built. It is easy to make, and it takes only a few minutes to assemble the ingredients, but the actual cooking time is lengthy.

There are very few things to remember about stock, but each one is important. First you must decide what kind of stock you will make. Naturally, you would use beef bones for a pure beef stock and chicken bones (backs and wings) for chicken stock. However, if you just want to have fine-tasting, all-purpose broth in the kitchen, you can combine beef and chicken bones.

The foundation of stock is a good bone. A good beef bone is one that has meat clinging to it and some marrow inside it. The beef will give the broth flavor, and the collagen content of the bone will cause the

Soup and fish explain half the emotions of life.
SYDNEY SMITH

stock to gel and give it body. (The marrow also tastes delicious!) It is best to use raw bones for stock; cooked meat bones and leftover chicken bones do not have enough flavor and make the stock cloudy. The vegetables must be fresh and of good quality. If you are in any doubt about whether to throw a vegetable into the garbage or the soup pot, let your conscience be your guide, and ignore all those tales about stock pots that simmer for generations.

The aromatic vegetables most often used in both beef and chicken stock are carrots, onions, and celery. Tomatoes and other fresh vegetables may be added, but don't use strong-tasting vegetables such as spinach and turnips unless you have a specific purpose for using the stock. After the vegetables, add the herbs—a few peppercorns, a bay leaf, parsley, and thyme. (It is neither necessary nor wise to add salt at this point; if the stock boils down too rapidly, it may become too salty.) Finally, fill the pot with cold water so that the ingredients are barely covered, place it over a gentle flame, and allow it to simmer slowly, partially covered, for 6 hours. Then strain the liquid and discard the meat bones and vegetables (they will no longer have any taste). Chill the liquid to make the fat rise, so that it can be skimmed off easily.

Stock will keep in the refrigerator for at least a week, but it should be boiled again every three days to prevent it from becoming sour. It can also be frozen. You can freeze the stock as it is or, if your freezer space is limited, boil it, uncovered, until it has reduced to a small quantity. Freeze the concentrated stock in ice-cube trays and reconstitute it with water as you need it. You will need to taste it to estimate how much water to add.

BROWN BEEF STOCK

Yield: approximately 2 quarts of stock, depending on how fast the stock is boiled. (Ideally, it should be maintained at the simmering point.)

2½ pounds beef bones, with meat clinging to the bones
2 onions, peeled and coarsely chopped
2 carrots, washed and chopped
2 stalks celery

3 quarts water
1 bay leaf
½ teaspoon thyme*
10 peppercorns
4 sprigs parsley

* Unless fresh herbs are specified, it is assumed that you will use the dried variety.

1. Place the bones in a heavy roasting pan and allow them to roast, uncovered, in their own fat in a preheated 350° F. oven for 20 minutes.

2. Add the vegetables and allow them to brown for 10 minutes.

3. Transfer the bones and vegetables into a large saucepan or casserole. Discard the fat from the roasting pan and add ½ cup cold water. Scrape the bottom of the pan with a spatula to release the browned pieces clinging to the surface. Add this flavored liquid to the casserole with the herbs and enough cold water to barely cover the ingredients.

4. Simmer over gentle heat for 6 hours. The lid should be adjusted so that it almost covers the pot. (Allow a little opening so that some evaporation and concentration of the broth will take place.)

5. Strain the stock and discard the vegetable pulp and the bones. Allow to cool to room temperature.

6. Chill in the refrigerator for 6 hours more to allow the fat to come to the surface and congeal. Skim off the fat. The stock is now ready to use or to freeze.

VEAL, LAMB, CHICKEN, OR FISH STOCK

Veal, lamb, and chicken stock are all made in almost exactly the same way as beef stock. However, it is not necessary to brown the bones and vegetables if you are not using beef. Simply eliminate this step and place the same quantity of bones, vegetables, and herbs in a large saucepan. Add enough water to barely cover all the ingredients. Simmer veal and lamb stock for 4 hours and chicken stock for 3 hours.

To make fish stock, use the head, bones, and skin of the fish and simmer with the vegetables and herbs for 20 minutes. Equal quantities of dry white wine and water may be used as the liquid.

These stocks, or flavored broths, become the liquid part of soups, stews, or sauces and may be served, thickened, with the meat, chicken, or fish or separately as a soup.

CHICKEN AND CLAM BROTH

Some soups are made simply by combining two flavored broths.

Serves 6

4 cups chicken broth
2 cups bottled clam juice

½ teaspoon dried basil or 6 fresh basil leaves, finely chopped

Pour the chicken broth and clam juice into a saucepan. Add the basil and simmer for 5 minutes. Serve in mugs with a sandwich.

CLARET CONSOMMÉ

This soup is a combination of two flavored liquids, with the added texture of vermicelli. It makes an excellent transition between cocktails and buffet dining. Double or triple the quantities to serve more guests.

Serves 6

½ cup vermicelli, broken into
   ½-inch pieces
4 cups beef broth
2 cups red wine

1 tablespoon lemon juice
2 tablespoons finely chopped
   chives

1. Cook the vermicelli in plenty of boiling salted water for 8 minutes. Drain.
2. Pour the beef broth, wine, and lemon juice into a saucepan. Bring to the simmering point and add the vermicelli. Simmer for 3 minutes until the vermicelli is hot.
3. Garnish with chives.

TOMATO CONSOMMÉ

A thin tomato soup is a good choice for serving before a substantial steak dinner. The base of the soup is chicken broth flavored with tomatoes, herbs, spices, and wine.

Serves 6

1 16-ounce can Italian plum
   tomatoes
4 cups chicken broth
½ teaspoon dried thyme
½ teaspoon allspice
1 teaspoon dried basil

1 teaspoon lemon juice
1 teaspoon tomato paste
2 tablespoons sherry or Madeira
   wine
2 tablespoons finely chopped
   parsley

1. Place the tomatoes with their juice from the can in a saucepan. Add all the remaining ingredients except the wine and the parsley. Cover and simmer for 20 minutes.
2. Strain the soup and return it to the saucepan. Add the wine.
3. Serve hot with a garnish of parsley.

JELLIED MADRILÈNE

This is a simple tomato-flavored broth. The gelatin enables it to "set." If you omit the gelatin, you can serve this soup in the winter and call it consommé madrilène.

Serves 6

4 cups chicken broth	2 packages unflavored gelatin
1 cup tomato purée	2 tablespoons finely chopped
1 tablespoon tomato paste	chives
¼ cup white wine or vermouth	

1. Pour the chicken broth and tomato purée into a saucepan. Add the tomato paste and simmer for 5 minutes.
2. Pour the wine into a small bowl. Sprinkle the surface of the wine with gelatin and allow it to stand undisturbed for 5 minutes, until the gelatin has softened. Stir the gelatin mixture into the simmering soup.
3. Remove the soup from the heat, allow to cool to room temperature, and chill for 4 hours.
4. Stir the jellied soup with a fork and spoon it into individual bowls. Garnish with chives.

ONION SOUP

Serves 6

2 tablespoons butter	Freshly ground black pepper to
4 large yellow onions, sliced	taste
1 tablespoon flour	6 slices French bread
6 cups simmering beef broth	¾ cup grated Swiss cheese
½ teaspoon salt	¼ cup grated Parmesan cheese

. . . this is every cook's opinion,
No savory dish without an onion,
But lest your kissing should be spoiled,
Your onions must be thoroughly boiled . . .

DEAN SMITH

1. Heat the butter in a skillet.

2. Add the onions and fry them over low heat for 7 minutes until they are softened but not browned.

3. Stir in the flour and cook for 2 minutes.

4. Add the onions to the broth, season with salt and pepper, and simmer the soup for 30 minutes.

5. Ladle the soup into individual bowls. Float a round of French bread in each bowl. (If you cannot find a good-quality French bread, use 3-inch circles of a firm-textured bread, toasting the bread before using.)

6. Divide the cheeses among the bowls and place the bowls under a preheated broiler until the cheese has browned lightly and formed a bubbling crust over the soup.

VEGETABLE SOUP WITH BEEF

This vegetable soup is a master plan for many clear soups, demonstrating how each ingredient is added in a sequence according to the length of time it must be cooked in order to become tender.

Serves 6

1 tablespoon butter
1 medium-sized onion, finely chopped
1 clove garlic, finely chopped
2 carrots, diced
2 stalks celery, finely chopped
4 cups beef broth
1 teaspoon thyme or savory
½ teaspoon salt
Freshly ground black pepper to taste

1 cup tomato purée
1 tomato, peeled, seeded, and chopped
1 cup cooked leftover beef, cut into small pieces
½ cup raw string beans, cut into small pieces
½ cup raw peas
2 tablespoons finely chopped parsley

1. Heat the butter until it is bubbling.

2. Fry the onion, garlic, carrots, and celery for 3 minutes until softened.

3. Add the beef broth, thyme or savory, salt, and pepper and simmer for 5 minutes.

4. Add the tomato purée, chopped tomato, beef pieces, beans, and peas. Simmer for 15 minutes, until the beans and peas are tender.

5. Serve, garnished with parsley.

CHICKEN SOUP WITH RICE

The flavors of the chicken, vegetables, and herbs pass into the water to form a flavored broth. Rice is added to the broth to make a substantial soup. A cup of carrots, peas, tomatoes, or any other vegetable may also be added to the soup along with the rice.

Serves 6

1 2-pound chicken, cut up
1 onion, sliced
1 carrot, peeled and sliced
1 stalk celery, sliced
1 bay leaf
½ teaspoon thyme
1 teaspoon peppercorns
4 sprigs parsley
8 cups water
½ cup uncooked rice

2 carrots, peeled and cut into strips 2 inches long and ⅛ inch wide
½ teaspoon sage
1 teaspoon salt
Freshly ground black pepper to taste
½ cup heavy cream (optional)
2 tablespoons finely chopped parsley

1. Place the chicken and the giblets, except for the liver, in a large saucepan. (Do not add the liver, because it will make the broth cloudy.) Add the onion, carrot, celery, bay leaf, thyme, peppercorns, parsley, and water. Adjust the lid so that the saucepan is three-quarters covered. Bring to the boiling point. Lower the heat and simmer for 45 minutes.

2. Remove the chicken from the broth and set it aside until it is cool enough to handle. Separate the chicken from the skin and bones. Cut the meat into bite-sized pieces and reserve. Return the skin and bones to the saucepan. Partially cover the pan and simmer for 1½ hours.

3. Strain the broth, cool a bit, and chill it in the refrigerator for 8 hours. Remove and discard the fat, which will have risen to the surface.

4. Pour the broth into a saucepan and bring it to the boiling point. Stir in the rice, carrot strips, sage, salt, and pepper. Lower the heat, cover the pan, and simmer for 15 minutes.

5. Add the reserved chicken meat and simmer for 5 minutes. Add the cream (if desired).

6. Serve the soup, garnished with parsley.

THICK SOUPS

There are several kinds of thick soup. One is really a clear soup that has been thickened by the addition of a starch in the form of flour, cornstarch, potatoes, rice, or beans. Another kind of soup is thickened by puréeing it in a blender. Soups are sometimes also thickened and enriched with egg yolks. And finally, soup will also become thicker if it is boiled to reduce the quantity of liquid.

It seems logical enough just to stir some flour into a thin soup and expect it to become thick miraculously. Unfortunately, it doesn't work that way. When flour or cornstarch is added to a hot liquid, it immediately forms itself into small lumps, which doggedly refuse to dissolve no matter how desperately you implore them simply to go away. Egg yolks behave in equally appalling fashion, spinning themselves off into long, yellow, stringy whines of protest. The whole procedure of thickening soups is somewhat like sending out wedding invitations. You cannot invite one relative without offending another who has not been so favored. Flour must be combined with butter, cornstarch needs to be mixed with cold water, and egg yolks crave the companionship of cream. Each ingredient has to be dealt with on its own terms and with its own chosen partner.

FLOUR

One tablespoon of flour combined with one tablespoon of butter or oil will thicken one cup of liquid to the consistency of a thin sauce.

This seemingly minor piece of information is of at least equivalent importance to knowing your own name. It is as difficult to operate in society without an identity as it is to function in the kitchen without this formula. Armed with the ability to make a simple sauce, you can make any group of ingredients into a sauce, a soup, or a stew. In fact, you can make virtually thousands of apparently unrelated dishes, from cheese and macaroni to a lobster soufflé. You can whip up a beef Stroganoff or devise a sauce for a roast lamb without opening a book. You can cleverly transform the leftover roast turkey into a succulent casserole dish or turn a handful of scallops into coquilles St. Jacques. Who would have guessed it? Anyway, in the meantime, you can also thicken a soup.

To return to the flour, when you stir one tablespoon of flour into one tablespoon of bubbling hot butter and add one cup of liquid, you will have made a thin sauce. When you stir one tablespoon of flour into one tablespoon of butter and add *four* cups of liquid, you will have made a thinner sauce—a soup. When you are making a soup, as witness the foregoing recipes, the first step is to cook the vegetables in a little butter, to enhance their flavor and soften them slightly. As the butter is already available, it seems (and is) logical to add the flour at this point and then the liquid. However, if you find that the soup is too thin when it has finished cooking, you can thicken it at the end of the preparation as well. Soften one tablespoon of butter in a cup, combine it with one tablespoon of flour, add the paste to the boiling soup, and the soup will thicken without lumps. If you prefer not to add more butter to the soup, you can make a last-minute adjustment in the thickness of the soup quickly and easily by adding cornstarch.

CORNSTARCH

One tablespoon of cornstarch stirred into two tablespoons of cold water added to one cup of boiling liquid has the same thickening quality as the butter-and-flour combination. Cornstarch is always added in the last few minutes before serving. If it is added at the beginning of a long cooking period, the starch breaks down and the liquid thins out again. *Cornstarch thickens any liquid as soon as it reaches boiling point.*

OTHER STARCHES

Potatoes, rice, dried beans, peas, barley, and lentils will also thicken soup in proportion to the amount that is added. One cup of regular long-grain rice, for instance, will completely absorb three cups of water. The rice must be added sparingly, for instead of having a bowl of chicken soup with rice, you may wind up with a plate of rice and chicken. Rice is added to the soup in the final twenty minutes of cooking.

Beans require a longer cooking period, so they are added at the beginning of the preparation of the soup.

PURÉEING THE SOUP

If you purée the completed soup in a blender or force it through a strainer, you will transform a clear soup into a thick soup. The greater the starchiness of the ingredients and the higher the proportion of solid to liquid ingredients, the thicker the puréed soup will be. If the soup is not thick enough, pour it back into a saucepan and bring it to the boiling point. Then stir in one tablespoon of flour mixed to a paste with one tablespoon of soft butter, or add one tablespoon of cornstarch dissolved in two tablespoons of cold water.

EGG YOLKS AND CREAM

Some soups are thickened by the addition of egg yolks and cream. This combination has a unifying effect on the soup, holding all the ingredients together in a smooth suspension. Egg yolks and cream also enrich the soup and improve the texture. Two egg yolks beaten lightly with two tablespoons of heavy cream are sufficient for six cups of soup. Add about one-quarter cup of hot soup to the egg yolks and cream and stir the mixture well. This will heat the egg yolks slightly. Then add the mixture to the hot soup. Do not let the soup boil after the egg yolks have been added or they will curdle.

HOW TO MAKE THICK SOUP

1. First heat butter in a saucepan until it is bubbling. Then fry onions, garlic, celery, and carrots for 3 minutes to release their flavor and to soften them. (The butter is also needed as a base for incorporating the flour.)
2. Stir in the flour, to thicken the soup very slightly and give it body. (*Body* is an elusive term. Perhaps the easiest way to define it is to think of the difference between instant and regular coffee: regular coffee seems to have more "body" than the instant variety.)
3. Add the liquid gradually, so as to obtain a smooth mixture.
4. Next add the principal ingredient—e.g., tomatoes, if you are making tomato soup—and the herbs and seasonings, and simmer, uncovered, for 20 minutes. (The principal ingredient added to the soup base gives the soup its character. The herbs and seasonings are selected to enhance and complement the primary flavor.)
5. Purée the soup in a blender to make it smooth. (After it has been puréed, it may need to be strained to remove seeds, skins, or other odds and ends.)
6. Strain the blended soup into a clean saucepan and reheat it.
7. Serve and garnish.

Tomatoes

As Edward Lear's headwaiter said when asked if a tomato was a fruit or a vegetable, "Turmarter, sir? Turmarters ha hextra!"

Tomatoes are one of the youngest of the commonly used vegetables. Part of the reason for their slow acceptance lies in their color. Colors have very definite connotations in relation to food: purple (as in eggplant) is regal; black is rare (as in truffles) or beautiful; white signifies purity and innocence (white vegetables grow beneath the soil and are not exposed to light); greens are unpopular with persons under fourteen for a variety of reasons; while red—red is for danger, poison, lust, and scarlet women. No wonder nobody ate tomatoes for hundreds of years except the Aztec Indians, and we all know what happened to them.

Though the Aztecs had cultivated tomatoes since A.D. 700, they guarded their secret crop jealously, and many generations passed before the tomato reached the Mediterranean. There, to judge by the cooking in Italian-American restaurants, it appears that a flood of tomatoes simply swamped a parched desert of spaghetti in a great deluge of sauce. One can imagine the dancing in the streets after centuries of pasta and no tomatoes!

Traveling on to France, the tomato was characteristically dignified by a new name, la pomme d'amour (the love apple), thus giving credence to the old rumors that it was an aphrodisiac and, even worse, that Eve seduced Adam not with an apple but with a tomato. After that idea bore fruit, the tomato was again regarded with deep suspicion and relegated to the flower bed, where its blossoms, resembling those of deadly nightshade, were viewed from a respectful distance. Even then they knew about digitalis.

Much later—in fact, in 1820—a French painter who had set up house and garden in Rhode Island decided to test the love-hate theory as it pertained to the tomato. He erected a platform, invited all his friends and neighbors to gather round, and publicly ate a home-grown tomato. He survived and so did the tomato, which soon became one of the most popular of vegetables, flavorings, and "hextras."

The bishop smiled approvingly, "A soup like this is not the work of one man," he said; "it is the result of a constantly refined tradition. There are nearly a thousand years of history in this soup."

WILLA CATHER

TOMATO SOUP

Serves 6

1 tablespoon butter
1 onion, finely chopped
1 clove garlic, finely chopped
1 carrot, finely chopped
1 stalk celery, finely chopped
1 tablespoon flour
4 cups chicken broth
4 large tomatoes, chopped
1 teaspoon basil or thyme

½ teaspoon salt
Freshly ground black pepper to taste
1 teaspoon tomato paste (if you are using winter tomatoes)
2 tablespoons finely chopped parsley, chives, or sour cream for garnish

1. Heat the butter until it is bubbling.
2. Fry the onion, garlic, carrot, and celery for 3 minutes.
3. Stir in the flour.
4. Add the chicken broth gradually.
5. Add the tomatoes, basil or thyme, salt and pepper, and tomato paste. Simmer, uncovered, for 20 minutes.
6. Purée the soup in a blender.
7. Strain the blended soup into a clean saucepan and reheat.
8. Garnish with parsley, chives, or sour cream and serve.

Almost all puréed soups are made in this way, but the substitution or addition of one or two ingredients results in entirely different soups, as you will see in the following recipes, which are almost identical to this one but taste quite different.

TOMATO AND CLAM SOUP

Serves 6

1 tablespoon butter
1 onion, finely chopped
1 clove garlic, finely chopped
1 carrot, finely chopped
1 stalk celery, finely chopped
1 tablespoon flour
2 cups chicken broth
2 cups clam broth (the liquid from the 2 cans of minced clams)
4 large tomatoes, chopped

1 teaspoon oregano
½ teaspoon salt
Freshly ground black pepper to taste
1 teaspoon tomato paste (if you are using winter tomatoes)
2 8-ounce cans minced clams, drained
2 tablespoons finely chopped parsley for garnish

1. Heat the butter until it is bubbling.
2. Fry the onion, garlic, carrot, and celery for 3 minutes.
3. Stir in the flour.
4. Add the chicken broth and clam broth gradually.
5. Add the tomatoes, oregano, salt and pepper, and tomato paste. Simmer, uncovered, for 20 minutes.
6. Purée the soup in a blender.
7. Strain the blended soup into a clean saucepan, add the drained clams, and reheat the soup.
8. Garnish with parsley and serve.

TOMATO SOUP WITH BEER AND DILL

Serves 6

1 tablespoon butter	4 large tomatoes, chopped
1 onion, finely chopped	1 teaspoon dill weed
1 clove garlic, finely chopped	½ teaspoon salt
1 carrot, finely chopped	Freshly ground black pepper to
1 stalk celery, finely chopped	taste
1 tablespoon flour	1 teaspoon tomato paste (if you
2 cups beef broth	are using winter tomatoes)
2 cups beer	1 teaspoon dill weed for garnish

1. Heat the butter until it is bubbling.
2. Fry the onion, garlic, carrot, and celery for 3 minutes.
3. Stir in the flour.
4. Add the beef broth and beer gradually.
5. Add the tomatoes, dill weed, salt and pepper, and tomato paste. Simmer, uncovered, for 20 minutes.
6. Purée the soup in a blender.
7. Strain the blended soup into a clean saucepan and reheat.
8. Garnish with dill weed and serve.

Rabbits, one story goes, will not cross a row of scallions to eat succulent lettuce lest their fur be contaminated with the smell of the onion.

TOMATO-ORANGE SOUP

Serves 6

1 tablespoon butter
1 onion, finely chopped
1 clove garlic, finely chopped
1 carrot, finely chopped
1 stalk celery, finely chopped
1 tablespoon flour
3 cups chicken broth
1 cup orange juice
4 large tomatoes, chopped

1 teaspoon basil
½ teaspoon salt
Freshly ground black pepper to taste
1 teaspoon tomato paste (if you are using winter tomatoes)
Rind of 2 oranges (colored part only, not the pith)

1. Heat the butter until it is bubbling.
2. Fry the onion, garlic, carrot, and celery for 3 minutes.
3. Stir in the flour.
4. Add 2 cups of the chicken broth and all the orange juice gradually.
5. Add the tomatoes, basil, salt and pepper, and tomato paste. Simmer, uncovered, for 20 minutes.
6. Cut the orange rind into very thin strips, discarding the bitter white pith, and chop the strips into tiny pieces, a little larger than a tomato seed. Simmer the pieces of rind in the remaining 1 cup of chicken broth for 10 minutes.
7. Purée the soup in a blender.
8. Strain the blended soup, add the chicken broth and rind, and reheat or chill.
9. Serve hot or cold.

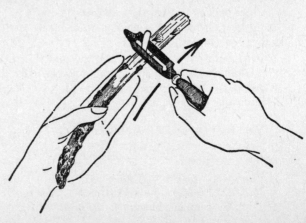

Asparagus

Asparagus is one of the few vegetables that still seems to have a season. The first glimpse of asparagus heralds spring, Hollandaise sauce, and happiness.

In selecting asparagus, choose the brightest, tallest, slenderest, and straightest of uniformly sized stalks. Run all the way home, and if the asparagus must be kept for a day, wrap it tightly in wet paper towels. Wash it very carefully to remove any sand or grit. If the asparagus is very fresh, the thick, rough ends can be snapped off. If you trim the lower quarter or so with a potato peeler rather than cutting it, there will be more to eat.

Asparagus can be steamed by immersing the stalks in two inches of water, so that the "flowers" are bathed in hot, moist vapor. It also does very well—contrary to tradition—totally immersed in water in an uncovered pan.

ASPARAGUS SOUP

Asparagus soup is made like tomato soup. The asparagus is simmered in chicken broth until it is tender, and the soup is then puréed in a blender.

Serves 6

1 tablespoon butter	1 pound fresh asparagus, washed
1 onion, finely chopped	and cut into small pieces
1 tablespoon flour	½ teaspoon salt
4 cups chicken broth	Juice and grated rind of 1 lemon

1. Heat the butter until it is bubbling.
2. Fry the onion for 3 minutes.
3. Stir in the flour.
4. Add the chicken broth gradually.
5. Add the asparagus and salt. Simmer, uncovered, for 20 minutes.
6. Purée the soup in a blender.

7. Strain the blended soup into a clean saucepan, stir in the lemon juice, and heat or chill.

8. Serve hot or cold, garnished with grated lemon rind. If the soup is served cold, you may need to add a little more salt, and a spoonful of whipping cream makes it even smoother and more sensual.

CAULIFLOWER SOUP

Serves 6

1 tablespoon butter
1 onion, finely chopped
1 clove garlic, finely chopped
1 carrot, finely chopped
1 stalk celery, finely chopped
1 teaspoon curry powder
1 tablespoon flour
5 cups chicken broth

1 medium-sized cauliflower, cut or broken into small pieces (4 cups cauliflower)
½ teaspoon salt
Freshly ground black pepper to taste
For garnish: a few cooked cauliflower sprigs, ½ cup toasted croutons, or ½ cup grated cheese

1. Heat the butter until it is bubbling.
2. Fry the onion, garlic, carrot, and celery for 3 minutes.
3. Stir in the curry powder and continue cooking for 1 minute.
4. Stir in the flour.
5. Add the chicken broth gradually.
6. Add the cauliflower, salt, and pepper, and simmer, uncovered, for 20 minutes.
7. Purée the soup in a blender, reserving a few cauliflower sprigs for garnish.
8. Strain the blended soup into a clean saucepan and reheat.
9. Garnish with cauliflower sprigs or croutons, or sprinkle with cheese and place under the broiler for 4 minutes or until the cheese is brown and bubbling.

Cauliflower is nothing but a cabbage with a college education.

MARK TWAIN

Leeks

At a time when wars were not the simple contests of good against evil that they are today, there sometimes was a danger that a soldier might inadvertently dispose of a friend in his rampage against the enemy. To prevent such tragedies, St. David instructed troops in the army of Wales to wear leeks in their hats for identification purposes. Needless to say, that day the Welsh won a resounding victory, and fourteen hundred years ago the leek became the national emblem of the thoughtful people of Wales.

POTATO SOUP

Soups containing potatoes, rice, barley, or beans are thickened by the starch contained in these ingredients, so it is not necessary to add any flour. The following recipe becomes a thick soup by mashing the potatoes into the broth.

Serves 6

4 cups chicken broth
½ teaspoon salt
4 medium-sized boiling potatoes, peeled and chopped into 1-inch cubes
3 leeks (white part only), washed and chopped
2 small yellow onions, chopped (or 3 onions if leeks are not available)

1 teaspoon chervil
½ cup heavy cream
1 tablespoon butter
Freshly ground black pepper to taste
2 tablespoons finely chopped parsley

1. Bring the chicken broth to the boiling point. Taste it and add salt if necessary.

2. Add potatoes, leeks, onions, and chervil. Cover and simmer for 20 minutes.

3. Partially mash the vegetables into the broth, using a potato masher. (Do not mash the potatoes completely but leave them in small, recognizable pieces.)

4. Add the cream and simmer for 3 minutes until the soup is very hot.

5. Add the butter and a dusting of freshly ground black pepper. Garnish with parsley and serve.

VICHYSSOISE

Vichyssoise is a variation of Potato Soup. Additional cream is needed because puréeing and chilling thicken the soup. Cold soups generally need a little more salt than hot soups, so taste the soup after it has chilled and add more salt if necessary.

Serves 6

4 cups chicken broth
½ teaspoon salt
4 medium-sized boiling potatoes, peeled and chopped into small pieces
3 leeks, washed and chopped
2 small yellow onions, chopped (or 3 onions if leeks are not available)

1 teaspoon chervil
1 cup light cream
½ teaspoon salt (optional)
2 tablespoons finely chopped chives
Freshly ground black pepper to taste

1. Bring the chicken broth to the boiling point. Taste it and add salt if necessary.

2. Add the potatoes, leeks, onions, and chervil. Cover and simmer for 20 minutes.

3. Purée the soup in a blender.

4. Stir in the cream.

5. Chill the soup for 4 hours.

6. Taste it and add more salt if necessary. Garnish with chopped chives and freshly ground black pepper and serve.

WATERCRESS VICHYSSOISE

Watercress Vichyssoise is prepared in the same way as Vichyssoise, except that 1 bunch of chopped watercress is substituted for 2 of the 4 potatoes, and the completed soup is garnished with a few reserved watercress leaves. Serve the soup hot or cold.

PEAR AND TURNIP SOUP

Pear and Turnip Soup is made in almost the same way as Potato Soup, with pears and turnips used to replace some of the potatoes and onions. The soup is garnished with finely chopped raw celery.

Serves 6

4 cups chicken broth
½ teaspoon salt
2 medium-sized boiling potatoes, peeled and chopped into small pieces
2 small yellow onions, chopped
2 firm, ripe Anjou pears, unpeeled, chopped and cored
1 small turnip, peeled and chopped
1 teaspoon dried winter savory or dill weed
1 cup light cream
Freshly ground black pepper to taste
½ cup finely chopped raw celery

1. Bring the chicken broth to the boiling point. Taste it and add salt if necessary.
2. Add potatoes, onions, pears, turnip, and winter savory or dill weed. Cover and simmer for 20 minutes.
3. Purée the soup in a blender.
4. Strain it into a clean saucepan to remove any fragments of the pear core and skin.
5. Add the cream and reheat.
6. Season with pepper and garnish with chopped celery.

CARROT SOUP

The Potato Soup foundation can be transformed into what seems to be an entirely different soup by substituting carrots for some of the potatoes. The soup may be served hot or cold.

Serves 6

4 cups chicken broth
½ teaspoon salt
2 medium-sized boiling potatoes, peeled and chopped into small pieces
7 carrots, peeled and chopped
3 leeks, washed and chopped

2 small yellow onions, chopped (or 3 onions if leeks are not available)
1 teaspoon marjoram
¼ cup dry (white) vermouth
¼ cup heavy cream
1 carrot, peeled and grated

1. Bring the chicken broth to the boiling point. Taste it and add salt if necessary.
2. Add potatoes, 7 carrots, leeks, onions, and marjoram. Cover and simmer for 20 minutes.
3. Purée the soup in a blender.
4. Stir in the vermouth and cream.
5. Garnish with the grated carrot, and serve hot or cold.

MUSHROOM AND BARLEY SOUP

Serves 6

1 tablespoon butter
1 onion, finely chopped
1 clove garlic, finely chopped
1 carrot, finely chopped
1 stalk celery, finely chopped
1 pound mushrooms, finely chopped

7 cups beef broth
½ cup barley, washed
½ teaspoon salt
Freshly ground black pepper to taste
2 tablespoons finely chopped parsley

1. Heat the butter until it is bubbling.
2. Fry the onion, garlic, carrot, and celery for 3 minutes.
3. Add the mushrooms. Lower the heat, cover the pan, and steam for 10 minutes.
4. Add the beef broth, barley, salt, and pepper. Simmer, uncovered, for 30 minutes.
5. Serve, garnished with parsley.

2. casserole cooking

Casserole cooking is a long, slow method of moist tenderizing. Cuts of beef that are recommended for cooking in a casserole include top round, bottom round, and chuck steak, which come from hard-working muscles and, because they contain little internal fat, are naturally tough and fibrous. The fibers are broken down when the meat is stewed, braised, or pot-roasted—the three methods of cooking in a casserole.

In *stewing*, the meat is usually cubed and browned in hot fat. Onions, other vegetables, and seasonings are added, along with enough liquid to cover the basic ingredients. The stew is cooked in a covered pot or casserole in the oven or on top of the stove, though it is preferable to cook it in the even heat of the oven. The cooking liquid may be thickened into a sauce either at the beginning or at the end of the preparation. Other meats such as veal, lamb, and chicken, as well as fish and vegetables, may also be stewed.

In the process of *braising*, a large piece of tough red meat is first browned in hot oil or fat and then placed on a bed of vegetables. In braising white meat, such as veal or chicken, this initial browning procedure is sometimes eliminated. Just enough liquid is added to keep all the ingredients moistened with steam rather than immersed. The meat is cooked in the oven or on top of the stove and becomes tender by a combination of steaming and baking. The braised meat is sliced at the end of the cooking period, and the juices are thickened into a sauce. Fish and vegetables may also be braised.

Pot-roasting is a method of cooking a small roast, a large piece of meat, or a whole chicken in a covered pot or casserole. Pot-roasted meat is first browned in hot oil or fat, and no other ingredients need be added. The meat is cooked on top of the stove or in the oven by a combination of frying and steaming. (The steam is generated from the moisture within the meat itself.) The terms *pot-roasting* and *braising* are often used interchangeably, and many pot roast recipes suggest adding vegetables, seasonings, and a small quantity of liquid.

Stewing and braising are very similar processes. One meat may be substituted for another meat, or chicken, fish, or even vegetables can be used instead of meat. (When one primary ingredient is exchanged for another, the cooking time may need to be altered. Chicken and fish need less cooking time than red meat, and the timing of vegetables varies widely.) The liquid in which the food is simmered may be water, broth, wine, or a combination of these ingredients. Beer can also be used very successfully in casserole cookery. As a rough guide, three-fourths of a cup of liquid is added for each pound of uncooked meat, chicken, or fish when preparing a stew. The quantity of liquid added to a vegetable stew depends on the water content of the vegetables themselves. Less liquid is used for braised than for stewed meats, and, as has been noted, sometimes no liquid is added to pot-roasted meats.

Once you have mastered a simple beef stew, you will be able to make a curry by adding curry powder and the traditional garnishings (chopped nuts, chutney, etc.). A Hungarian goulash is made in the same way as a beef stew, but paprika and sour cream are added. A Belgian Carbonnade of Beef is also a beef stew in which the beef is cooked in beer rather than beef broth. Chicken and fish stews follow the same pattern, differing from beef stew only in the addition or deletion of one or more ingredients. All are served with starchy vegetables, potatoes, rice, or noodles, which soak up the hearty and robust sauce from the casserole.

THE CASSEROLE POT

You may, of course, use a pretty china casserole as a serving dish, but for cooking, it is preferable to choose a heavy iron or enameled iron casserole. Lightweight casseroles with poorly fitting lids allow the liquid to escape rapidly in the form of steam, and the food becomes dry and tasteless. If you cook in a heavy iron pot, the meat can be browned in the same utensil in which it will later be cooked in the oven. When the cooking has been completed, you can adjust the consistency of the sauce by adding a thickening agent and heating the sauce over surface heat.

A heavy metal casserole can also go directly from the refrigerator to the stove for reheating. (Bring the sauce back to the simmering point before returning the casserole to the oven to reheat the meat.) Such a casserole may also be brought to the table as a serving dish or chilled if the stew is to be frozen.

MAKING STEWS

The preparation of a stew is very similar to the preparation of a soup. In fact, the only difference is that the stew is cooked for a longer period of time, and less liquid is added.

1. Cut the meat or other principal ingredient into serving-sized pieces (about 2-inch cubes) and ruthlessly trim off all fat and gristle. Dry the meat on paper towels.

2. Heat the oil in a heavy skillet until it is almost smoking, then add about one-fourth of the beef cubes.

3. Brown the meat quickly on all sides in a large, heavy skillet and transfer it to a casserole as soon as it is browned. (It is always tempting to throw all the beef into the pan at one time, in the hope of getting the browning part done more quickly. However, if you do this, the temperature of the oil will drop very rapidly and the beef will steam rather than fry. No matter how long it cooks, it will never become brown and firm but will remain limp and gray. The vegetables will also refuse to brown when they are added. The reason is that as the steam collects and condenses in the pan, the cooking oil becomes watery. Later, the flour tends to protest the presence of water and turns lumpy, and the resulting sauce is a dull, miserable catastrophe. So, all in all, it is probably worth taking a little extra time at the outset.) The initial browning makes the meat firm and gives a rich brown color to the sauce. (The meat may be browned directly in the casserole, but it is quicker to use a large skillet.)

4. Add the vegetables.

5. Stir in the flour.

6. Add the liquid.

7. Season with salt and pepper, herbs, or spices.

8. Cover the casserole and cook in a moderate oven (350° F.) until the main ingredient—meat, chicken, fish, or vegetables—is soft and tender. (The cooking time will vary from 1½ hours for a beef stew to as little as 20 minutes for a fish or vegetable stew.) The stew can be served as soon as it is cooked, it may be reheated later in the day or even two or three days later, or it may be frozen and reheated when desired.

FREEZING STEWS

If you are fortunate enough to own a freezer, it is certainly worthwhile doubling the recipe for a stew. Meats, chicken, or fish prepared with a sauce freeze very well, and it is always comforting to know that there is a complete dinner all ready to pop into the oven. It does not take twice as long to make a stew for twelve as for six, there is only one set of utensils to wash, and all the cooking can be done at the same time.

Be sure to chill the stew and remove any surface fat before committing it to the freezer. If you put a warm dish in the freezer, it takes too long to freeze and ice crystals will form, which eventually change the taste, texture, and color of the food.

If you can spare the dish for the freezer, you can freeze the stew and store it in its original casserole. If not, freeze the stew and, when it has become solidly frozen, stand the casserole in a bowl of hot water for a few minutes until the edges begin to defrost. Then unmold the stew, wrap it tightly in freezer wrap, and put it back in the freezer. Wrap frozen food very carefully, making sure that all the air is excluded, or white freezer-burn spots will develop and cause the food to deteriorate. Label and date each package and store at 0° F. in the freezer for not more than two months.

When you are ready to serve it, thaw the stew slowly in the coolest part of the refrigerator. If there is too rapid a change in the temperature, the meat loses its character.

The guests retired with thankful hearts
And even fuller other parts
They were not seen for several days.
Alas, the gourmet always pays.

BASIC BEEF STEW

Serves 6
Preheat oven to 350° F.

2½ pounds boneless chuck
3 tablespoons oil
2 onions, finely chopped
1 clove garlic, finely chopped
2 carrots, finely chopped
2 stalks celery, finely chopped
1 green pepper, seeded and finely chopped
2 tablespoons flour
2 cups beef broth

3 sprigs parsley
1 teaspoon dried thyme
1 bay leaf
1 teaspoon peppercorns
½ teaspoon salt
4 carrots, sliced and cooked
1 cup cooked peas
2 tablespoons finely chopped parsley

1. Trim the beef to remove any fat and cut into 2-inch cubes.
2. Fry the cubes in a large heavy skillet, a few at a time, in very hot oil. Transfer the beef to a casserole as soon as it has browned on all sides, or brown the beef in the casserole itself.
3. Fry the vegetables in the same oil for 3 minutes until softened.
4. Stir in the flour.
5. Gradually add the beef broth to the vegetables.
6. Add the sauce and vegetables to the beef in the casserole.
7. Tie the herbs in a cheesecloth bag. Add this plus the salt to the casserole.
8. Cover and cook in a preheated oven for 1½ hours.* Discard the herb bag.

9. Add the cooked carrots and peas† and garnish with chopped parsley. Serve with boiled potatoes, rice or noodles, a vegetable, and a tossed salad.

* May be prepared in advance to this point. Reheat the stew on top of the stove until the sauce is simmering. Cover and place in a preheated 350° F. oven for 20 minutes until the stew is very hot.

† The cooked carrots and peas are added at the end of the preparation and simply reheated so that they retain their bright color and attractive appearance.

Cooking with Wine

> Drink no longer water, but use a little wine for thy stomach's sake, and thine often infirmities. [St. Paul's advice to Timothy.]
>
> 1 Tim. 5:23

Some people, in spite of St. Paul's admonition, hesitate to add a few drops of wine to their food, regarding the very idea as either wantonly wasteful or a flirtation with the devil. Certainly nobody will dispute that wine costs more than water. On the other hand, some wines taste better than water. As for the association with sin, even Christ is reputed to have turned water into wine and the Church has at one time or another owned some of the finest vineyards in France. In England it established a legally sanctioned monopoly over the brewing of beer. Surely Ben Jonson's suggestion that one's lover should "drink to me only with thine eyes" was not meant to be taken literally? Apart from those totally irrelevant remarks, the alcohol content of beer, wine, and brandy evaporates as soon as they are heated.

Wine is added to many foods to give them added strength and character. Tough meats become tender and flavorful if they are left to relax in a bath of wine for a day or two. (Wouldn't we all?)

Beware those noxious fluids called cooking wines. Cooking wines are those that the bottler has designated as unfit to drink, though the implication is that they are all right to eat.

The whole idea of cooking wines came about because the wines that were used in medieval kitchens were heavily salted to prevent the rowdy cooks from satisfying their own private thirst at their masters' expense. (In retaliation, the cooks saved their potato peelings, apple cores, and all manner of herbs and odds and ends and distilled them into much more potent spirits. Even the monks went in for this recycling scheme.) The so-called cooking wines that are available today do not bear any resemblance to the salted wines of the Middle Ages. Unfortunately, in spite of the many miracles associated with wine, it is a fact that when a poor wine is heated or reduced in volume by boiling, that which was not palatable to begin with will predictably taste worse as its flavor becomes concentrated. On the other hand, it is not necessary or even desirable to use the best or most expensive wines for cooking. A medium-priced American jug wine is perfectly adequate for most culinary purposes.

If there is some wine remaining in a bottle that you have served with dinner, the best way to store it is to transfer it to a container with a tightly fitting stopper and keep it in the refrigerator. Do not keep it for more than a day or two unless you plan to use it for vinegar.

BEEF IN RED WINE (BOEUF BOURGUIGNON)

Serves 6
Preheat oven to 350° F.

2½ pounds boneless chuck
4 slices bacon
2 tablespoons brandy (optional)
2 onions, finely chopped
1 clove garlic, finely chopped
2 tablespoons flour
1½ cups red wine
½ cup beef broth
3 sprigs parsley

1 bay leaf
½ teaspoon thyme
1 teaspoon peppercorns
½ teaspoon salt
2 tablespoons butter
½ pound mushrooms, quartered
2 tablespoons finely chopped
   parsley

1. Trim the beef and cut it into 2-inch cubes.
2. Fry the bacon until it is almost crisp and all the fat has been rendered. Drain the bacon and reserve 3 tablespoons of fat.
3. Fry the beef cubes, a few at a time, in very hot bacon fat. Transfer the cubes to a casserole as soon as they have browned on all sides.
4. Heat the brandy in a small saucepan. Remove it from the fire, ignite and pour it, flaming, over the beef. (The brandy will light more readily if it is warm.)

5. Fry the onions and garlic in the same fat that was used for the beef for 3 minutes, until softened.

6. Stir in the flour.

7. Add the red wine and beef broth gradually.

8. Add the sauce, onions, and garlic to the beef in the casserole. Add the herbs, tied in a cheesecloth bag, and the salt. Cover and cook in a preheated oven for 1½ hours.* Discard the herb bag.

9. Heat the butter and fry the mushrooms for 4 minutes until lightly browned. Add the mushrooms to the casserole.

10. Garnish with parsley and serve with buttered noodles.

* May be prepared in advance to this point and frozen. To serve, thaw and reheat the casserole on top of the stove until the sauce is simmering. Cover and place in a preheated 350° F. oven for about 20 minutes until very hot.

CHICKEN IN WHITE WINE

Follow the recipe for Beef in Red Wine, substituting a 3½-pound chicken, cut into serving pieces, for the beef, white wine for the red wine, and chicken broth for the beef broth. All the remaining ingredients are the same. Reduce the total cooking time to 50 minutes.

Beer

Noah, a wise and thoughtful man, took heed of all that water, and for forty days and forty nights he stayed in the ark and drank his beer. So says a Syrian tablet that was unearthed in Nineveh. Beer, unlike water, not only travels well but tastes good on sea or land and at home, too.

In fact, beer was known long before Noah took it on his cruise. The people of Egypt and Mesopotamia were busily fermenting their brews more than 6,200 years ago. Actually, beer is believed to be the oldest fermented drink known to man, although hundreds of genera-

It is said that Lord Byron, during his lifetime, drank gallons and gallons of vinegar in the unpoetic belief that it would keep his weight down.

tions of refining the techniques have resulted in a brew that has little resemblance to the beer of ancient civilizations. The beer we drink today is considerably weaker than that which accompanied the bier in the funeral processions of long ago. ("Here's beer to your ghost" was a commonly offered toast upon hearing of the death of a friend; to cheer each other up a bit, the mourners would solicitously drink the beer themselves.)

Beer making has traditionally been women's work. Egyptian women added bitter herbs to their brews, just as, much later, hops were used to intensify the flavor. The Babylonians staffed their taverns with barmaids who kept a record of the customers' drinks on wet clay tablets. When the grain was harvested at the end of the year, the plate was passed around for collection. Interest charges were thought of much later.

The Egyptians taught the art of brewing to the Greeks, and from the Greeks their knowledge traveled to the Romans and on to England, where it eventually passed into the hands of the Church. The records of St. Paul's Cathedral indicate that at one time it brewed 60,000 gallons of ale a year, with all due reverence. Canterbury Cathedral, situated among the hop fields, produced the finest beer of all. The ecclesiastic breweries gradually developed a total trading monopoly; although every household possessed its own small vat for brewing ale, no beer could be marketed until the monasteries and churches had disposed of their own production.

Ale was once the accepted drink for special events. To distinguish it from the everyday types, special brews were concocted. Private blends were created for certain families and craftsmen's guilds. Bride ale, or bridals as they came to be known, were made for weddings, just as the universities had their own college ales, or collegials.

The German people did as much to develop their beer as the French did to develop their wine. The Germans were, in fact, the first people to add hops to beer, and it was the presence of hops that first distinguished beer from ale. Not only did the Germans improve the taste of the beer, but instead of drinking it immediately, they decided to age it. Lagern means "to store"; thus lager is an aged (and, theoretically, a better) beer.

Like Noah, the Pilgrims brought plenty of beer for their long journey across the sea. They decided to settle in New England primarily because their supplies were running low. Later the Dutch established a brewery in New York, followed closely in time by a sugar refinery. *The brewing of beer and the refining of sugar were the first two industries in America and are as important today as they were in those times.*

BELGIAN CARBONNADE OF BEEF

Beer tenderizes the beef as well as flavoring the entire dish.

Serves 6
Preheat oven to 350° F.

2½ pounds boneless chuck
3 tablespoons oil
4 medium-sized yellow onions, sliced
1 clove garlic, finely chopped
2 tablespoons flour
1½ cups beer
1 cup beef broth
3 sprigs parsley
1 bay leaf
½ teaspoon thyme
1 teaspoon peppercorns
¼ teaspoon nutmeg
½ teaspoon salt
1 teaspoon sugar
1 teaspoon mild French mustard
6 small (3-inch) rounds of French bread (or other firm-textured bread, toasted)
2 tablespoons mild French mustard

1. Trim the beef and cut it into 2-inch cubes.
2. Fry the cubes, a few at a time, in very hot oil. Transfer the beef to a casserole as soon as it has browned on all sides.
3. Fry the onions and garlic in the same oil for 3 minutes until softened.
4. Stir in the flour.
5. Add the beer and beef broth gradually.
6. Add the sauce, onions and garlic to the beef in the casserole. Add the herbs, tied in a cheesecloth bag, the nutmeg, salt, sugar, and mustard. Cover the casserole and cook it in a preheated oven for 1½ hours.* Discard the herb bag.

* May be prepared in advance to this point. To serve, reheat the casserole on top of the stove until the sauce is simmering. Cover and place in a preheated 350° F. oven for 20 minutes until very hot.

7. Coat one side of each bread round with mustard. Place the bread, mustard side down, on top of the meat, pushing the bread partially into the sauce.

8. Return the casserole to the oven and continue cooking for 15 minutes, until the bread is crusty brown.

HUNGARIAN GOULASH

Serves 6
Preheat oven to 350° F.

2½ pounds boneless chuck	1 bay leaf
3 tablespoons oil	½ teaspoon thyme
1 onion, finely chopped	3 sprigs parsley
1 clove garlic, finely chopped	1 teaspoon peppercorns
1 carrot, finely chopped	½ teaspoon salt
1 stalk celery, finely chopped	1 cup sour cream
1 tablespoon paprika	2 tablespoons finely chopped
2 tablespoons flour	parsley
1½ cups beef broth	

1. Trim the meat and cut it into 2-inch cubes.

2. Fry the cubes, a few at a time, in very hot oil. Transfer the meat to a casserole as soon as it has browned on all sides.

3. Fry the vegetables in the same oil for 3 minutes until softened. Fry the paprika with the vegetables for 2 minutes.

4. Stir in the flour.

5. Add the broth gradually.

6. Add the sauce and vegetables to the meat in the casserole. Add the herbs, tied in a cheesecloth bag, and the salt. Cover the casserole and cook in a preheated oven for 1½ hours. Discard the herb bag.*

7. Set the casserole over a low flame on top of the stove and stir in the sour cream. Do not let the sour cream boil or it will curdle.

8. Garnish with parsley and serve with wide buttered noodles.

This dish can also be made with stewing veal instead of chuck, in which case chicken broth is used instead of beef broth. If veal is used, cook for 1 hour at step 6 instead of 1½ hours.

---

* May be prepared in advance to this point. Reheat the casserole on top of the stove until the sauce is simmering. Cover and place in a preheated 350° F. oven for 20 minutes until very hot. Then proceed with step 7.

Mushrooms

Julius Caesar's friends, Romans, and countrymen believed that mushrooms were created by bolts of lightning from heaven. By some obscure and undemocratic reasoning, it was decided that this gift of the Gods had been provided for the exclusive delectation of the patricians. So the plebeians went without.

VEAL STEW WITH MUSHROOMS AND TOMATOES

Serves 6
Preheat oven to 350° F.

2½ pounds stewing veal
3 tablespoons oil
1 onion, finely chopped
1 clove garlic, finely chopped
1 carrot, finely chopped
1 stalk celery, finely chopped
6 mushrooms, finely chopped
2 tablespoons flour
1 cup white wine
½ cup chicken broth
2 teaspoons tomato paste
1 bay leaf

½ teaspoon thyme
3 sprigs parsley
1 teaspoon peppercorns
½ teaspoon salt
2 tablespoons butter
12 button mushrooms
2 tomatoes, peeled, seeded, and chopped
1 teaspoon dried basil or oregano
2 tablespoons finely chopped parsley

1. Trim the veal and cut it into 2-inch cubes.
2. Fry the cubes, a few at a time, in very hot oil. Transfer the veal to a casserole as soon as it has browned lightly on all sides.
3. Fry the vegetables and chopped mushrooms in the same oil for 3 minutes until softened.
4. Stir in the flour.

5. Add the wine and chicken broth gradually. Stir in the tomato paste.

6. Add the sauce, vegetables, herbs (tied in a cheesecloth bag), and salt to the casserole. Cover and cook in a preheated oven for 50 minutes.* Discard the herb bag.

7. Heat the butter and fry the remaining mushrooms until lightly browned.

8. Add the mushrooms, tomatoes, and basil or oregano to the casserole and continue cooking for 10 minutes.

9. Garnish with parsley and serve with rice.

* May be prepared in advance to this point. Reheat the casserole on top of the stove until the sauce is simmering. Cover and place in a preheated 350° F. oven for 20 minutes until very hot.

VEAL STEW WITH ONIONS AND CREAM (BLANQUETTE DE VEAU)

This is a "white" stew, so the usual browning of the meat is omitted. Frying chicken cut into pieces and pork loin cut into 1½-inch cubes can be prepared in exactly the same way.

Serves 6
Preheat oven to 350° F.

2½ pounds veal, cut from shoulder or leg
1 onion, chopped
1 clove garlic, finely chopped
2 carrots, chopped
2 stalks celery, chopped
1 bay leaf
3 sprigs parsley
1 teaspoon peppercorns
1½ cups chicken broth
½ pound mushrooms, quartered

4 tablespoons butter
1 1-pound jar white onions, drained
2 tablespoons flour
½ teaspoon salt
Freshly ground black pepper to taste
2 egg yolks
½ cup heavy cream
2 tablespoons finely chopped parsley

1. Trim veal and cut it into 2-inch cubes.

2. Place veal in a saucepan, cover it with cold water, bring to the simmering point, and continue simmering for 5 minutes.

3. Drain veal and place in a casserole.

4. Add the onion, garlic, carrots, and celery. Add the herbs, tied in a cheesecloth bag.

5. Add the chicken broth.

6. Cover the casserole and simmer for 1½ hours, until veal is tender.

7. Remove veal from the liquid and keep it warm. Discard the herb bag.

8. Fry mushrooms in 3 tablespoons butter until lightly browned. Add white onions and cook until heated through. Add to veal.

9. Melt remaining 1 tablespoon butter in a small saucepan. Stir in the flour, and gradually add the cooking liquid in which the veal was simmered. Season with salt and pepper.*

10. Combine egg yolks and cream. Add to the sauce. (Do not let the sauce boil or the egg yolks will curdle.)

11. Pour the sauce over the veal and garnish with parsley. Serve with rice.

* May be prepared in advance to this point. To serve, reheat the casserole on top of the stove until the sauce is simmering. Cover and place in a preheated 350° F. oven for 15 minutes until hot.

OSSO BUCO

Serves 6
Preheat oven to 350° F.

3½ pounds veal knuckles (from lower part of leg) with bone in the center, cut into 1½-inch pieces

½ cup flour, seasoned with ½ teaspoon salt and freshly ground black pepper to taste

2 tablespoons butter

1 tablespoon oil

1 onion, finely chopped

2 cloves garlic, finely chopped

1 carrot, diced

2 stalks celery, diced

1½ tablespoons flour

½ cup white wine

1 cup chicken broth

½ cup tomato purée

1 1-pound can Italian tomatoes, drained and chopped

1 teaspoon oregano

½ teaspoon salt

Freshly ground black pepper to taste

1. Dredge veal in seasoned flour.

2. Fry in a casserole over high heat in combined butter and oil.

3. Remove veal from casserole and fry onion, garlic, carrot, and celery until softened.

4. Stir in flour.

5. Add wine, broth, tomato purée, tomatoes, oregano, and salt and pepper.

6. Return the veal to the casserole. Cover and cook in a preheated oven for 1 hour until the meat is tender.* Serve with rice.

* May be prepared in advance. To serve, reheat the casserole on top of the stove until the sauce is simmering. Cover and place in a preheated 350° F. oven for 15 minutes until very hot.

LAMB STEW

Serves 6
Preheat oven to 350° F.

2½ pounds stewing lamb	1 teaspoon tomato paste
2 tablespoons butter	1 teaspoon rosemary
1 tablespoon oil	1 bay leaf
2 onions, finely chopped	½ teaspoon salt
2 cloves garlic, finely chopped	Freshly ground black pepper to
2 carrots, chopped	taste
2 stalks celery, chopped	1 cup peas, cooked
2 tablespoons flour	1 1-pound can white beans
1 cup white wine (optional)	2 tablespoons finely chopped
1 cup chicken broth (or 2 cups if	parsley
wine is omitted)	

1. Trim lamb and cut it into 2-inch cubes.

2. Fry lamb in combined butter and oil until lightly browned. Transfer to a casserole.

3. Fry onions, garlic, carrots, and celery in the same butter and oil for 3 minutes until softened.

4. Stir in the flour.

5. Add wine and broth (or 2 cups broth).

6. Add tomato paste, rosemary, bay leaf, salt, and pepper.

7. Cover casserole and place it in a preheated oven for 1½ hours, until lamb is tender.*

8. Add peas and drained beans. Continue cooking for 5 minutes until the peas and beans are hot. Garnish with parsley.

* May be prepared in advance to this point. To serve, reheat the casserole on top of the stove until the sauce is simmering. Cover and place in a preheated 350° F. oven for 15 minutes until very hot.

SOUPY STEW OF LAMB SHANKS

Because lamb shanks are very large and bulky, it is necessary to add more than the usual quantity of liquid to ensure that the meat is completely covered. To compensate for the additional liquid, an increased amount of flour is added. The paprika gives the sauce an extremely attractive color as well as a distinctive flavor. This is a very hearty "country" supper.

Serves 6

5 pounds lamb shanks	1 tablespoon paprika
3 tablespoons oil	3 tablespoons flour
2 onions, chopped	4 cups beef broth
2 cloves garlic, finely chopped	2 bay leaves
6 carrots, peeled and cut into 2-inch pieces	1 tablespoon rosemary
6 stalks celery, cut into 2-inch lengths	1 teaspoon salt
	1 8-ounce can tomato purée

1. Brown the lamb shanks, one at a time, on all sides in very hot oil. Transfer to a casserole.
2. Fry the vegetables in the same oil for 3 minutes until softened. Fry the paprika with the vegetables for 2 minutes.
3. Stir in the flour.
4. Add the beef broth gradually.
5. Add the bay leaves, rosemary, salt, and tomato purée. Cover and simmer over a low flame on top of the stove for 1½ hours, or until the lamb is tender and almost falling from the bone.*

* May be prepared in advance. To serve, reheat the stew over low heat until it is very hot. Do not let it boil or the lamb *will* fall off the bone and will not look so beautiful.

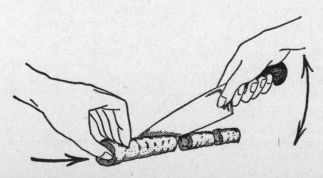

The Monk's Chicken

It was in medieval times that a monk visited a baron's home and sat down to dinner with the family. When the chicken was brought out on a platter, the monk offered to carve the splendid bird according to scriptural precepts. The baron was delighted and agreed enthusiastically. The monk thereupon offered the head, neck, wings, and drumsticks to the baron and his family and took the rest of the bird onto his own plate. When the baron questioned the seemingly disparate division of the chicken, the monk explained: "Since the master is head of the house, he should get the head. The baroness, being closest to the head, should receive that part of the bird closest to the head—namely, the neck. The wings symbolize the flighty thoughts of the young daughters and so constitute their portion. The drumsticks go to the sons to remind them that they are the support of the house even as the legs hold up the chicken." Having delivered himself of this edifying piece of logic, the monk proceeded to devour his handsome portion, while the baron and his family were left to nourish themselves mainly on his wisdom.

CURRIED CHICKEN

Serves 6
Preheat oven to 350° F.

2 2-pound chickens, cut into serving pieces
3 tablespoons oil
2 small yellow onions, chopped
1 green pepper, chopped
1 tablespoon good Indian (Madras) curry powder
1 tablespoon paprika
2 tablespoons flour
2 tablespoons tomato purée
1½ cups chicken broth
Juice of ½ lemon

1. Fry chicken pieces in hot oil until lightly browned.
2. Remove the chicken and place in a casserole.
3. Fry onions and green pepper in the oil remaining in the skillet for 3 minutes.

4. Stir in the curry powder and paprika and cook over moderate heat for 2 minutes.

5. Stir in the flour and add tomato purée, chicken broth, and lemon juice.

6. Pour the sauce over the chicken, cover the casserole, and cook 50 minutes in a preheated oven until chicken is tender.*

7. Serve with traditional curry accompaniments: rice, chutney, pappadums (Indian bread), chopped peanuts, chopped cucumbers, and yogurt.

* May be prepared in advance. To serve, reheat the casserole on top of the stove until the sauce is simmering. Cover and place in a preheated 350° F. oven for 20 minutes until very hot.

LAMB AND BEEF CURRIES

Lamb and beef curries are prepared in exactly the same way as chicken curry, except that 2½ pounds of either meat substitutes for the chicken, and beef broth is used instead of chicken broth. Select stewing lamb or boneless chuck and increase the cooking time to 1½ hours.

SHRIMP CASSEROLE WITH GREEN PEPPER, TOMATOES, AND HERBS

Serves 4

2 tablespoons butter
1 yellow onion, finely chopped
1 clove garlic, finely chopped
1 green pepper, chopped
2 tablespoons flour
½ cup tomato purée
½ cup white wine or chicken broth
2 tomatoes, peeled, seeded, and chopped

2 pounds raw shrimp, shelled and deveined
½ teaspoon tarragon
1 bay leaf
½ teaspoon salt
Freshly ground black pepper to taste
2 tablespoons finely chopped parsley

1. Heat the butter in a skillet. Add onion, garlic, and green pepper and fry for 3 minutes until softened.

2. Stir in the flour. Add tomato purée and all remaining ingredients except parsley.

3. Simmer for 10 minutes over moderate heat.

4. Garnish with parsley and serve with rice.

BRAISED CHICKEN WITH TARRAGON

Serves 4
Preheat oven to 350° F.

1 3½-pound chicken, whole	3 sprigs parsley
3 tablespoons oil	1 teaspoon peppercorns
1 onion, finely chopped	1 teaspoon tarragon
1 clove garlic, finely chopped	½ teaspoon salt
1 carrot, finely chopped	2 teaspoons cornstarch, dissolved
1 stalk celery, finely chopped	in 2 tablespoons cold water
1 cup chicken broth	2 tablespoons finely chopped
1 bay leaf	parsley
½ teaspoon thyme	

1. Truss the chicken and brown it, breast side first, in hot oil in a casserole. Remove the chicken.

2. Fry the vegetables in the same oil for 3 minutes until they are softened.

3. Place the chicken on top of the vegetables in the casserole, add the chicken broth, the herbs (tied in a cheesecloth bag), and the salt. Cover the casserole and cook in a preheated oven for approximately 50 minutes.*

4. Remove the chicken and cut into serving pieces. Discard the herb bag.

5. Set the casserole over a low flame on top of the stove. Add the cornstarch, dissolved in water, to the boiling liquid in the casserole. Cook, stirring 1 minute, until thickened.

6. Replace the chicken pieces in the thickened sauce, garnish with parsley, and serve with rice.

* May be prepared in advance to this point. Reheat the casserole on top of the stove until the sauce is simmering. Cover and place in a preheated 350° F. oven for 20 minutes until very hot.

SAUERBRATEN

Serves 6
Preheat oven to 350° F.

2½ pounds top round steak in one piece
1 tablespoon oil
1 onion, finely chopped
1 clove garlic, finely chopped
1 carrot, finely chopped
1 bay leaf

1 tablespoon pickling spice
½ teaspoon ginger
1 cup red wine
½ cup red wine vinegar
½ cup water
3 tablespoons oil
¾ cup crushed gingersnaps

1. Place the beef in an enamel casserole with all the remaining ingredients except the 3 tablespoons of oil and the gingersnaps. Cover the casserole and leave in the refrigerator for four days, turning the beef every day.
2. Remove the beef from the marinade and pat it dry on paper towels. (If you do not dry it, it will not brown.)
3. Brown the beef in hot oil in a heavy skillet.
4. Heat the marinade mixture in the casserole and return the meat to the marinade. Cover and cook in a preheated oven for 1½ hours.*
5. Remove the beef and strain the sauce into a clean saucepan. Add the gingersnaps and cook over low heat for two minutes, stirring until the sauce has thickened.
6. Slice the beef and serve with the sauce. Dumplings are the perfect accompaniment.

* May be prepared in advance to this point. Reheat the casserole on top of the stove until the sauce is simmering. Cover and place in a preheated 350° F. oven for 20 minutes until very hot.

BRAISED VEGETABLE CASSEROLE

Serves 6
Preheat oven to 350° F.

6 medium-sized carrots
1 small turnip
4 tender stalks celery
2 small onions
2 tablespoons butter

⅓ cup white wine (or dry vermouth)
½ teaspoon salt
2 tablespoons finely chopped parsley

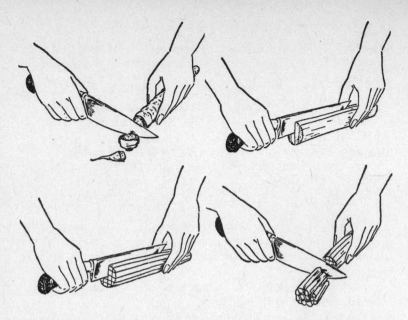

1. Cut the vegetables into thin strips, 2 inches long by ¼ inch thick.

2. Melt the butter in a small casserole. Add the vegetables, wine, and salt. Cover them with a piece of wax paper cut to fit the casserole. (This will prevent the steam from escaping.) Add the lid.

3. Cook in a preheated oven for 40 minutes until the vegetables are tender. Discard the wax paper.

4. Garnish with finely chopped parsley and serve.

Celery

Celery is a member of the parsley family and is as old as time itself, or nearly so. It was mentioned in the Odyssey, *though not as a food. In Homer's time, celery was used only for medicinal purposes, to "purify the blood." In the 1600s, the leaves began to be used for flavoring stocks and soups. It was not until two hundred years later, however, that the blanched celeriac, or celery root, became popular in Europe and America. The root has a delicate yet distinctive taste and is frequently braised in a small amount of liquid or served as a salad with an oil-and-vinegar dressing.*

In America, Pascal celery has become far more popular than the celery root. Unlike the white European variety, Pascal celery has a light green tinge to its stalks. It was first cultivated in Kalamazoo, Michigan, in 1874. The crisp stalks were sold to the passengers who passed through on trains. They must have spread the word well, for it is now the second most important salad crop in America and is grown in every state of the Union.

BRAISED CELERY

Serves 6
Preheat oven to 375° F.

3 bunches celery hearts
1 onion, finely chopped
1 carrot, finely chopped
1 cup boiling beef broth
1 teaspoon tomato paste

1 tablespoon cornstarch, dissolved in 2 tablespoons cold water
2 tablespoons finely chopped parsley

1. Separate celery stalks and wash to remove soil.
2. Cut lengthwise into thin strips and then into pieces about 3 inches long.
3. Place celery in a saucepan. Cover it with cold water. Simmer 15 minutes and drain.
4. Place drained celery in a baking dish and add remaining ingredients except cornstarch and parsley.
5. Cover and place in a preheated oven for 1 hour until soft and tender.
6. Combine cornstarch with water and stir into hot liquid surrounding celery. Heat liquid 1 minute until thickened.
7. Serve hot, with chopped parsley.

POT-ROASTED BEEF

Serves 6

3 pounds beef shoulder, in one piece, tied with string at 1-inch intervals
3 tablespoons oil
1 onion, finely chopped
1 clove garlic, finely chopped
1 carrot, finely chopped
1 stalk celery, finely chopped

½ cup red wine
½ cup beef broth
½ cup tomato juice (optional)
1 bay leaf
½ teaspoon thyme
3 sprigs parsley
1 teaspoon peppercorns
½ teaspoon salt

1. Dry the beef on paper towels and brown it on all sides in hot oil. Remove the beef.

2. Fry the vegetables in the same oil for 3 minutes until softened.

3. Place the beef on top of the vegetables. Reduce the heat.

4. Add the wine, beef broth, tomato juice, herbs (tied in a cheese-cloth bag), and salt. Cover the casserole with a tight-fitting lid and simmer over very low heat for 2 hours. Discard the herb bag.

5. Slice the beef thinly and serve with horseradish, boiled potatoes, and broiled tomato halves.

FISH STEW
Serves 4

1½ pounds haddock, sea bass, or cod, cut into 1-inch-thick fillets	4 carrots, peeled and sliced
½ teaspoon salt	1 green pepper, cut into 2-inch pieces
Head and bones of the filleted fish	1 cup peas
2½ cups water	1 teaspoon paprika
3 tablespoons olive oil	½ teaspoon coriander
1 onion, finely chopped	¼ teaspoon caraway seeds
4 cloves garlic, peeled	2 tablespoons lemon juice

1. Sprinkle the fish fillets with salt on both sides and set aside in the refrigerator.

2. Place the head and bones of the fish in a saucepan. Add the water and bring to a boil. Lower the heat and simmer for 20 minutes. Strain the broth. (If fish trimmings are not available, substitute equal quantities of bottled clam juice and water.)

3. Heat the olive oil in a large pan and fry the fish fillets over moderately high heat until nicely browned. Remove the fish.

4. Fry the onion and garlic in the same oil for 3 minutes until softened. Pour off the oil and place the softened onion in a saucepan. Discard the garlic cloves. Add the carrots, green pepper, and the strained fish broth. Cover and simmer for 15 minutes.

5. Add the peas and continue cooking for 5 minutes.

6. Add the fish fillets, paprika, coriander, and caraway seeds. Simmer for 7 minutes until the fish is white and opaque and flakes easily.

7. Add the lemon juice and serve hot or cold in soup bowls, with crusty bread.

BRAISED BEEF WITH PICKLED FRUITS

This extraordinary combination of ingredients produces a magnificent range of taste and texture. Served with a cauliflower mousse, it makes a memorable meal.

Serves 6
Preheat oven to 350° F.

2½ pounds top round of beef
3 tablespoons oil
1 large onion, finely chopped
1 clove garlic, finely chopped
12 ounces beer
3 sprigs parsley
1 teaspoon peppercorns
1 bay leaf
1 teaspoon salt
1½ tablespoons butter

1½ tablespoons flour
1 cup (total) pickled watermelon
    rind and sour and sweet
    pickles, chopped
2 tablespoons Dijon mustard
½ cup chili sauce
1 tablespoon tomato paste
1 cup mayonnaise
1 teaspoon thyme

1. Tie the beef at 2-inch intervals so it will retain its shape as it cooks. Brown the beef on all sides in hot oil.

2. Remove beef from the pan and fry the onion and garlic. Place vegetables in a casserole with the beef.

3. Add the beer, parsley, peppercorns, bay leaf, and salt. Cover and cook in a preheated oven for 1½ hours until the beef is tender when pierced with the tip of a knife. Remove the beef and strain the broth.*

4. Heat the butter in a saucepan. Stir in the flour and add the strained broth gradually until thickened into a sauce. Stir all the remaining ingredients into the sauce.

5. Slice the beef and reheat it in the sauce. Serve on Cauliflower Mousse.

* May be prepared in advance to this point.

CAULIFLOWER MOUSSE

Serves 6

1 head cauliflower
1½ tablespoons butter
1½ tablespoons flour
1½ cups milk

½ teaspoon salt
Dash of nutmeg
Freshly ground black pepper to
    taste

1. Break the cauliflower into flowerets and discard the heavy stem. Simmer, covered, in boiling salted water for 20 minutes until just tender. Drain the cauliflower.

2. Melt the butter in a small saucepan. Add the flour and cook over low heat for 1 minute. Stir in the milk and add the salt, nutmeg, and pepper. Stir until thickened into a smooth sauce.

3. Place half of the hot sauce in a blender and add a third of the drained cauliflower. Continue adding cauliflower and sauce until a purée is formed.

4. Return the mixture to a large buttered skillet and cook over low heat, stirring constantly to prevent it from sticking, until it is very hot. Serve on hot plates as a foundation for Braised Beef with Pickled Fruits.

VEGETABLE STEW (RATATOUILLE)

Ratatouille may be served hot or cold. As you can see, no liquid is added to this stew. There is sufficient moisture from the eggplant, tomatoes, and zucchini to keep the vegetables bathed in steam.

Serves 8

1 medium-sized eggplant
1 tablespoon salt
4 tablespoons olive oil
2 onions, sliced
3 cloves garlic, finely chopped
1 green pepper, cut into strips
2 medium-sized zucchini, sliced
2 medium-sized ripe tomatoes, peeled, seeded, and chopped

½ teaspoon salt
Freshly ground black pepper to taste
1 teaspoon dried basil (or 1 tablespoon fresh basil), finely chopped
2 tablespoons parsley, finely chopped

1. Cut the eggplant into slices ½-inch thick. Then cut into bite-sized pieces. Place the eggplant on a wire rack, sprinkle with 1 tablespoon salt, and allow to stand for 15 minutes to drain the bitter juices. Dry the eggplant on paper towels.

2. Heat the oil in a large skillet and fry the onions and garlic for 3 minutes until softened.

3. Add the eggplant and fry for 5 minutes until lightly browned.

4. Add all the remaining ingredients except the parsley. Cover and continue cooking for 20 minutes until all the vegetables are soft and tender. Garnish with parsley and serve.

3. sauces

SIMPLE WHITE SAUCE (BÉCHAMEL) · ENRICHED WHITE SAUCE ·
CHEESE SAUCE (SAUCE MORNAY) · SAUCE VELOUTÉ · SAUCE
ALLEMANDE · SAUCE AURORE · CAPER SAUCE · ONION SAUCE · CHAUD-
FROID SAUCE · TURKEY CASSEROLE · SCALLOPS IN WHITE WINE SAUCE
· CURRIED SHRIMP · CLASSIC BROWN SAUCE · SAUCE ITALIENNE ·
SAUCE MADEIRA · HERB SAUCE · GIBLET SAUCE · MUSHROOM SAUCE
· CURRY SAUCE · SAUCE FOR ROAST BEEF OR LAMB · TOMATO SAUCE ·
SPAGHETTI SAUCE · MAYONNAISE · GREEN MAYONNAISE · HOT
MAYONNAISE · TARTAR SAUCE · SAUCE AIOLI · MAYONNAISE CHAUD-
FROID · HOLLANDAISE SAUCE · MOUSSELINE · MALTAISE SAUCE ·
SAUCE BÉARNAISE · SAUCE CHORON · OIL AND VINEGAR DRESSING ·
SAUCE VINAIGRETTE

If French fries were called *pommes alumettes,* do you suppose we
would eat so many of them? One of the problems with sauces is that
many of them have French names, which automatically makes them
sound difficult to make. Yet, as most of the famous sauces originated in
France, it seems reasonable enough to give credit where it is due. Even

the word *sauce* is Gascon in origin. It is a corruption of the Latin word for salt, which was used to preserve the meat in a marinade. The marinade was then used as a sauce. Before forks were invented, all sauces were thickened with bread crumbs so they could be scooped up with the fingers. But gradually all this changed.

The original Béchamel sauce, the ubiquitous white sauce, is said to have been created by Louis de Béchamel, marquis de Nointel, financier and gentleman at large, although jealous contemporaries whispered that he merely claimed credit for a concoction that was first made by the chefs in the kitchen of Henri IV, where the nobility used to romp. Henri's prime minister, Philippe de Mornay, threw a handful of cheese into the Béchamel sauce and thus achieved immortality. Sauce Béarnaise is not native to Béarn but was named by a nostalgic chef from that region, then laboring at the Pavillon Henri IV at St. Germain-en-laye, Paris, in 1835.

Some claim that sauce-making is not an exact science but an art, a gift mysteriously bestowed by the good fairy at birth. Fortunately, however, there are many sauces that can be made by combining precise quantities of ingredients.

There are three principal families of sauces: white, brown, and oil- or butter-based (emulsified) sauces. The foundation of each of these families is known as a "mother" because it gives birth to a number of children, each a little different from the others.

WHITE SAUCES

1 tablespoon butter + 1 tablespoon flour + 1 cup milk = 1 cup thin Béchamel, or White Sauce. This is the "mother" sauce of this particular group, white sauce in its simplest form.

1 tablespoon butter + 1 tablespoon flour + 1 cup milk + ¼ cup cheese = 1¼ cups Sauce Mornay.

1 tablespoon butter + 1 tablespoon flour + 1 cup chicken broth = 1 cup Sauce Velouté.

1 tablespoon butter + 1 tablespoon flour + 1 cup chicken broth + 2 teaspoons curry powder = 1 cup Curry Sauce.

These ingredients are combined in a two-step process:

1. The butter is melted and flour is added to form a paste, or *roux*.
2. Cold liquid is added slowly to the roux, stirred gently and constantly with a wire whisk.

There are a number of ways of achieving a sauce that is of the correct consistency—not grainy, greasy, or lumpy but smooth, subtly flavored, and glossy. If you decide to add hot liquid to a cold roux, instead of following step 2 as described, you will achieve essentially the same sauce. The same consistency will be obtained if you decide to substitute a different liquid, e.g., replacing the milk with the equivalent quantity of chicken broth, veal stock, fish stock, or white wine. Similarly, if you decide to add herbs, spices, or another sauce of the same consistency, the ultimate thickness will remain the same; only the flavor will be changed. However, if you add cheese or egg yolks, the sauce will be thicker.

If you add more than one cup of liquid to the roux and then simmer the sauce until it has been reduced to one cup, it will have the same consistency as if you had added one cup in the beginning, but the flavor will be more concentrated. Milk will taste creamier as part of the water content evaporates. Concentrated stocks and wine will give the sauce a more dominant character.

SIMPLE WHITE SAUCE (BÉCHAMEL)

This is a simple, all-purpose white sauce that may be used over vegetables.

Yield: 2 cups

2 tablespoons butter	¼ teaspoon salt
2 tablespoons flour	White pepper to taste
2 cups milk	

1. Heat the butter until it is sizzling, but do not let it brown. Stir in the flour and cook it over low heat, stirring constantly, for 2 minutes.
2. Add the milk gradually, stirring constantly with a wire whisk until a smooth sauce is formed. Season the sauce with salt and pepper.

ENRICHED WHITE SAUCE

For chicken, fish, eggs, vegetables, and pasta.

Yield: 2 cups

2 tablespoons butter	3 cups milk
1 small onion, thinly sliced	1 bay leaf
1 small carrot, sliced (roughly	2 sprigs parsley
⅓ cup)	Pinch of nutmeg
½ stalk celery, sliced	¼ teaspoon salt
3 tablespoons flour	White pepper to taste

1. Heat the butter and fry the onion, carrot, and celery for 3 minutes until softened but not brown.
2. Stir in the flour and continue cooking over low heat for 5 minutes.
3. Add the milk gradually, stirring constantly with a wire whisk. Add the bay leaf, parsley, nutmeg, salt, and pepper.
4. Simmer uncovered over very low heat for about 40 minutes, until the milk has reduced to 2 cups. Stir the sauce occasionally to be sure it is not sticking to the pan.
5. Strain the sauce. If you don't wish to use the sauce immediately, cover it with a film of melted butter or transparent wrap to prevent a skin from forming. It will keep for a week in the refrigerator but does not freeze well.

CHEESE SAUCE (SAUCE MORNAY)

For poached fish, eggs, vegetables, and pasta dishes.

Prepare the Simple White Sauce or Enriched White Sauce. Add ½ cup grated Swiss cheese and ¼ cup grated Parmesan cheese, or ¾ cup other grated firm cheese, while sauce is simmering.

SAUCE VELOUTÉ

For chicken and fish.

For chicken dishes, prepare the Simple White Sauce or Enriched White Sauce but substitute 3 cups chicken broth for the milk.
For fish, substitute 2 cups fish stock and 1 cup dry white wine.

SAUCE ALLEMANDE

For chicken breasts and poached fish.

Prepare the Simple White Sauce or Enriched White Sauce. Combine 2 egg yolks with ¼ cup heavy cream. Stir ⅛ cup of the hot sauce into the egg yolk and cream and return the mixture to the saucepan. Heat until hot, but do not let the sauce boil or the egg yolks will separate.

SAUCE AURORE

For poached fish or eggs.

Prepare the Simple White Sauce or Enriched White Sauce and add ½ cup tomato purée just before serving. Mix well.

CAPER SAUCE

For poached fish or boiled beef.

Prepare Simple White Sauce or Enriched White Sauce and add ¼ cup capers and 1 tablespoon finely chopped parsley or fresh dill before serving.

ONION SAUCE (SOUBISE)

For roast veal.

Chop 1 cup onions and place in saucepan with 2 tablespoons butter. Cover with a round of buttered wax paper. Place the lid on the pan and steam or "sweat" the onions in butter for 10 minutes until soft but not brown. Discard the wax paper. Proceed with the Simple or Enriched White Sauce, omitting the carrot and celery. Do not strain the sauce.

CHAUD-FROID SAUCE

For coating poached chicken and fish.

Prepare the Simple or Enriched White Sauce. Sprinkle 1 package unflavored gelatin on the surface of ¼ cup dry white wine. Leave undisturbed for 5 minutes until the gelatin has softened. Stir gelatin into hot sauce and allow the sauce to cool. Spoon sauce over the food and then chill in the refrigerator.

TURKEY CASSEROLE

This recipe is a Simple White Sauce added to noodles, turkey, and vegetables to form a complete dish.

Serves 4
Preheat oven to 350° F.

1½ tablespoons butter	1 cup mixed vegetables, cooked
1½ tablespoons flour	½ teaspoon salt
1½ cups milk (or chicken broth)	Freshly ground black pepper to
2 cups noodles	taste
3 cups turkey, cooked	¼ cup grated Parmesan cheese
1 tomato, peeled, seeded, and chopped	

1. To make sauce, heat the butter in a small saucepan. Stir in the flour and cook over low heat for 1 minute. Add the milk (or chicken broth) gradually, stirring with a wire whisk to form a smooth sauce.
2. Cook the noodles in plenty of boiling salted water for 6 minutes. Drain the noodles and place them in a buttered casserole.
3. Combine the turkey, tomato, and vegetables in a bowl. Season with salt and pepper and place on top of the noodles.
4. Pour the sauce over the turkey and vegetables. Sprinkle the surface of the sauce with Parmesan cheese. Place the casserole, uncovered, in a preheated oven and cook for 30 minutes until a bubbling brown crust has formed over the sauce. Serve with a crisp salad.

Scallops

The scallop has two shells, like the oyster and the clam, but, unlike them, it swims in the water or moves along on the ocean floor. The shell is rounded and has a wavy "scalloped" edge. A large muscle, sometimes called the eye, controls the movement of the shell as the scallop propels itself along. It is this muscle, or eye, that opens and closes the shell to see if you are coming for dinner! The white muscle is the only part of the scallop that is commonly eaten in America.

There are two kinds of scallops, bay scallops and sea scallops, and they come from the two localities that give them their names. The bay scallop is small and is taken from the inshore waters of the New England and Middle Atlantic coast. The larger sea scallop inhabits the offshore banks and deep waters of these areas and is harvested from the sea by scallop draggers.

The flavor of the bay scallop is sweeter and the "meat" more tender than that of the larger sea scallop. Both kinds of scallop can be cooked in various ways. When used for sautéing or broiling, they are best poached for a few minutes first to prevent shrinkage.

SCALLOPS IN WHITE WINE SAUCE
(COQUILLES ST. JACQUES)

Coquilles St. Jacques consists of scallops in a fish broth that is thickened into a white sauce. They can be served as an elegant first course.

Serves 6
Preheat oven to 350° F.

2 pounds scallops, preferably bay scallops
½ cup bottled clam juice
1 cup white wine
1 bay leaf
½ teaspoon tarragon
3 sprigs fresh parsley
1 teaspoon peppercorns
1 tomato, chopped and seeded (optional)
1 avocado, chopped (optional)

Sauce:
2 tablespoons butter
2 tablespoons flour
2 egg yolks
¼ cup heavy cream
½ cup freshly grated Parmesan cheese
1 tablespoon butter

1. Place the scallops in a saucepan with the clam juice and wine. Tie the herbs in a cheesecloth bag and bury the bag among the scallops. Cover and simmer for 8 minutes until scallops are firm, white, and opaque.

2. Drain the scallops, reserving the broth and discarding the herbs. Cut the scallops into small pieces if sea scallops are used. Replace the broth on high heat and boil until only half of the original quantity remains. The color will be an undistinguished gray, but it improves later in the preparation.

3. To prepare the sauce, heat 2 tablespoons of butter in a saucepan. Stir in the flour and add the broth, which should have been reduced to ¾ cup. Combine the egg yolks and cream and add the mixture to the hot sauce, stirring with a wire whisk. Do not let the sauce boil or the egg yolks will curdle.

4. Remove the sauce from the heat and add the scallops. Tomato and avocado may be added at this point to supply additional taste, texture, and color. (If you decide to make a Shrimp Coquille, prepare it in exactly the same way but add 2 teaspoons of tomato paste to the sauce before adding the shrimp.)

5. Divide the mixture among individual dishes or scallop shells. Sprinkle each with Parmesan cheese and dot with butter. Place shells on a cookie sheet. Coquilles can be frozen at this point.

6. Reheat the Coquilles in a preheated oven for 5 minutes until very hot and bubbly.

CURRIED SHRIMP

This recipe is prepared in the same way as Coquilles St. Jacques in that the shrimp receive a preliminary cooking in a liquid, which is flavored both by the shrimp and the spices, and then becomes thickened into a sauce. Serve this dish as an appetizer in pastry shells or scallop shells, or over toast points.

Serves 6

2 pounds raw shrimp, unpeeled
1½ cups chicken broth
1 onion, finely chopped
1 clove garlic, finely chopped
2 cinnamon sticks
4 thin slices fresh ginger root
Dash of cayenne pepper
⅛ teaspoon turmeric
½ teaspoon salt

Curry Sauce:
2 tablespoons oil
1 tablespoon curry powder
2 tablespoons flour
2 tablespoons lime juice
1 teaspoon sugar

1. Place the shrimp in a saucepan with the chicken broth. Tie the onion, garlic, cinnamon sticks, and ginger root in a cheesecloth bag and bury the bag among the shrimp. Add the cayenne pepper, turmeric, and salt. Cover and simmer the shrimp for 8 minutes, until firm and pink.

2. Drain the shrimp, reserving the broth and the spices. Peel the shrimp and cut into ½-inch pieces if large shrimp are used.

3. Replace the broth and bag of spices on high heat and boil until only half of the original quantity remains. Discard the bag of spices.

4. To prepare the sauce, heat the oil in a saucepan. Add the curry powder and cook for 1 minute to release the flavor of the curry. Stir in the flour and add the broth, which has been reduced to ¾ cup.

5. Add the lime juice, sugar, and shrimp. Continue cooking over moderate heat until the shrimp are hot.

BROWN SAUCES

Brown sauces are made in much the same way as white sauces, except that vegetables, giblets, or wines are added and the roux—consisting of butter, oil, or animal fat (rendered bacon fat, drippings from a roast etc.) plus flour—is browned slightly before the liquid is added.

Classic brown sauce is a mother sauce from which an infinite variety of other sauces are derived. The flavor of the sauce is wholly dependent on the quality of the beef stock. Although commercially prepared canned beef broth or dehydrated cubes may be used, it is preferable to make your own stock.

There are four steps in the preparation of a brown sauce:

1. The butter is heated until it is sizzling but not brown. An equal quantity of flour is stirred into the butter to form a roux. The roux is stirred over low heat for two or three minutes until the flour is thoroughly cooked.

2. The stock is added very slowly while stirring constantly with a wire whisk to obtain a smooth blend. Making a brown sauce requires double or even triple the quantity of liquid used for a white sauce:

> 1 tablespoon butter + 1 tablespoon flour + 1 cup milk = 1 cup white sauce.
> 1 tablespoon butter + 1 tablespoon flour + 3 cups beef stock = 1 cup brown sauce.

3. The sauce is simmered, uncovered, over very low heat for an hour or even longer, until it has reduced in quantity to the correct consistency. During this long, slow cooking period, the flavor becomes more and more concentrated and the starch in the flour thickens the sauce to a velvety smoothness.

4. The sauce is strained to remove any particles of skin that may have formed. It is then ready to use. It may be served in this form, or other ingredients or flavorings can be added. It will keep in the refrigerator for at least a month and can also be frozen.

CLASSIC BROWN SAUCE (ESPAGNOLE)

For red meat and game.

Yield: 2 cups

2 tablespoons butter	1 bay leaf
1 onion, finely chopped	½ teaspoon thyme
½ cup chopped carrots	3 sprigs parsley
½ cup sliced celery	1 teaspoon peppercorns
2 tablespoons flour	½ cup tomato purée
4 cups beef stock	½ teaspoon salt

1. Heat the butter and fry the onion, carrots, and celery for 5 minutes over low heat until softened and lightly browned. Stir in the flour and continue cooking for 2 minutes.

2. Stir in the beef stock gradually. Add the bay leaf, thyme, parsley, and peppercorns.

3. Simmer over very low heat for 1½ hours, stirring occasionally, until the sauce has reduced to 2 cups. Add the tomato purée and salt. Simmer for 10 minutes more.

4. Strain the sauce.

SAUCE ITALIENNE

For broiled meats.

Prepare Classic Brown Sauce. Simmer 4 chopped scallions (white part only) and ¼ cup chopped mushrooms in ½ cup wine for 15 minutes, until the vegetables are cooked and the wine has reduced to ¼ cup. Stir in 1 chopped, peeled, and seeded tomato, 1 tablespoon chopped parsley, and 1 teaspoon lemon juice. Stir all these ingredients into the strained sauce.

SAUCE MADEIRA

For roast beef, beef Wellington, and broiled filet steaks.

Prepare Classic Brown Sauce and add ⅓ cup Madeira to the strained sauce.

HERB SAUCE

For roast chicken, boiled beef and game, and roast lamb.

Prepare Classic Brown Sauce. Simmer 4 chopped scallions (white part only) and 2 tablespoons mixed dried herbs (or 5 tablespoons mixed fresh herbs) in ½ cup wine for 10 minutes. (The herbs may be parsley and one or more of the following: tarragon, basil, oregano, or rosemary.) Reduce the wine to ¼ cup and add to the hot sauce.

GIBLET SAUCE

Yield: 2 cups

2 tablespoons butter	1 bay leaf
2 onions, finely chopped	½ teaspoon thyme
2 carrots, finely chopped	2 sprigs parsley
2 stalks celery, finely chopped	1 teaspoon peppercorns
2 tablespoons flour	½ teaspoon salt
2½ cups chicken broth	Freshly ground black pepper to
2 cups giblets (excluding the liver)	taste

1. Melt the butter in a saucepan. Add the onions, carrots, and celery and fry over low heat for 3 minutes until softened.
2. Stir in the flour and allow it to brown lightly.
3. Add the chicken broth slowly. Add all the remaining ingredients. Partially cover with a lid. (Do not cover completely so that some evaporation and concentration of the chicken broth can take place.) Simmer for 30 minutes and strain the sauce, discarding the giblets.
4. Purée the sauce in a blender.

MUSHROOM SAUCE

Yield: 2 cups

2 tablespoons butter (or oil)
2 onions, finely chopped
1 clove garlic, finely chopped
1 carrot, finely chopped
1 stalk celery, finely chopped
12 mushrooms, finely chopped
2 tablespoons flour
1 cup red wine (optional)

1 cup beef broth (or 2 cups beef
  broth if wine is eliminated)
1 tablespoon lemon juice
1 tablespoon tomato paste
½ teaspoon salt
Freshly ground black pepper to
  taste
2 tablespoons finely chopped
  parsley

1. Heat the butter (or oil) and fry the onions, garlic, carrot, and celery for 3 minutes.
2. Add the mushrooms. Cover and steam over low heat for 10 minutes.
3. Remove the lid and stir in the flour. Allow the flour to brown lightly for 2 minutes.
4. Add the liquids gradually.
5. Add the remaining ingredients and simmer, uncovered, for 10 minutes.

CURRY SAUCE

For leftover chicken, lamb, or beef.

Yield: 2 cups

4 slices bacon, cut into small
  pieces
2 onions, finely chopped
1 clove garlic, finely chopped
2 carrots, finely chopped
2 stalks celery, finely chopped

1 unpeeled apple, chopped
2 tablespoons curry powder
2 tablespoons flour
2½ cups chicken (or beef) broth
1 tablespoon lemon juice
1 teaspoon sugar

1. Fry the bacon until all the fat has been rendered. Measure 2 tablespoons bacon fat into a saucepan. Drain and reserve the bacon.
2. Fry the onions, garlic, carrots, celery, and apple* in the bacon fat

* One-quarter cup dried apricots may be substituted for the apple. If apricots are used, add them *after* the chicken broth (step 3).

for 3 minutes until softened. Stir in the curry powder and flour and cook 1 minute until lightly browned.

3. Add the broth gradually. Add lemon juice and sugar. Simmer over low heat for 30 minutes until sauce is reduced to a medium-thick consistency.

4. Strain the sauce and add the reserved bacon pieces.

SAUCE FOR ROAST BEEF OR LAMB

2 tablespoons fat, rendered from the roast
1 cup red wine
1 cup beef (or chicken) broth
½ teaspoon dried herbs—thyme for beef, rosemary for lamb
2 tablespoons Madeira
1 tablespoon cornstarch, dissolved in 2 tablespoons red wine (or cold water)
1 tablespoon butter

1. Discard all but 2 tablespoons (roughly) of fat.

2. Place the pan over direct heat and add 1 cup of wine. Stir over low heat, scraping up the pieces clinging to the bottom of the pan. Transfer to a saucepan; it will be easier to handle.

3. Add the broth, herbs, and Madeira and simmer, uncovered, for 10 minutes.*

4. Add the cornstarch dissolved in cold liquid. Stir 2 minutes until the sauce has thickened.

5. Add the butter and cook 1 minute to make the sauce shine.

* A teaspoon of tomato paste will give the sauce additional flavor if the broth is not as good as you would like. Stir in the tomato paste with the herbs.

TOMATO SAUCE

Yield: 2 cups

1 tablespoon butter
1 onion, finely chopped
1 clove garlic, finely chopped
1 carrot, finely chopped
1 stalk celery, finely chopped
1 tablespoon flour
½ cup chicken broth
4 large tomatoes, chopped
1 teaspoon dried basil (or thyme)
1 teaspoon tomato paste (if you are using winter tomatoes)
½ teaspoon salt
Freshly ground black pepper to taste

1. Heat the butter until it is bubbling.
2. Fry the onion, garlic, carrot, and celery for 3 minutes.
3. Stir in the flour.
4. Add the chicken broth, tomatoes, basil (or thyme), tomato paste, and the salt and pepper. Simmer, uncovered, for 1½ hours, stirring frequently to prevent the tomatoes from scorching.
5. Purée the sauce in a blender.
6. Strain the blended sauce. Serve it over pasta, fish, chicken or vegetables (e.g., stuffed green peppers or eggplant).

SPAGHETTI SAUCE WITH MEAT

Double the recipe for Tomato Sauce and brown 1 pound ground chuck in the frying pan after the vegetables have softened (step 2). Pour off the excess fat, if any, before adding the flour.

TOMATO SOUP

1 tablespoon butter
1 onion, finely chopped
1 clove garlic, finely chopped
1 carrot, finely chopped
1 stalk celery, finely chopped
1 tablespoon flour
4 *cups chicken broth*
4 large tomatoes, chopped
1 teaspoon dried basil (or thyme)
1 teaspoon tomato paste (if you are using winter tomatoes)
½ teaspoon salt
Freshly ground black pepper to taste

TOMATO SAUCE

1 tablespoon butter
1 onion, finely chopped
1 clove garlic, finely chopped
1 carrot, finely chopped
1 stalk celery, finely chopped
1 tablespoon flour
½ *cup chicken broth*
4 large tomatoes, chopped
1 teaspoon dried basil (or thyme)
1 teaspoon tomato paste (if you are using winter tomatoes)
½ teaspoon salt
Freshly ground black pepper to taste

As can be seen from these lists of ingredients, the only difference between Tomato Soup and Tomato Sauce is in the quantity of liquid added. Any sauce can be made into a soup by increasing the liquid—and, conversely, a soup can become a sauce if the liquid is decreased.

EMULSIFIED SAUCES

An emulsified sauce is achieved as a result of the slow but steady in-sistence of egg yolks on drinking and digesting such a huge quantity of butter or oil that they almost burst or, as it is phrased, "break." If this critical point is inadvertently passed, another yolk is called in to remedy the situation.

All the sauces whose names end in -aise, and some that have different names, march to the beat of the same drummer and are made according to the same principles:

> 3 egg yolks + 3 tablespoons vinegar + 1½ cups oil = 2½ cups Mayonnaise.

> Mayonnaise + garlic = Garlic Mayonnaise (or "Aioli Sauce," if there are guests for dinner).

> 3 egg yolks + 3 tablespoons lemon juice + 1½ sticks butter (12 tablespoons) = Hollandaise Sauce.

> 3 egg yolks + 1 tablespoon lemon juice + 2 tablespoons orange juice + 1½ sticks butter = Maltaise Sauce.

> Hollandaise + ½ cup heavy cream = Mousseline (not, annoyingly, Mousselaise).

> 3 egg yolks + 3 tablespoons scallions + ¼ cup each vinegar and wine = Sauce Béarnaise.

> Béarnaise + 3 tablespoons tomato paste = Sauce Choron.

Although mayonnaise is a sauce based on egg yolks, it does not fit neatly into the category of other egg-based sauces such as Hollandaise, Maltaise, or Béarnaise. Mayonnaise differs from these preparations in that it is the only major sauce that is not cooked. In addition, the prin-cipal ingredient is oil rather than butter. In fact, more than three-quarters of the sauce is oil.

Mayonnaise made only with egg yolks will be richer in color, more delicate in taste, and lighter in texture than mayonnaise made with whole eggs. If you were to measure mayonnaise made by hand and a blender mayonnaise made by using exactly the same quantities of the same ingredients, you would be surprised to see how much smaller the yield of the blended variety would be. If you put 3 egg yolks and 1½ cups of oil in the blender, you will end up with 1½ cups of mayonnaise. If you put the same ingredients in a bowl and whisk it by hand, you will get 2 cups. Nor will the blender mayonnaise taste the same as the handmade one! The point is, obviously, that although the blender is a wonderful help in the kitchen, it doesn't do everything quite as well as a French maid!

MAYONNAISE

Yield: 2½ cups

3 egg yolks
¼ teaspoon dry mustard
    (Dijon-type)
½ teaspoon salt

Freshly ground black pepper to
    taste
3 tablespoons lemon juice (or
    white wine vinegar)
1½ cups olive oil (or salad oil)

1. Place the egg yolks in a bowl. Using a hand or standard electric mixer or (preferably) a wire whisk, beat the yolks until they are thick and creamy.

2. Beat in the mustard, salt, pepper, and 1 tablespoon lemon juice (or vinegar).

3. Add the oil in a slow, steady, continuous stream of drops, beating constantly until all the oil is used and the mayonnaise is thick. Be sure not to add the oil too quickly or the mayonnaise may curdle.

4. Beat in the remaining lemon juice (or vinegar).

Rescuing Mayonnaise in Distress

If you add insufficient lemon juice or vinegar to the mayonnaise or pour in too much oil too quickly, it may curdle or thin to a watery consistency. Simply put another egg yolk and one teaspoon of prepared (Dijon-type) mustard into a bowl. Beat it for a few seconds and add one-half cup of the curdled mayonnaise, a teaspoon at a time. The mayonnaise will straighten itself out. You can then add the remaining curdled sauce more quickly without fear of further separation.

Note: Dijon mustard can also be used as a thickening agent for hot sauces, such as sauces for pork, ham, kidneys, and game. This technique, however, works only with Dijon mustard, because the powder forming the base of the mustard has been ground more finely than is true of other commercial varieties. Incidentally, the Dijon mustard made in America has a completely different taste from the more pungent variety made in the Dijon area of France, which is mixed with white wine and aged.

GREEN MAYONNAISE

For hard-boiled egg and cold fish dishes.

Yield: 2 cups

¼ package frozen chopped spinach
¼ cup parsley
¼ cup watercress leaves
1 tablespoon fresh (or frozen) chives
½ teaspoon dried tarragon

1 egg
2 egg yolks
½ teaspoon salt
Freshly ground pepper to taste
Grated rind and juice of 1 lemon
¾ cup salad oil

1. Bring ½ cup water to the boiling point in a small saucepan. Add frozen spinach and cook for 3 minutes until thawed.
2. Add parsley, watercress, chives, and tarragon. Simmer for 2 more minutes.
3. Drain and pat ingredients dry on paper towels. Place in a blender or mixing bowl.
4. Add egg, egg yolks, salt, pepper, grated lemon rind, and lemon juice. Blend to form a purée.
5. Add the oil in a slow, steady stream, beating continuously until all the oil has been absorbed.

HOT MAYONNAISE

Mayonnaise may be added to casserole preparations such as Braised Beef to give them extra flavor.

A little grated Swiss (or Cheddar) cheese added to mayonnaise makes an excellent quick sauce. When placed under a broiler, the sauce will turn a beautiful golden brown and will not separate.

TARTAR SAUCE

1 cup mayonnaise
2 teaspoons capers

2 sweet gherkins, finely chopped
2 tablespoons finely chopped parsley

Combine all the ingredients in a small bowl and refrigerate for 1 hour. Serve with fried fish.

Garlic

In ancient times, when an oath was sworn before a public notary, the oath-taker held a clove of garlic in his mouth so that the notary could then tell if he was telling the truth. If the garlic was immediately detectable on his breath, he was obviously lying!

It was said that after the Devil left Paradise, garlic sprang up in his footprints. Some few generations later, the Provençal poet Mistral wrote of garlic that it "gently intoxicates, charges the body with warmth, [and] bathes the soul in rapture," which only goes to prove that if you look hard enough, even Satan had his good points. If you have a hard time differentiating the strength of the onion family, remember:

> Shallots are for babies,
> Onions are for men, and
> Garlic is for heroes.

SAUCE AIOLI (BLENDER GARLIC MAYONNAISE)

For fish and as a dip for raw vegetables.

Yield: 2 cups

¼ cup bread crumbs
1 tablespoon white wine vinegar
6 cloves garlic, crushed
¼ teaspoon salt
3 egg yolks

1½ cups salad oil
¼ cup bottled clam juice (or white wine)
3 tablespoons lemon juice

1. Place the bread crumbs, vinegar, garlic, and salt in a blender. Add the egg yolks and turn on the motor.
2. Add the oil *very slowly*, drop by drop in a continuous steady

stream. (Do not add the oil too quickly or the aioli will not thicken.)
Add the clam juice (or wine) and lemon juice.

MAYONNAISE CHAUD-FROID

Two teaspoons of gelatin, dissolved in ¼ cup of water, may be added
to the mayonnaise recipe for use as a coating for cold fish or stuffed
hard-boiled eggs. If the mayonnaise is stiffened with gelatin, it will hold
its shape and not roll off the completed dish.

OTHER VARIATIONS OF MAYONNAISE

As you peer into your refrigerator, you may find all sorts of interesting odds and ends of other sauces—prepared commercially or, perhaps, your own. A tablespoon or two of a sauce left over from a chicken
dinner may be added to some mayonnaise and used to accompany cold
meats, vegetables, or hors d'oeuvres, or to 1 cup of mayonnaise add one
of the following:

- 1 or 2 tablespoons of Hollandaise, for asparagus or broccoli
- A little chili sauce, for shrimp
- Chutney, for cold lamb
- Horseradish, for cold sliced beef
- Mashed anchovies, for hard-boiled eggs

I don't think I need give exact proportions. Taste the result and see
how you like it. If it tastes right to you, it *is* right.

HOLLANDAISE SAUCE

1½ sticks butter (12 tablespoons)   Pinch of salt
3 egg yolks   Dash of cayenne pepper
Juice of 1 lemon (3 tablespoons)

1. Reserving 2 tablespoons butter, melt the remainder in a small
saucepan over low heat until almost boiling. Remove from the heat.
2. In another small saucepan, combine egg yolks, lemon juice, and
salt and place over low heat.
3. Add 1 tablespoon of reserved butter immediately and stir con-

stantly until it has almost melted. Add remaining 1 tablespoon butter and stir until melted.

4. Remove saucepan from heat and add first saucepan of melted butter slowly, stirring with a wire whisk.

5. Taste for seasoning, adding cayenne pepper, salt, and lemon juice if necessary.

MOUSSELINE

To Hollandaise Sauce add ½ cup heavy cream and stir well.

MALTAISE SAUCE

Make Hollandaise Sauce, substituting 1 tablespoon lemon juice and 2 tablespoons orange juice for the 3 tablespoons lemon juice.

SAUCE BÉARNAISE

The difference between Hollandaise and Sauce Béarnaise lies in their flavoring. The method of preparation is the same for both sauces.

¼ cup wine vinegar
¼ cup red or white wine (or white vermouth)
3 scallions, finely chopped

1 teaspoon tarragon
1½ sticks butter (12 tablespoons)
3 egg yolks

1. Place wine vinegar, wine (or vermouth), scallions, and ½ teaspoon tarragon in a small saucepan. Simmer 5 minutes, until the original quantity of liquid is reduced by half.

2. Strain liquid and discard scallions and tarragon.

3. Reserving 2 tablespoons butter, heat the remainder until hot but not boiling. Remove from heat.

4. Add egg yolks to reduced vinegar and wine mixture, stirring with a wire whisk. Place over gentle heat.

5. Add 1 tablespoon reserved butter and stir until dissolved. Add remaining 1 tablespoon butter and stir until dissolved. Remove saucepan from the heat.

6. Add first saucepan of melted butter gradually, stirring constantly to form a thick sauce. Add remaining tarragon. Serve with broiled meats and fish.

SAUCE CHORON

To Sauce Béarnaise add 3 tablespoons of tomato paste and stir well.

Olive Oil

Olive trees were first planted in the south of France more than 2,500 years ago. The blazing sun has been filling the olives with delicately flavored oil ever since. Olive trees live to a great age. Some, in fact, are known to be more than 500 years old. The twisted and gnarled wood of the olive tree, with its tortuous whorls and tight graining, makes an ideal salad bowl. With each libation of oil, the graining of the wood becomes more pronounced. Eventually the bowl acquires a fragrance and life of its own.

OIL AND VINEGAR DRESSING

When tomatoes are bursting with flavor, one of the joys of summer is to slice them and marinate them in a simple Oil and Vinegar Dressing with 1 tablespoon freshly chopped basil.

Pinch of salt
Freshly ground black pepper to
 taste
1 clove garlic, finely chopped

½ teaspoon mild (Dijon)
 mustard
2 tablespoons vinegar
6 tablespoons light olive oil

Combine ingredients in the order listed above.

Lettuce

Persian kings ate lettuce 2,500 years ago. All the types of lettuce that are known today were eaten in the Middle Ages; Chaucer, who was born in 1340, "had a friend who loved eating garlic, onions, and lettuce," though it is not known whether his friend embellished his salad with a dressing.

SAUCE VINAIGRETTE

A Sauce Vinaigrette is sublime not only with artichokes or asparagus but also with cold beef, hot chicken, or crab salad.

Serves 6

3 tablespoons finely chopped parsley

3 tablespoons finely chopped chives, preferably fresh

1 tablespoon finely chopped capers

1 tablespoon finely chopped sweet gherkins

1 hard-boiled egg, finely chopped

To prepare Sauce Vinaigrette, make an Oil and Vinegar Dressing and add to it the ingredients listed above.

4. soufflés

CHEESE SOUFFLÉ · CHEESE AND HERB SOUFFLÉ · HAM AND CHEESE
SOUFFLÉ · SPINACH SOUFFLÉ · CURRIED CHICKEN SOUFFLÉ · CRAB
SOUFFLÉ · TOMATO AND ANCHOVY SOUFFLÉ · ROLLED MUSHROOM
SOUFFLÉ · STRAWBERRY SOUFFLÉ · RASPBERRY SOUFFLÉ · PEACH
SOUFFLÉ · BLACK CHERRY SOUFFLÉ · CHOCOLATE SOUFFLÉ · GRAND
MARNIER SOUFFLÉ · CRÊPE SOUFFLÉ · MELBA SAUCE · OMELETTE
SOUFFLÉ · FROZEN MOUSSE SOUFFLÉ

A hot soufflé is just a flavored thick white sauce, enriched with egg yolks and lightened with beaten egg whites. The air incorporated into the egg whites causes the soufflé to expand as it cooks. A soufflé is a fragile castle in the air which will not linger while its architecture is admired. It has to be eaten immediately, at the very height of its full-blown glory, or it will crumple and collapse into a dejected ruin.

SOUFFLÉ DISHES

A soufflé can be made in any dish with straight sides. The dish, if you are interested in the dramatic arts, should be just large enough to contain the unbaked soufflé. As it cooks, the soufflé will rise two or three inches above the level of the dish. This is why a paper collar is used to support the rising soufflé. The collar is removed just before serving, and the soufflé supports itself on tiptoe until the air trapped inside it escapes. At this point it gently subsides.

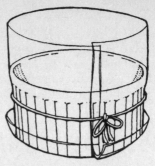

PREPARATION OF THE SOUFFLÉ DISH

1. Butter the soufflé dish and sprinkle it with cheese, fine bread crumbs, or flour.
2. Tear off a piece of wax paper large enough to encircle the dish and allow a 2-inch overlap.
3. Fold the paper in half lengthwise and make a ½-inch fold at the folded edge for additional rigidity.
4. Butter the top third of the paper, including the overlap, and sprinkle with cheese, fine bread crumbs, or flour.
5. Tie the paper around the outside of the dish with a piece of string.

ENTRÉE SOUFFLÉS

CHEESE SOUFFLÉ

Serves 4
Preheat oven to 375° F.

2 tablespoons butter	Dash of cayenne pepper
3 tablespoons flour	Dash of nutmeg
1¼ cups milk	6 egg whites
4 egg yolks	¼ teaspoon salt
1 cup grated cheese	⅛ teaspoon cream of tartar
1 teaspoon mustard	3 tablespoons grated cheese

1. Prepare a 1½-quart soufflé dish. Heat the butter in a saucepan until it is hot and bubbling.
2. Stir in the flour and cook over low heat for 1 minute, stirring constantly.

3. Stir in the milk gradually with a wire whisk to obtain a smooth sauce. Remove the pan from the heat.

4. Stir in the egg yolks, cheese, mustard, pepper, and nutmeg.

5. In a bowl, beat the egg whites with the salt and cream of tartar until they stand in soft peaks.

6. Stir about 1 cup of the beaten egg whites into the hot cheese sauce. Pour the sauce over the remaining egg whites and fold them lovingly together, using a rubber spatula. With every stroke, some of the

air in the egg whites will escape, so fold the mixture over and over but do not try to incorporate every puff of egg white. The small clouds will disappear by the time the soufflé is baked.

7. Pile the soufflé into the prepared dish. It should come to just below the rim. (If it doesn't, there is nothing you can do about it now. You probably did not believe the bit about folding in the egg whites gently. Add an extra egg white next time just to be sure.)

8. Sprinkle the top of the soufflé with the remaining cheese. Place the soufflé in a preheated oven. Close the door gently and creep quietly away.

9. In 30 minutes,* come back and the soufflé will have risen to the top of the oven. Remove the collar and carry it, with appropriate immodesty, to the table. Serve it immediately for Sunday lunch with a simple tossed green salad and cool white wine.

* If you prefer to make 4 individual servings, reduce the baking time from 30 minutes to 20 minutes.

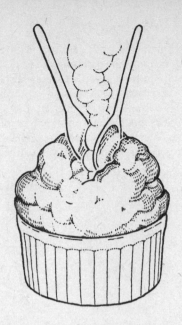

SOUFFLÉ FOR FOUR

Now that you can make a Cheese Soufflé, you can make any other soufflé you wish. The proportions of the ingredients and the method of cooking remain the same:

2 tablespoons butter
3 tablespoons flour
1¼ cups liquid (milk, chicken broth, beef broth, beer, or wine)
4 egg yolks
1 cup flavoring (cheese, cooked meat, fish, or vegetables)

Seasonings to enhance the principal ingredient (herbs, spices, mustard, horseradish, tomato paste, chutney, etc.)
6 egg whites
¼ teaspoon salt
⅛ teaspoon cream of tartar

Bake in a preheated oven for 30 minutes.

CHEESE AND HERB SOUFFLÉ

Add ¾ cup grated cheese and ¼ cup freshly chopped herbs. In the place of the milk, substitute 1¼ cups chicken broth or beer.

HAM AND CHEESE SOUFFLÉ

Add ½ cup diced boiled ham and ½ cup grated cheese.

SPINACH SOUFFLÉ

Add 1 cup chopped or puréed cooked spinach to replace the cheese.

CURRIED CHICKEN SOUFFLÉ

Fry 1 tablespoon curry powder (to release its full flavor) in the 2 tablespoons butter. Replace the cheese with 1 cup diced, cooked chicken.

CRAB SOUFFLÉ

Replace cheese with ¾ cup crabmeat and ¼ cup diced green pepper. Boil the pepper for 5 minutes to soften before adding the soufflé. Substitute 1¼ cups beer for the milk or use ¾ cup white wine and ½ cup chicken broth.

TOMATO AND ANCHOVY SOUFFLÉ

Replace cheese with 1 cup peeled, seeded, and chopped tomatoes and 6 chopped anchovy fillets. Substitute 1¼ cups chicken broth for the milk.

A SOUFFLÉ FOR SIX

To make a soufflé for six people, use a 2-quart dish, increase the ingredients as indicated below, and follow the instructions for Cheese Soufflé.

3 tablespoons butter
4 tablespoons flour
1½ cups liquid (milk, chicken broth, beef broth, beer, or wine)
6 egg yolks
1½ cups flavoring (cheese, meat, fish, or vegetables)

Seasonings to enhance the principal ingredient (herbs, spices, mustard, horseradish, tomato paste, chutney, etc.)
8 egg whites
¼ teaspoon salt
⅛ teaspoon cream of tartar

Bake in preheated 375° F. oven for 35 minutes.

ROLLED MUSHROOM SOUFFLÉ

Even if you do not have a soufflé dish, you can still have a soufflé. Make it in the form of a jelly roll instead. The proportions of the ingredients have been changed slightly from those of a regular soufflé to make it easier to roll. This makes an elegant lunch.

Serves 6
Preheat oven to 325° F.

Soufflé:
4 tablespoons butter
½ cup flour
2 cups milk
4 eggs, separated
¼ teaspoon salt
⅛ teaspoon cream of tartar
1 cup toasted bread crumbs

Sauce:
1 cup sour cream
½ cup finely chopped chives

Filling:
2 tablespoons butter
1 onion, finely chopped
1 pound mushrooms, finely chopped
1 cup diced boiled ham
2 tablespoons chopped pimento
2 tablespoons lemon juice
½ teaspoon salt
Freshly ground black pepper to taste
3 tablespoons sour cream

1. Oil a 15-by-10-inch jelly-roll pan. Line the pan with wax paper, allowing 2 inches of overlap at each short end of the pan. Oil the paper lightly and dust with flour. Shake out the excess flour.

2. To prepare the soufflé, melt the butter in a saucepan. Stir in the flour and add the milk gradually.

3. Remove the pan from the heat and stir in the egg yolks.

4. In a bowl, beat the egg whites with the salt and cream of tartar until they stand in soft peaks.

5. Stir 1 cup of the egg whites into the hot sauce. Pour the sauce over the remaining egg whites and fold the mixture gently, over and over, until it is barely combined.

6. Spread the mixture into the prepared pan and bake for 40 minutes until it is lightly firm and the edges pull away from the side of the pan. (Be careful not to overcook the soufflé or it will crack when it is rolled. It will crack slightly anyway, but not as much as if it is overcooked.)

7. While the soufflé is baking, prepare the filling. Heat the butter in a frying pan, add the onion, and fry for 3 minutes until softened.

8. Add the mushrooms and continue cooking for 5 minutes.

9. Stir in the ham, pimento, lemon juice, salt, pepper, and sour cream.

10. Sprinkle the surface of the baked soufflé with bread crumbs.

11. Cover with a piece of wax paper cut 4 inches longer than the jelly-roll pan. Cover with the back of a cookie sheet and invert the soufflé onto the cookie sheet.

12. Peel off the paper on which the soufflé was baked. Spread surface with the mushroom mixture and roll onto a jelly-roll board from the longest side, as if you were rolling a jelly roll.

13. Serve immediately with a sauce of sour cream combined with chopped chives and a tossed salad.

Note: Any of the other suggested soufflé combinations may also be used instead of this mushroom and ham filling.

DESSERT SOUFFLÉS

Many hot dessert soufflés are made in exactly the same way as entrée soufflés except that the inside of the dish and the collar are sprinkled with sugar, and ¼ cup sugar is added to the basic mixture. As the base of a soufflé is a neutral vehicle, be sure to select very flavorful fruits and enhance their flavor with liqueurs. Any of the following fruits may be substituted for the cheese in the basic mixture, prepared in a 1½-quart soufflé dish. All are served with a light dusting of sifted powdered sugar and mounds of whipped cream.

STRAWBERRY SOUFFLÉ

Add 1 cup sliced strawberries sprinkled with 1 tablespoon sugar and 2 tablespoons Grand Marnier.

RASPBERRY SOUFFLÉ

Add 1 cup whole raspberries and 2 tablespoons of Framboise. Three drops of red food coloring make this a more beautiful soufflé.

PEACH SOUFFLÉ

Add 1 cup sliced, peeled peaches and 2 tablespoons white rum.

BLACK CHERRY SOUFFLÉ

Add 1 cup canned, pitted, and chopped black cherries and 2 table-spoons brandy.

CHOCOLATE SOUFFLÉ

Chocolate soufflés tend to sink in the middle because the chocolate makes the mixture heavy. To prevent this from happening, the ingredients for this soufflé have been adjusted slightly.

Serves 4
Preheat oven to 375° F.

1 teaspoon butter	¼ cup sugar
2 tablespoons flour	1 teaspoon instant coffee
6 ounces sweet chocolate	4 egg yolks
2 tablespoons rum	5 egg whites
2 tablespoons butter	¼ teaspoon salt
3 tablespoons flour	⅛ teaspoon cream of tartar
1¼ cups milk	

1. Prepare a 1½-quart soufflé dish following the directions on page 74. Unlike the other dessert soufflés, this one requires that you butter the dish and the upper third of the collar and sprinkle with flour rather than sugar.

2. Break the chocolate into small pieces and put them on a plate. Put

the plate over a pan of simmering water and cover with another plate. Place the pan over low heat for approximately 10 minutes until the chocolate has melted. Stir in the rum with a rubber spatula.

3. Heat the butter in a saucepan until it is hot and bubbling.

4. Stir in the flour and cook over low heat for 1 minute, stirring constantly.

5. Stir in the milk gradually, add the sugar and instant coffee, and continue stirring with a wire whisk to obtain a smooth sauce. Remove the pan from the heat.

6. Stir in the egg yolks and the melted chocolate and rum mixture.

7. In a bowl, beat the egg whites with the salt and cream of tartar until they stand in soft peaks.

8. Stir about ¾ cup of the egg whites into the hot chocolate sauce. Pour the sauce over the remaining egg whites. Fold gently over and over. Do not try to mix in every island of egg white. They will disappear in the cooking, and too much mixing will make the mixture deflate. Transfer the mixture to the prepared soufflé dish.

9. Set the soufflé dish in a pan of hot water and bake in a preheated oven for 45 minutes until firm. Remove the collar. Dust with sifted powdered sugar and serve with whipped cream.

GRAND MARNIER SOUFFLÉ I

Serves 4
Preheat oven to 375° F.

2 tablespoons butter	1 teaspoon vanilla extract
3 tablespoons flour	4 egg yolks
1 cup milk	6 egg whites
2 tablespoons Grand Marnier	¼ teaspoon salt
Grated rind of 1 orange	⅛ teaspoon cream of tartar

1. Prepare a 1½-quart soufflé dish. Heat the butter in a saucepan until it is hot and bubbling.

2. Add the flour and cook over low heat for 1 minute, stirring constantly.

3. Stir in the milk gradually with a wire whisk to obtain a smooth sauce. Remove the pan from the heat.

4. Stir in the Grand Marnier, grated orange rind, vanilla extract, and egg yolks.

5. In a bowl, beat the egg whites with the salt and cream of tartar until they stand in soft peaks.

6. Stir about 1 cup of the beaten egg whites into the hot sauce. Pour the sauce over the remaining egg whites and fold them together, using a rubber spatula; do not try to incorporate every puff of egg white.

7. Pile the soufflé into the prepared dish and place in a preheated oven. Close the door gently. Bake for 30 minutes.

8. Remove the collar and serve the soufflé immediately.

GRAND MARNIER SOUFFLÉ II (CRÊPE SOUFFLÉ)

When you are able to grasp the idea that a soufflé is just a pretentious white sauce, you need not stand in awe of it any more. You can also say to yourself that *crêpe* is just a word used to enable a restaurant to charge four dollars for a couple of pancakes. Reducing the concept to absurdity should not, however, discourage you from preparing this triumphant dessert—a Grand Marnier soufflé served *inside* individual crêpes!

Serves 8
Preheat oven to 375° F.

1. Butter two 10-by-12-inch baking dishes (or individual dishes).

2. Prepare 16 crêpes using the Basic Crêpe Batter recipe, and prepare the Grand Marnier Soufflé I mixture using only 4, instead of 6, egg whites.

3. Place 4 tablespoons of the soufflé mixture on half a crêpe and fold the other half over to cover the soufflé.

4. Place the filled crêpes in the baking dishes, leaving about ½ inch of space between them to allow the soufflés to expand and puff in the oven.

5. Bake in the center of the oven for 15 minutes until the soufflé mixture has set. Serve immediately with Melba Sauce.

MELBA SAUCE

Yield: 1 cup

1 package frozen raspberries
Grated rind and juice of 1 orange
Juice of ½ lemon

1 tablespoon Kirsch or Grand Marnier

1. Thaw the raspberries and place with their juice in a blender. Add grated orange rind and juice and lemon juice. Blend for a minute.
2. Strain the sauce to remove the raspberry seeds and add the liqueur.

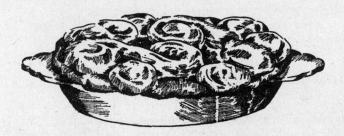

GRAND MARNIER SOUFFLÉ III (OMELETTE SOUFFLÉ)

Sometimes a preparation acquires a name because it seems to bear some resemblance to another dish. This glorious dessert is not a soufflé, made in a traditional soufflé dish, but the *idea* of a light, airy dessert resembles a soufflé. It is a spectacularly elegant and ethereal dish, but it is surprisingly easy to make, and you cannot go wrong. Spirits, as you know, have a tendency to rise, so they carry the soufflé with them.

If you have a large pastry bag, fit it with a No. 6 plain tube and decorate the unbaked soufflé with part of the mixture, making curlicues and arabesques all over the top. As it bakes, the decoration will stand out in relief like the carving on a Victorian table.

Serves 4
Preheat oven to 400° F.

1 teaspoon butter	2 tablespoons brandy
1 teaspoon sugar	8 egg whites
6 egg yolks	¼ teaspoon salt
¾ cup sugar	⅛ teaspoon cream of tartar
2 tablespoons Grand Marnier	

1. Butter a 10-by-12-inch baking dish or large oval baking dish. Sprinkle with 1 teaspoon sugar and a few drops of brandy.
2. Beat the egg yolks and ¾ cup sugar until very, very thick.
3. Add the Grand Marnier and brandy gradually and continue beating for 5 minutes.
4. In another bowl, beat the egg whites with the salt and cream of tartar until they stand in soft peaks.
5. Fold the egg yolks into the egg whites very gently. This soufflé will rise as the air which is beaten into it expands in the oven. If you stir the mixture rather than folding it over and over, you will lose all the air.
6. Pour three-quarters of the mixture into the prepared dish. Use the remaining quarter to decorate the surface, using a pastry bag.
7. Bake in a preheated oven for 18 minutes. Serve with whipped cream or Melba Sauce or both.

GRAND MARNIER SOUFFLÉ IV (FROZEN MOUSSE SOUFFLÉ)

So-called cold soufflés are not soufflés at all but mousses that are lightened with air and molded with gelatin. Then there is this soufflé, which is also not a true soufflé made from a white sauce. The recipe is included to show that there are exceptions to all rules, and a rose is not always a rose . . . but it tastes scrumptious nevertheless!

Serves 6

4 egg yolks
½ cup sugar
Grated rind of 1 orange
2 tablespoons Grand Marnier
1 cup heavy cream

1. Beat the egg yolks and sugar together until they are very, very thick.

2. Add the grated rind and the Grand Marnier. Continue beating for 2 minutes until the mixture is thick again.

3. Beat the cream until it is the same consistency as the egg mixture and combine with the egg mixture.

4. Freeze in individual dishes or in scooped-out orange halves.

5. poaching

POACHED EGGS · EGGS FLORENTINE · EGGS BENEDICT · POACHED
CHICKEN BREASTS WITH CREAM SAUCE · NEW ENGLAND BOILED
DINNER · POACHED BLUE FISH WITH BUTTER SAUCE · FLOUNDER WITH
WHITE GRAPES (VÉRONIQUE) · POACHED SALMON STEAKS · RED
SNAPPER WITH TOMATOES · LOBSTER MAYONNAISE

To poach food is to cook it in a liquid until it becomes tender, but without losing its firmness. Poached food is comforting to body and soul. It is uncomplicated, unhurried, and undemanding. The aim is to maintain the poaching liquid at a Mona Lisa smile rather than an uproarious Franz Hals belly laugh. The technique remains the same whether you poach an egg or a chicken breast, a salmon steak, a "boiled" lobster, or a New England "boiled" dinner.

POACHED EGGS
Serves 4

- 1 teaspoon salt
- 1 teaspoon vinegar (or lemon juice)
- 8 fresh eggs

- 3 tablespoons butter (for toast)
- 8 pieces buttered toast, freshly made

> *There is nothing more simple than greatness.*
> RALPH WALDO EMERSON

1. Fill a very large saucepan with water. Add salt and vinegar (or lemon juice).* Bring water to the simmering point.

2. Stir the water with a spoon so it is swirling gently around the pan.

3. Break open the eggs and lower them one at a time into the slowly revolving water. The whites will immediately encase the yolks to form a tidy package.

4. Lower the heat until no bubbles expire on the surface of the water and poach eggs for 4 to 5 minutes, until set. If you decide to serve the eggs later, remove them from the poaching water and place them in a bowl of warm water. They will stay hot as long as the water remains hot, but the yolks will stay soft and not continue to cook.

5. Serve eggs on hot buttered toast.

* The addition of vinegar or lemon juice makes the water slightly acid and causes the eggs to become firmer and hold their oval shape.

EGGS FLORENTINE

An inspired breakfast, brunch, lunch, or midnight supper dish.

Serves 4
Preheat oven to 425° F.

2 tablespoons butter
1 pound fresh spinach, cooked
Salt and pepper to taste
1 tablespoon butter
1 tablespoon flour
¾ cup milk

⅓ cup grated Swiss (or Gruyère) cheese
8 poached eggs
3 tablespoons grated Parmesan cheese
¼ cup bread crumbs
1 tablespoon butter

1. Add 2 tablespoons butter to the hot spinach and season with salt and pepper. Place in a baking dish and keep it warm in the oven.

2. Melt 1 tablespoon butter, stir in flour, and add milk gradually. Add Swiss (or Gruyère) cheese to sauce.

3. Place hot poached eggs on bed of spinach. Coat with cheese sauce. Add Parmesan cheese and bread crumbs and dot with butter.

4. Place in oven for 6 to 8 minutes until very hot.

EGGS BENEDICT

Serves 6

6 poached eggs
4 egg yolks
Salt and pepper to taste
Dash of cayenne pepper
Juice of 1 lemon (3 tablespoons)
3 whole English muffins

1½ sticks butter (12 tablespoons)
6 slices Canadian bacon (or boiled ham)
6 slices black truffle (or dash of paprika)

1. Remove eggs from poaching liquid. Place in a bowl of warm water.

2. To prepare Hollandaise Sauce, use the recipe on page 69, or heat butter in a small saucepan until hot but not boiling. Place egg yolks, salt, pepper, cayenne, and lemon juice in a blender. Turn on motor and add melted butter in a slow stream. Turn off motor as soon as all the butter has been absorbed.

3. Split and toast muffins and broil bacon. Place a slice of bacon (or ham), then a poached egg, on each muffin half.

4. Coat each egg with warm Hollandaise Sauce. Garnish with a slice of truffle or a dash of paprika.

POACHED CHICKEN BREASTS WITH CREAM SAUCE

Serves 6

6 whole chicken breasts, cut in half
Salt and pepper to taste
Juice of 1 lemon
2 tablespoons butter
⅓ cup chicken broth
2 tablespoons butter
½ cup chicken broth

½ cup white wine
½ cup heavy cream
Salt and pepper to taste
2 teaspoons cornstarch, dissolved in 1 tablespoon cold water
3 truffles, sliced (or 2 tablespoons finely chopped parsley)

1. Remove skin and bones from chicken breasts and arrange in a buttered baking dish. Season with salt and pepper, sprinkle with lemon juice, and dot with butter. Pour the chicken broth around the breasts. Cover with aluminum foil.

2. Simmer over very low heat for 15 minutes until the breasts are white and tender.

3. In the meantime, prepare the cream sauce. Place butter, broth, wine, cream, salt, and pepper in a small, heavy saucepan. Simmer over low heat until reduced to half of the original quantity.

4. Check seasoning, adding more salt and pepper if necessary.

5. Pour juices from chicken into the saucepan.

6. Thicken sauce with cornstarch, dissolved in cold water.

7. To serve, prepare a ring of rice; fill the ring with hot cooked chopped spinach (or any other vegetable); arrange chicken breasts around the rice ring and on top of the spinach; spoon sauce over the chicken. Garnish with sliced truffles (or finely chopped parsley).

NEW ENGLAND BOILED DINNER

This should properly be called New England poached dinner but the Pilgrims, who invented the dish, did not consider "poaching" to be proper.

Serves 6

2½ pounds corned beef (or beef brisket)
1 bay leaf
1 teaspoon dried thyme
3 sprigs parsley
1 teaspoon peppercorns
2 onions, sliced
2 carrots, sliced
2 stalks celery, sliced

Accompaniments:
1 small cabbage, cut into wedges
5 carrots, sliced
6 potatoes, halved
3 parsnips, cut into cubes
1 small turnip, cut into cubes

Dressing:
1 cup heavy cream
3 tablespoons prepared white horseradish
Juice of ½ lemon

1. Place the beef in a casserole, adding enough water to cover the beef, herbs, and the first group of vegetables. Cover and simmer over low heat for 2½ hours until the beef is tender.

2. Tie each cabbage wedge with a piece of string so it will retain its shape.

3. Cook the accompaniment vegetables in separate saucepans in salted simmering water for 15 to 20 minutes until each is cooked.

4. Drain the vegetables and remove the string from the cabbage wedges.

5. Whip the cream and combine with horseradish and lemon juice.

6. Slice beef and serve, with vegetables and horseradish dressing on the side.

Poaching Fish

Large and small whole fish, fish steaks, and fish fillets are poached by total immersion in a liquid. This liquid can be water, a combination of water and wine, fish stock, or milk. Aromatic vegetables, such as onions, carrots, and celery, may also be added to the liquid along with a sprig or two of parsley or other herbs.

Fish may be poached either on top of the stove or in the oven. As a general rule fish one inch or less in thickness is cooked in eight to ten minutes. When cooking fish steaks and whole fish, allow ten minutes poaching time for each inch of thickness.

The cooking time for fish is surprisingly short, and there is a greater likelihood of overcooking rather than undercooking. It becomes tough if it is overcooked.

The fish is ready for eating when it flakes and separates easily at the touch of a fork and has become opaque all the way through.

POACHED BLUE FISH WITH BUTTER SAUCE

Serves 6
Preheat oven to 300° F. (optional)

3 pounds blue fish in one piece
½ onion, thinly sliced
Juice of ½ lemon
3 stalks parsley
1 bay leaf
Pinch of salt
4 scallions, finely chopped

½ teaspoon tarragon
1 tablespoon white vinegar
½ cup white wine
12 tablespoons butter
Juice of ½ lemon
Salt and pepper to taste

1. Place fish in a poacher or large skillet. Cover with water and add onion, lemon juice, parsley stalks, bay leaf, and salt.
2. Simmer over low heat or in a preheated oven, allowing 10 minutes for each inch of thickness, until the fish is white, opaque, and flaky.
3. Simmer scallions and tarragon in vinegar and wine for 5 minutes.
4. Strain liquid and discard scallions and tarragon.
5. Heat butter until hot but not boiling.
6. Using a wire whisk, beat the hot butter into the flavored vinegar

and wine. Add the butter gradually and beat continuously to form a medium-thin butter sauce. Add lemon juice, salt and pepper.

7. Spoon sauce over fish. Serve with broiled tomato halves, green beans, and boiled potatoes.

FLOUNDER WITH WHITE GRAPES (VÉRONIQUE)

Serves 4
Preheat oven to 350° F.

1½ pounds flounder fillets
Salt and pepper to taste
½ cup white wine
½ cup water
1 tablespoon cornstarch, dissolved in 2 tablespoons cold water

2 egg yolks
½ cup heavy cream
½ cup white seedless grapes, canned

1. Cut each fish fillet in half lengthwise. Season with salt and pepper. Roll each fillet and fasten with a toothpick.

2. Stand fish rolls in a buttered baking dish. Add wine and water. Cover with a piece of foil. Bake in a preheated oven for 10 minutes until fish is white and opaque. Transfer the fish to a hot serving plate.

3. Boil poaching liquid until reduced to ¾ cup.

4. Thicken liquid with cornstarch, dissolved in cold water.

5. In a bowl, combine egg yolks and cream and add to the sauce.

6. Drain grapes and heat in hot water for 3 minutes.

7. Spoon sauce over fish. Garnish with grapes.

POACHED SALMON STEAKS

Serves 4

4 salmon steaks (or 1 piece
  salmon weighing 1½ pounds)
½ onion, thinly sliced
1 teaspoon whole peppercorns
1 bay leaf

4 sprigs parsley
½ teaspoon thyme
1 teaspoon salt
Juice of ½ lemon

1. Place the salmon in a skillet or a fish poacher and cover with cold water.

2. Tie the onion, peppercorns, bay leaf, parsley, and thyme in a cheesecloth bag. Add the herb bag, salt, and lemon juice to the skillet.

3. Simmer, uncovered, allowing 10 minutes over low heat for each inch of thickness. The water should be barely moving, not boiling.

4. Lift salmon from the water and drain on a wire rack.

5. Serve with small potatoes, garnished with parsley and fresh green peas.

RED SNAPPER WITH TOMATOES

Serves 4

1½ pounds red snapper
2 tablespoons butter
½ onion, chopped
1 cup dry white wine (or ½ cup
  white vermouth and ½ cup
  water)
Juice of ½ lemon
½ teaspoon salt

4 tomatoes, peeled, seeded, and
  chopped
½ teaspoon finely chopped
  parsley
1 tablespoon cornstarch, dissolved in 2 tablespoons cold
  water
2 egg yolks
¼ cup heavy cream

1. Place fish in a shallow pan just large enough to hold it. Add butter, onion, wine (or vermouth and water), lemon juice, and salt.

2. Cover and simmer over low heat, allowing 10 minutes of cooking time for each inch of thickness.

3. Transfer fish to a serving dish.

4. Strain the poaching liquid into a saucepan and boil it until it is reduced to about ¾ cup. Add tomatoes and parsley.

5. Thicken into a sauce by adding cornstarch, dissolved in water.

6. In a bowl, combine egg yolks with cream and stir into the sauce. (The egg yolks and cream will enrich the sauce and give it a golden color.)

7. Spoon sauce over fish.

Lobster

The lobster cavorts in the waters of the Atlantic Ocean, where he spends five years gobbling up clams, mussels, flounder, mackerel, and tuna to become the king of the sea himself. All this effort is expended to make 1¼ pounds of lobster meat—enough to serve one person for one meal, accompanied by a drop or two of melted butter. What a magnificent gesture! During this time the lobster has changed his shell-coat twenty to twenty-five times in an unequal struggle against nature, lobstermen, and poachers to bring his shell to just the right size, color, and weight for the table.

BUYING A LOBSTER

Lobster meat is perhaps the choicest of the fruits of the sea, but it still must be purchased with extreme care. Unless you buy your lobster directly from the fisherman, the chances are that you will have to peer into a seaweedy aquarium and trust to luck. If you have the chance, before you buy find out how long the lobster has been in the tank. Deprived of its natural food, the lobster lives off its own meat, and the quality of its dinner will inevitably be better than yours!

An experienced person can weigh the lobster in his hand and know whether the shell is too heavy in relation to the meat. However, this takes a considerable amount of experience; just knowing the date the lobster arrived in the tank is as much of a guarantee as most of us can get. The less time that has elapsed since it was in its natural habitat, the more active and hence better-tasting the lobster will be. Select the most active lobster you see. If the lobster has actually died, regard it with extreme suspicion and leave the market without it. If it dies in your care, do not wait more than twenty-four hours to cook it, and keep it under refrigeration until you do. If you buy a lobster that has already been cooked, check its tail. If it is tightly curled under the body, it will snap back when extended and it will be fine. A flaccid tail indicates that the poor thing was long gone—so strike it from your dinner plans immediately.

Incidentally, the female, egg-bearing lobster is considered to have even tenderer meat than the narrow, swivel-hipped male varieties. It is difficult to tell the male or "cock" lobster from the hen unless they are lying on a chopping block side by side. The hen is slightly smaller and has a shade broader tail than the cock. The coral, or red egg sac, of the female lobster is prized as a delicacy. It is the "caviar" of the lobster and is used to give color and richness to lobster sauces, butters, and mayonnaise.

The easiest way to keep a live lobster is to take home some seaweed from the tank too. Lay the lobster on a bed of seaweed and let it explore the refrigerator for a while. (Impede its curiosity by keeping it inside the bag in which it was purchased.) If you decide to be motherly and fill up the sink with tap water to give it a bath to frolic in, it will drown. Tap water contains all the wrong things for lobsters; and fluorides, though no doubt remarkable for preventing cavities, do nothing to prolong the life of a lobster. It is probably best just to come home and pop it into a pot right away and deal with the partially or completely cooked lobster meat later in the day.

COOKING THE LOBSTER

They say that lobsters are silly creatures and feel no pain because their nervous system is so primitive. Winston Churchill once made a speech in the House of Commons proposing that the Ministry of Fisheries be linked with the Ministry of Agriculture because, in the minds of the English people, fish and chips were always considered together! From this reasoning, it will not surprise you to know that the gentle people of England, being concerned about the possibility of prolonged and needless agony of the lobster, commissioned the Royal Society for the Prevention of Cruelty to Animals to perform a study on the least painful way in which the lobster can meet its fate.

It is quite difficult to assess the validity of their conclusions, for no norm can possibly be established to serve as a control. Nevertheless, it was decided that it seemed most sportsmanlike to lower the lobster into the pot head first so it could at least see where it was going! Some say that the lobster screams as it goes into the pot; others hasten to assure you that this is merely the escape of air under high pressure. Yet, other people prefer to make an approach from the rear and cut the lobster up alive—after first severing the spinal cord—and then broil it. Lobsters prepared in this manner tend to thrash about rather alarmingly, but disregard these imbecilic movements and be the master of your own kitchen. The results will undoubtedly prove you were right, as usual.

LOBSTER MAYONNAISE

Serves 6

> 3 3-pound lobsters or 6 1½-pound
> live lobsters

1. Bring a large pot of salted water to the boiling point, adding a few strands of seaweed if available. There should be sufficient water to cover the lobster by 2 inches.

2. Lower the lobsters into the water head first. Do not cover the pot and maintain the water at the simmering point for 15 minutes. Adding more water if it boils away too rapidly (if you are using larger lobsters add 4 minutes cooking for each additional pound), time the lobsters from the moment they are put in the pot.

3. Remove the lobsters from the pot and allow them to cool for 5 minutes.

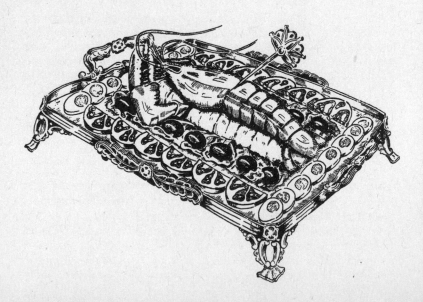

4. Turn a lobster onto its back with its legs in the air. Extend the tail and hold it down with a kitchen towel.

5. Cut the membrane to which the legs are attached on each side of the back shell. Remove and discard the membrane and lift the tail meat out in one piece. Cut the meat into slices. (The tail meat will come out very easily.)

6. Remove and discard the stomach sac and contents of the head cavity. The green "tomalle" is used to enrich hot sauces but cannot be used in this recipe. However, keep a watch for the red coral found at the top of the tail meat. Put the coral to one side to be added to the mayonnaise. (Gentlemen lobsters will, of course, not have coral.)

7. Wrap each claw in a kitchen towel and crack the shell with a heavy rolling pin, a lobster-cracking utensil, or a hammer. Remove the lobster meat and cut into bite-sized pieces.

8. When you come to the third lobster, leave the head meat inside the cavity and simply fold the membrane back over the body when the tail meat is removed. Remove the claws and extract the meat. This lobster will be used to garnish the dish and will become the centerpiece while the dinner is eaten.

9. On a large oval or rectangular serving tray, lay a trough of freshly washed Boston or bibb lettuce leaves. Let the shape of the bed of lettuce conform roughly to the long Y shape of the lobster. Pile the lobster meat on top of the lettuce, putting a greater quantity at the top of the Y to give the presentation some height. Brush the shell of the third (garnishing) lobster with oil to make it shine and lay it over the meat, placing the head over the elevation of the pile. Fold the membrane and legs back over the empty tail shell and extend the legs over the lobster meat. Garnish the tray with alternating slices of cucumber, tomato, and hard-boiled egg quarters. Serve with homemade Mayonnaise, crusty bread, and chilled white wine.

An epicure is . . . one who gets nothing except the cream of everything but cheerfully makes the best of it.

OLIVER HERFORD

6. roasting

ROAST PRIME RIBS OF BEEF · ROAST LEG OF LAMB · ROAST
BUTTERFLIED LEG OF LAMB · ROAST RACK OF LAMB · ROAST PORK
LOIN · ROAST CHICKEN WITH CANADIAN BACON AND COTTAGE CHEESE
· STUFFED HONEY-GLAZED DUCKLING · GLAZED BAKED HAM · BAKED
STUFFED STRIPED BASS · BAKED SEA BASS

Roasting is one of the two methods of cooking large pieces of meat,
whole chickens, turkeys, ducks, or whole fish with dry heat. (Fish and
ham are said to be *baked* rather than roasted, but the two terms are synonymous.) The purpose is to obtain a firm exterior while the interior
becomes tender and remains moist. The ideal way to cook a roast is to
suspend it on a rack so that the hot air can circulate freely around it. If
you don't have a roasting rack, you can place the roast on a wire cake-
cooling rack over a baking pan. This will prevent the underside of the
roast from frying and stewing in its own fat.

All roasts are cooked uncovered. Large cuts of meat that are covered
with a layer of fat, such as prime ribs, pork loin, or leg of lamb, do not
need to be basted; its own melting fat will keep the meat bathed in moisture. Smaller roasts, those weighing less than three-and-one-half pounds,
are improved if they are basted every thirty minutes with their own

drippings to prevent the meat from becoming dry. The larger the roast, the moister it will be. It is best not to cook less than two ribs of beef; a smaller roast, with a large exposed surface, will dry out before it is completely cooked.

There is less shrinkage of the meat if it is roasted at 350° F. or even 300° F. rather than at higher temperatures. Searing the meat at an initially high temperature of 450° F. for fifteen minutes, as some experts recommend, causes a considerable loss of moisture and an almost immediate shrinkage. In addition, the fat drippings burn and give an unpleasant taste to the developing pan juices; they then cannot be used to form a sauce.

TIMING THE ROAST

A rigid rule of cooking meat demands that roasted beef, pork, lamb, chicken, and turkey be cooked for twenty minutes per pound. This would be an excellent guide if every piece of meat was of the same age, quality, and shape and every oven matched every other oven in efficiency and accuracy. Since life is made up of many variables, however, it may be wiser to trust a meat thermometer than an arbitrarily dogmatic statement. Insert the meat thermometer into the deepest part of the meat, being careful to see that it does not rest against the bone; otherwise you will not be taking the temperature of the meat but of the bone—a matter of passing scientific interest but of gastronomical irrelevance.

Even with the most conscientious use of a thermometer some degree of judgment is still required. A twelve-pound roast of aged prime ribs will take less time to cook than a twelve-pound roast of unaged beef. This is because top-quality aged beef is marbled with fat, which makes the meat less dense; the fat itself conducts the heat more quickly than the compact meat. A tough shoulder roast requires a longer cooking time than a tender filet of beef of the same weight and shape. A rolled leg of lamb without a bone takes longer to cook than meat containing a bone because the bone acts as an additional internal source of heat. A thin, flat piece of meat will be cooked in a much shorter period of time than a square, chunky block of meat, even though the actual weights of the two cuts are identical. Remember, too, that meat continues to cook for at least five minutes after it has been removed from the oven as a result of its own internal temperature. This extension of the cooking will result in raising the internal temperature by two or three degrees and may mean the difference between rare and medium-rare. Err on the side of having the meat very slightly underdone rather than over-done.

CARVING THE MEAT

If the meat is carved immediately after it is taken from the oven, the juices spill out in great profusion. In theory, it would seem that if you simply spoon them back over the meat, all will be well. Unfortunately, the result of this tactic is a dry, leathery slice of meat afloat in liquid. The liquid cools rapidly, making the roast potatoes soggy and giving the plate a generally unappetizing and mildly barbaric appearance. When, however, the meat is allowed to rest peacefully for fifteen minutes, the juices settle themselves in the meat, making it firmer and easier to carve. Keep the meat covered with foil during the resting period so that it doesn't get cold.

A standing rib roast is easier to carve if the short ribs have been removed by the butcher. You can roast them at the same time as the long ribs, using them as a rack to elevate the roast. The roasted short ribs can then be reheated and used at another meal.

ROAST PRIME RIBS OF BEEF

If the roast is larger than you need for a single meal, remove it from the oven while it is still very rare in the center. (The thermometer reading should be 120° F.) Carve the beef from both ends and reserve the center for preparing new dishes—for example, Beef Stroganoff.

Serves 12
Preheat oven to 350° F.

1 8-rib standing roast of beef

1. Stand the beef fat side up on a roasting rack in a shallow roasting pan, or use the short ribs to form a rack. Do not salt the roast before it is cooked; the flavor of the salt will not penetrate the meat and tends to draw out the meat juices.
2. Insert a meat thermometer into the center of the beef, making sure the tip does not touch the bone.
3. Roast the beef in the lower third of a preheated oven until it reaches the correct degree of doneness.

> For rare beef: allow 18 minutes to the pound
> (internal meat-thermometer reading 130° F.)
>
> For medium beef: allow 20 minutes to the pound
> (internal meat-thermometer reading 140° F.)
>
> For well-done beef: allow 25 minutes to the pound
> (internal meat-thermometer reading 150° F.)

4. Let the beef rest for 15 minutes before carving. The traditional accompaniment is, of course, Yorkshire Pudding (page 175).

Salt

The Greeks consecrated it to the gods, and Plutarch called it the condiment of condiments. Although the Romans mistakenly thought it occurred naturally as a single element, like iron, they were right in recognizing the worth of the salt of the earth! It was the commodity on which trade was built between the Aegean and southern Russia. In fact, the road on which the salt traveled was named Via Celaria. A daily ration of salt was given to the Roman soldiers. The portion allotted was known as the salarium, *from which our modern word* salary *is derived.*

Even before these times, salt was being traded in Tibet and Abyssinia. Marco Polo wrote long, long ago about the value of salt in the financial manipulations of Mongolian emperors.

We tend to think of salt as being used to flavor and preserve food, but at one time it was used to preserve people, too! The soldiers of ancient times wore quilted jackets padded with salt to insulate themselves against the cold . . . as well as the slings and arrows of outrageous fortune.

Long ago the wealth of a household could be easily gauged by the size of the block of salt kept at the entrance. If a robber should fall over the salt, he would have to leave immediately (and empty-handed) because his clumsiness would result in a change of his luck!

With our increasing consumption of "convenience" foods, we are tending to add more and more salt in a futile effort to achieve some taste—any taste. In medieval England, those who were seated "below the salt" were not privileged to have salt at all, and perhaps in the long run they were the fortunate ones! Remember the old adage about he who laughs last? And by the way, what ever happened to Lot's wife?

Cooking with Herbs

Everybody must know by now that if it is good to cook with herbs, it is positively inspired to cook with fresh herbs. "Oh yes," they say, "I always use herbs" and, allying themselves with the angels, shake some garlic salt into the stew, smack their lips, and enroll themselves confidently in the brotherhood of gourmet folk. How much better it would be to use an honest pinch of salt (though even salt contains additives, to keep it flowing in the dampest of weather).

The art of cooking with herbs is as old as time itself and maybe even older. This does not mean, though, that there are such things as vintage herbs. Herbs and wine have a limited lifespan, so it is best not to keep them until they die or you do. If you are still using the same pot of thyme that has been in the kitchen for as long as you can remember, it might be worth examining it critically. Raise the lid suspiciously and take an explorative sniff. If the aroma is feeble and the color has faded, the taste will undoubtedly have diminished too. Throw it out as if it were a vase of dead flowers, for you may as well add a pinch of dust from the vacuum cleaner. Buy a new supply of freshly dried herbs and keep them in a temperate zone in your kitchen. Do not store them in one of those cute racks over the stove where they will marginally cook and cool every day.

Be bold with herbs and spices. Try new ones that you have never tasted before. Basil is as fine (and as Italian) as oregano, and chervil— good for your memory—is excellent in potato soup. Coriander, which once grew in the Hanging Gardens of Babylon, is now used principally to flavor gin, but it can also add an interesting flavor to a cake. Cumin

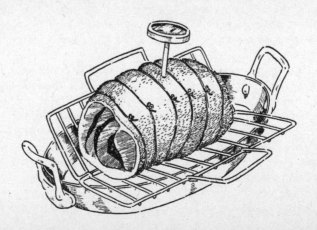

will keep your lover faithful, and if you have any left over, you can add it discreetly to the stew. Err on the side of being miserly with herbs rather than overgenerous. If somebody remarks on how clever it was of you to think of putting dill in the tomato soup, you have overdone it.

> Rosemary has become the symbol of remembrance because it was once used as a cure for forgetfulness.

ROAST LEG OF LAMB

A roast without a bone is very quick to cook and easy to carve, although the cooking time is slightly longer than a roast with the bone in.

Serves 6
Preheat oven to 350° F.

6 slices firm-textured bread with crusts removed
3 tablespoons finely chopped parsley
3 tablespoons chopped chives
2 teaspoons thyme
1 teaspoon rosemary
2 cloves garlic, finely chopped

1 teaspoon salt
Freshly ground black pepper to taste
¾ cup whole shelled pistachio nuts
1 4-pound leg of lamb, weighed with bone removed
2 tablespoons butter, melted

1. Place 2 slices of the bread, the herbs, garlic, salt, and pepper in a blender and blend until bread crumbs are formed and the herbs are finely chopped. Add the pistachio nuts and spread onto the inner surface of the lamb. Roll the lamb tightly and tie with string at 2-inch intervals.

2. Make bread crumbs from the remaining bread. Roll the lamb firmly on all sides in the crumbs, covering the surface evenly.

3. Place the lamb on a roasting rack over a shallow baking dish. Drizzle the melted butter over the bread crumbs. Insert a meat thermometer into the center of the lamb.

4. Roast, uncovered, in a preheated oven, allowing 30 minutes to the pound (internal meat-thermometer reading, 160° F.). (The meat will be medium-rare.)

5. Wrap the lamb in aluminum foil and allow it to rest for 15 minutes before slicing.

ROAST BUTTERFLIED LEG OF LAMB

Butterflied lamb can also be broiled over charcoal on an outdoor grill or under a preheated broiler, allowing 10 minutes for each side.

Serves 6
Preheat oven to 350° F.

1 4-pound leg of lamb, weighed with bone removed and cut butterfly-style by the butcher
4 cloves garlic, cut into fine slivers

3 tablespoons butter, softened
1 teaspoon rosemary
2 tablespoons finely chopped parsley

1. Spread the lamb out. Make several small incisions in the lamb and insert the garlic slivers into the cuts. Combine the butter, rosemary, and parsley and spread over the inner surface of the lamb.

2. Place the lamb on a broiler pan, buttered side up, and roast, allowing 10 minutes to the pound. Allow the lamb to rest for 10 minutes before slicing.

Serve with buttered corn, broiled tomatoes, and a jug of red wine.

Little lamb, who made thee?
Does't thou know who made thee,
Gave thee life,
And bid thee feed,
By the streams and o'er the mead?
WILLIAM BLAKE

ROAST RACK OF LAMB

There is always an occasional recipe that violates the pattern. Although all the other roasts are cooked at a moderate temperature, this one is better cooked by the following method.

Serves 6
Preheat oven to 425° F.

2 2½- to 3-pound racks of lamb with bones cracked to facilitate carving
3 tablespoons butter, melted
2 tablespoons finely chopped parsley
1 teaspoon thyme
2 teaspoons chopped chives
1 clove garlic, finely chopped
¾ cup freshly made bread crumbs
½ teaspoon salt
Freshly ground black pepper to taste

1. Brush the lamb with part of the melted butter. Place on a roasting rack and roast, uncovered, in a preheated oven for 15 minutes.
2. Meanwhile, combine the remaining ingredients. Press the mixture over the lamb. Return the lamb to the oven and continue roasting at 350° F. for 20 minutes. Allow the lamb to rest for 10 minutes and carve between the ribs.

Serve with asparagus with Hollandaise Sauce and roasted new potatoes.

ROAST PORK LOIN

Serves 6
Preheat oven to 325° F.

2 teaspoons salt
1 tablespoon dry mustard
2 teaspoons thyme
½ cup brown sugar
2 tablespoons butter, melted
1 4-pound boneless pork loin, tied at 2-inch intervals
2 cups apple juice

1. Combine salt, mustard powder, thyme, sugar, and butter in a bowl. Press the mixture firmly over the top and sides of the pork loin.
2. Place the pork on a rack over a roasting pan. Insert a meat thermometer into the center of the pork. Pour the apple juice into the roasting pan.

3. Roast, uncovered, allowing 35 minutes to the pound (internal meat-thermometer reading 180° F.).

4. Wrap the pork in aluminum foil and allow it to rest for 15 minutes before slicing.

Serve the pork with a garnish of peach halves or applesauce, mashed potatoes, and Brussels sprouts. It is also very good cold, accompanied by mustard-flavored mayonnaise and a salad.

> But I will place this carefully fed pig within the crackling oven, and I pray what nicer dish can e'er be given to man?
>
> AESCHYLUS

ROAST CHICKEN WITH CANADIAN BACON AND COTTAGE CHEESE

An odd combination, yet it is surprisingly good and a particularly valuable recipe when using a chicken taken from the freezer, which may be a little dry.

Serves 4
Preheat oven to 350° F.

1 3-pound roasting chicken	½ teaspoon salt
8 slices Canadian bacon	Freshly ground black pepper to
1 cup cottage cheese	taste
2 tablespoons butter	

1. Beginning at the neck of the chicken, run your finger beneath the skin to lift it from the chicken meat. Slide a piece of Canadian bacon beneath the skin. Use four slices for the breast, making sure each slice is flat and smooth. Arrange the remaining slices beneath the thigh skin.

2. Fill the cavity of the chicken with cottage cheese. Truss the chicken or secure the cavity with poultry lacers.

3. Place on a rack in a roasting pan, breast side up. Insert a meat thermometer into the thigh.

4. Dot the surface with butter and season with salt and pepper.

5. Bake in a preheated oven for 60 minutes (internal meat-thermometer reading 175° F.). When the thigh is pricked with the point of a paring knife and yields juice that is clear, without any trace of blood, the chicken is done.

STUFFED HONEY-GLAZED DUCKLING

This dressing can be used for turkey, chicken, or Rock Cornish hen as well as for duck. Double the recipe to stuff a turkey; halve it for a smaller bird. Leftover dressing can be frozen either cooked or uncooked.

Serves 4
Preheat oven to 350° F.

Dressing:
2 tablespoons butter
1 cup chopped walnuts
1 onion, finely chopped
3 cups freshly made bread crumbs
Grated rind of 1 lemon
½ teaspoon cinnamon
1 teaspoon sage

½ teaspoon salt
Freshly ground black pepper to taste
2 eggs, lightly beaten

1 4-pound duck
3 tablespoons butter, softened
3 tablespoons honey

1. To prepare the dressing, heat the butter in a skillet. Add the nuts and fry over moderately high heat for 3 minutes, until they are browned. Add the onion and fry with the nuts for 3 minutes until softened. Remove the pan from the heat and stir in the remaining ingredients.

2. Fill the duck cavity with the stuffing and secure it with trussing string or poultry lacers.

3. Place the duck, breast side up, on a rack in a roasting pan. Prick the skin with a fork to allow the fat to escape.

4. Combine the butter and honey and spread it over the duck.

5. Insert a meat thermometer into the plumpest part of the thigh, making sure the tip does not touch the bone. Roast the duck in a preheated oven for 1½ hours (internal meat-thermometer reading 190° F.).

6. Cut the duck into quarters with poultry shears or carve it into slices.

GLAZED BAKED HAM

For no apparent reason, roast ham is described as being "baked." The two methods of cooking are the same.

Serves 12
Preheat oven to 350° F.

1 6-pound oven-ready, fully cooked ham, with skin removed	*Glaze:*
	1 cup apricot preserves
	2 tablespoons sherry
2 cups orange juice (or cider)	2 tablespoons mild prepared mustard

1. Score the fat in a diamond pattern and place the ham, fat side up, on a roasting rack in a shallow baking dish. Insert a meat thermometer into the center of the ham, making sure the top does not touch the bone.

2. Pour the orange juice (or cider) into the baking dish and bake, uncovered, in a preheated oven. Allow 15 minutes to the pound (internal meat-thermometer reading 140° F.).

3. Prepare apricot glaze by heating the apricot preserves in a small saucepan and forcing it through a fine strainer to remove the skins. Stir in the sherry and mustard.

4. After the ham has cooked for 1½ hours, remove it from the oven and brush the surface with apricot glaze. Return the ham to the oven. Glaze the ham every 15 minutes until the total cooking time (approximately 2 hours) has elapsed. The ham is ready when it can be pierced easily with a fork.

5. Let the ham rest for 15 minutes before slicing.

Serve hot with sweet potatoes and puréed or braised vegetables or cold with a salad. Have a bottle of chilled rosé wine ready to pour.

BAKED STUFFED STRIPED BASS

This stuffing can be used for other fish, such as red snapper.

Serves 6
Preheat oven to 325° F.

1 4-pound striped bass, whole, with the head on
1 tablespoon oil
1 small onion, finely chopped
½ cup chopped celery leaves
2 tablespoons finely chopped parsley
1 tablespoon finely chopped fresh oregano or basil (or 1 teaspoon dried herbs)
1 cup freshly made bread crumbs
¼ cup white vermouth

Basting ingredients:
4 tablespoons butter, melted
½ teaspoon salt
Freshly ground black pepper to taste
1 tablespoon finely chopped fresh oregano or basil (or 1 teaspoon dried herbs)
2 teaspoons lemon juice

1. Wash and dry fish thoroughly.

2. To prepare the stuffing, heat the oil in a skillet. Fry the onion for 3 minutes until softened. Remove the pan from the heat and stir in the remaining stuffing ingredients. Fill the fish cavity with the hot stuffing and secure the opening with toothpicks or poultry lacers.

3. Brush a baking dish with oil to prevent the fish from sticking.

4. Combine the melted butter with the remaining basting ingredients and brush over the fish.

5. Bake the fish, uncovered, in a preheated oven for 18 minutes. Baste frequently with the remaining flavored butter as it is cooking.

BAKED SEA BASS

Serves 6
Preheat oven to 350° F.

1 4-pound whole bass
Juice of 1 lemon
½ teaspoon salt
Freshly ground black pepper to
taste
½ teaspoon dried chervil,
tarragon, or dill
2 tablespoons butter, melted

Sauce:
2 cups milk
½ onion, sliced
½ carrot, chopped
1 stalk celery, chopped
1 bay leaf
¼ teaspoon salt
½ teaspoon peppercorns
3 tablespoons butter
2 tablespoons flour
Juice of ½ lemon

1. Have the fish cleaned. Remove the head if you wish but leave the tail intact.

2. Season fish inside and on the surface with lemon juice, salt, pepper, and herbs. Brush the butter on the skin and place the remaining butter inside the fish.

3. Butter a baking dish and bake the fish, covered with a piece of aluminum foil, in a preheated oven for 20 minutes.

4. To prepare the sauce, simmer milk with onion, carrot, celery, bay leaf, salt, and peppercorns for 25 minutes, until the milk has reduced slightly. Strain.

5. Reserving 1 tablespoon of butter, melt the remainder and stir in flour. Add milk gradually, stirring with a wire whisk.

6. Stir in lemon juice and the reserved 1 tablespoon of butter.

7. Spoon sauce over fish and serve with mixed garden vegetables and boiled potatoes.

7. broiling

MUSHROOM-STUFFED SIRLOIN STEAK · TERIYAKI · BROILED MARINATED
FLANK STEAK · BROILED CHICKEN WITH MUSTARD · BROILED
BARBECUED SPARERIBS · BROILED HAM WITH GREEN PEPPERS ·
BROILED STRIPED BASS · BROILED TROUT · BROILED SALMON WITH
DILL SAUCE

The most succulent of broiled foods are those that contain a high
proportion of natural fat, such as thick, tender steaks and fatty fish. Thin
steaks must be broiled quickly under very high heat or they become dry
and tasteless. Tough beef, such as flank steak, is immeasurably improved
if it is marinated before it is broiled. The marinade ingredients form a
relaxing bath for the meat, soothing it into tenderness. Chicken needs
a blanket of butter to protect the delicate meat as it is broiled. The butter diffuses through the chicken and keeps it moist.

HOW TO BROIL

1. Preheat the broiler to the highest temperature possible for 10 minutes and brush the broiler rack or ridged broiling pan with oil to prevent
the food from sticking. A rack or ridged pan allows the fat to drain. If
the food stands in its own fat, it will fry as it broils.

2. Score the edges of the meat in several places to prevent them from
curling their toes under the sudden shock of intense heat. This step is
particularly important when cooking thin steaks and ham. Brush all

meats, poultry, and fish with oil or melted butter and season with pepper. Do not add salt to red meats; it causes them to bleed.

3. Place all beef steaks as close to the broiler as possible. Steaks more than 2½ inches thick should be lowered one notch after 3 minutes to prevent the outside from burning before the inside has a chance to know what is happening. Broil thin steaks as close to the heat as possible throughout the cooking time. Broil chicken, spareribs, veal, ham, and fish at least 4 inches from the heat or they become dry.

4. When the meat is ready for turning, it will tell you. Red blood spots will appear on the surface. Turn steaks with tools that do not puncture the surface, allowing the juices to escape.

5. You can tell when the meat is done by intuition, a risky method that is not highly recommended, or by smell, which is a help but not always infallible. Another method involves a certain level of initial courage but is the truest test. Press the meat with your index finger in an authoritative way. The more "done" it is, the greater will be the resistance. (Compare it mentally with the texture of raw meat.) If you do not trust your judgment, cut a piece of the meat or flake away part of the fish and look at it. The food should surprise the guests, not the cook.

Charcoal broiling takes longer than oven broiling because even on the hottest day the surface of the meat is cooled by the surrounding air.

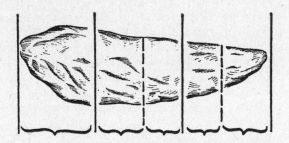

Châteaubriand

The tenderloin is the most expensive and perhaps the least flavorful of all cuts of beef. It needs a sauce or a flavorful topping to bring out its moist goodness. The tenderloin is divided into sirloin, Châteaubriand, filet tournedos, and filet mignon steaks. The filet mignon is cut from the narrowest part of the loin and the Châteaubriand from the thickest part.

The *Châteaubriand* cut is named for Monsieur Châteaubriand, a famous name dropper who used to open conversations with such phrases as "Napoleon and I . . . ." Napoleon is remembered for his pastries, among other things, but Monsieur Châteaubriand has left an even more indelible mark on gastronomic history with his steak.

The Châteaubriand steak received its name at a lunch given in honor of the gentleman himself, Vicomte François René de Châteaubriand, who had just completed a learned treatise on the origins of Christianity. Eager to please the good man who chose such exalted subjects for study, the patron of the Paris restaurant at which he was dining announced a new dish—the Châteaubriand. It consisted of a juicy piece of filet, protected on both sides by two flank steaks, symbolizing Christ between the two thieves. The outer steaks were seared under the broiler and discarded. The filet was served rare, triumphant and alone. And Monsieur Châteaubriand ate it.

MUSHROOM-STUFFED SIRLOIN STEAK

This is a good deal more interesting than the traditional sirloin steak. The steak can be stuffed in advance and left in the refrigerator until just before it is cooked. The stuffing increases the thickness of the steak, so it needs an extra couple of minutes' cooking time.

Serves 4
Preheat broiler for 10 minutes

4 sirloin steaks at least 1 inch thick
1 tablespoon vegetable oil
Freshly ground black pepper to taste

Stuffing:
2 tablespoons butter
1 onion, finely chopped
1 clove garlic, finely chopped
8 small mushrooms, finely chopped
2 slices boiled ham, diced
1 teaspoon lemon juice
2 tablespoons finely chopped parsley
½ cup freshly made bread crumbs

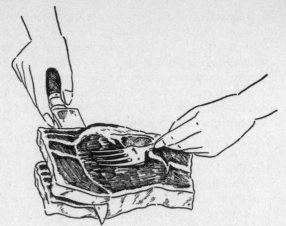

1. Cut the steak horizontally to form a pocket for the stuffing.

2. To prepare the stuffing, heat the butter in a skillet. Fry the onion and garlic for 3 minutes. Add the mushrooms and continue frying for 3 minutes more until the mushrooms are tender. Remove pan from heat and stir in ham, lemon juice, parsley, and bread crumbs.

3. Stuff the mixture into the pocket in each steak and sew the sides together or close the openings with toothpicks.

4. Brush the top of the steaks with oil and season with pepper. Oil the broiler rack. Broil close to the heat for 7 minutes on each side for rare beef, 8 minutes on each side for medium, and 10 minutes on each side for well-done beef. Serve with baked potatoes and a huge salad.

Tenderizers and Marinades

All cuts of beef have the same nutritional value. A whole steer is a miniature society, ranging from the soft, pampered filet to the hardworking chuck. The more movement a particular part of the animal has made, the more character it develops. The leaner shoulder meat is stronger, more flavorful, and tougher than a T-bone steak. In order to tenderize the tougher meats, you must either cook them slowly in a liquid or tenderize them before cooking in a relaxing bath, or marinade.

The meat tenderizers on the market are made from a papaya extract. When this substance is sprinkled on the meat, it instantly acquires a life of its own and greedily devours all the tough connective tissue in the meat. It digests your dinner for you to save you the trouble, and when it has satisfied itself, it leaves behind a flabby artifice for you to sup on.

TERIYAKI

Serves 4

1½ pounds lean round steak
   (or sirloin tip)
½ cup soy sauce
3 tablespoons brown sugar
1 tablespoon minced ginger root

1 onion, finely chopped
2 cloves garlic, finely chopped
2 tablespoons peanut oil
½ cup sake (or dry sherry)

1. Cut the beef across the grain into thin slices and place in a shallow dish.
2. Combine all the remaining ingredients and pour over the beef. Cover the dish and marinate the beef for 12 hours, turning the beef occasionally.
3. Thread the beef slices on skewers and broil over a charcoal fire or under the broiler, allowing 5 minutes on each side.

Serve with rice, broccoli, asparagus, or whatever you deem to be Japanese vegetables. Make a salad of sliced cucumbers and radishes.

BROILED MARINATED FLANK STEAK

Serves 4
Preheat broiler for 10 minutes

2 pounds flank steak
2 tablespoons soy sauce
½ cup red wine

1 tablespoon freshly ground
   black pepper to taste
1 onion, finely chopped
1 clove garlic, finely chopped

1. Draw crisscross lines $\frac{1}{16}$-inch deep in the steak to cut the surface fibers.
2. To prepare the marinade, combine all the ingredients in a shallow enamel or glass baking dish. Place the steak in the marinade. Cover and refrigerate for 12 hours. (The longer it stays, within reason, the more tender and flavorful it will be.) Turn the beef in the marinade once (or more often if you remember it).
3. Remove the beef from the marinade and dry it on paper towels. Broil it as close to the broiler as possible for 4 minutes on each side. Even if you do not think it will be done then, it will be. Flank steak is very thin and it gets tough if you overcook it.

4. To carve the steak, hold the knife almost flat and parallel to the beef. Cut long, thin slices across the grain.

Serve with cherry tomatoes, small roast potatoes, and garlic bread.

BROILED CHICKEN WITH MUSTARD

Serves 4
Preheat broiler for 10 minutes

1 2½-pound broiling chicken, cut into serving pieces

1 tablespoon vegetable oil

Basting sauce:
4 tablespoons butter, melted
2 tablespoons Dijon-style mustard

2 tablespoons finely chopped parsley
2 tablespoons chopped chives
1 tablespoon chopped fresh mint (or 1 teaspoon dried marjoram)
1 tablespoon lemon juice

1. Dry the chicken thoroughly on paper towels.

2. Brush broiling rack with oil to prevent the chicken from sticking.

3. Combine butter with all remaining ingredients and brush chicken with part of the flavored butter.

4. Broil chicken 6 inches from the heat for 20 minutes on each side, basting every 5 minutes with the remaining flavored butter.

Serve with braised vegetables and rice.

BROILED BARBECUED SPARERIBS

Serves 6
Preheat broiler for 10 minutes (or broil over charcoal)

6 pounds country-style
  spareribs
1 tablespoon vegetable oil
½ cup cider vinegar
¼ cup water (or pineapple
  juice)
½ cup sugar

1 clove garlic, finely chopped
3 tablespoons sherry
3 tablespoons soy sauce
1 tablespoon cornstarch, dissolved in 2 tablespoons cold
  water

1. Trim the spareribs of any excess fat.
2. To prepare the marinade, place the vinegar, water (or juice), and sugar in a small saucepan. Simmer until the sugar has dissolved.
3. Add the garlic, sherry, and soy sauce and simmer for another 3 minutes.
4. Add the cornstarch, dissolved in water, and stir until the mixture has thickened into a sauce. Let the sauce cool.
5. Marinate the spareribs in the sauce for 2 hours.
6. Brush the broiler rack with oil and broil the spareribs 6 inches from the heat, allowing 20 minutes on each side. Baste the ribs with barbecue sauce every 6 minutes.

Children love barbecued spareribs. Why not let them have everything they enjoy at the same meal? Serve with French fries, cherry tomatoes, and cole slaw, with chocolate ice cream for dessert.

The marinade can also be used for chicken and pork chops.

BROILED HAM WITH GREEN PEPPERS

Serves 4
Preheat broiler for 10 minutes

4 ham steaks, cut from a fully
  cooked ham
4 tablespoons light olive oil
  (or salad oil)

4 cloves garlic, finely chopped
4 green peppers, cut into wide
  strips

1. Snip the outer edges of the ham steaks every inch or so to prevent them from curling. Brush ham on both sides with some of the oil. Broil, allowing 4 minutes on each side.

2. In the meantime, heat the remaining oil in a skillet. Fry the garlic for 2 minutes and add the green peppers. Fry over moderately high heat for 8 minutes until the peppers are tender.

3. Spoon the peppers over the ham slices and serve with buttered noodles, string beans, and rosé wine.

BROILED STRIPED BASS

All fish recipes are best made with fresh rather than frozen fish. Be very careful not to cook fish too long. As soon as it has become firm and opaque and flakes easily with a fork, it is ready for the table.

Serves 4
Preheat broiler for 10 minutes

2 pounds striped bass fillets	1 tablespoon finely chopped
2 tablespoons oil	fresh oregano or fresh basil
½ teaspoon salt	(or 1 teaspoon dried herbs)
Freshly ground black pepper to taste	2 teaspoons lemon juice

1. Wash and dry fish thoroughly.

2. Brush the broiler rack with some of the oil to prevent the fish from sticking.

3. Combine the remaining oil with the remaining ingredients. Brush the surface of the bass with flavored oil.

4. Broil bass 4 inches from the broiler, allowing 5 minutes on each side. Baste the bass frequently with the remaining flavored oil as it is cooking.

Serve with boiled potatoes and peas.

BROILED TROUT

Serves 4
Preheat broiler for 10 minutes

4 small (¾ pound each) whole trout, cleaned	2 tablespoons lemon juice
1 tablespoon oil	2 tablespoons finely chopped parsley
4 tablespoons butter, melted	

1. Wash and dry trout thoroughly.

2. Brush broiler rack with oil to prevent fish from sticking.

3. Combine butter, lemon juice, and parsley. Brush cavity and surface of the trout with flavored butter.

4. Broil trout 4 inches from broiler, allowing 6 minutes on each side. Baste the trout with the remaining flavored butter frequently as it is cooking.

Serve broiled trout with candlelight, boiled potatoes, and the finest, freshest vegetable you can find. Sauce Béarnaise for the trout and a little white wine for the diners will complete the entrée. Serve a bowl of strawberries and cream for dessert.

BROILED SALMON WITH DILL SAUCE

Serves 4
Preheat broiler for 10 minutes

1 tablespoon oil
4 salmon steaks, ¾ inch thick
3 tablespoons butter, melted
Salt and pepper to taste

Dill Sauce:
1 cup sour cream
Juice of ½ lemon
2 scallions, finely chopped
½ teaspoon dill weed

1. Brush the broiler rack with oil. Brush fish with melted butter. Season with salt and pepper.

2. Broil 4 inches from the source of heat for 4 minutes on the first side. Turn and brush salmon with butter on the second side. Broil for another 4 minutes.

3. Combine sauce ingredients in a small saucepan. Heat until just warm but not hot.

4. Spoon sauce over salmon steaks and garnish plate with watercress and lemon wedges.

Serve with boiled potatoes and asparagus or peas.

8. frying and sautéing

PAN-FRIED POTATOES · PEPPER STEAK FLAMED IN BRANDY · FLAMING STEAK WITH MUSHROOMS · BEEF STROGANOFF · LOBSTER NEWBURG · PORK WITH NUTS AND SEASONINGS · VEAL SCALLOPINI WITH LEMON AND BRANDY · DEVILED VEAL KIDNEYS · CALVES' LIVER WITH LEMON AND THYME SAUCE · CRISP-FRIED TURKEY BREAST · FRIED CHICKEN WITH HERBS · CHICKEN LIVERS WITH APPLE · CHICKEN AND HAM À LA KING · HAM IN SHERRY SAUCE · SHRIMP WITH TOMATOES · FLOUNDER WITH BROWN BUTTER AND ALMONDS · FROGS' LEGS

Both frying and sautéing are quick methods of cooking food in fat or oil. Sautéing uses a smaller quantity of fat than frying—strictly speaking, only one to three tablespoons compared with four to six for frying. However, the terms are often used interchangeably. In both cases the purpose is to cook the food quickly, until it is lightly browned. Deep-fat frying, on the other hand, involves *immersion* of the food in very hot fat to seal in the juices while the outside becomes crisp and crusty.

Sometimes sautéing is the first step in making a more complicated dish, such as Beef Stroganoff. (Beef Stroganoff is made in exactly the same way as Beef Stew, but because the beef is, one hopes, very tender, only a short cooking time is necessary. The beef strips are first browned in a combination of very hot oil and butter. Flour is added to form a thickened base. Finally, liquid is stirred into the butter to make a sauce to surround the beef.)

There are literally hundreds of dishes that follow this familiar pattern and come under a general classification of sautés. They are all very quickly and easily made. As you will see from the following recipes, if you can make one, you can make them all.

These recipes, like most of the recipes in this book, have been selected to emphasize the similarities in the preparation of several dishes. Most are classic French dishes that have stood the test of time. However, if you delve into the cooking of many other countries, you will see that the methods of cooking are the same although specific ingredients may be unfamiliar.

HOW TO FRY MEAT

1. Use a heavy pan appropriate in size to the food being cooked. (If you use a lightweight pan, the cooking fat will be likely to burn.)

2. Use a combination of butter and oil rather than butter alone for frying meat. Butter alone burns at a lower temperature than a combination of butter and oil. You can, of course, use oil alone, preferably vegetable oil. Most olive oils have a distinctive flavor and are used only when this flavor is sought as an ingredient in the completed dish. Pure olive oil burns at a lower temperature than vegetable oils and is therefore not suitable for use as a frying oil.

3. Make sure the fat is very hot before you add the meat or it will not brown.

4. Do not salt meat before it is fried; salt draws out the juices and they evaporate during the cooking process. Make sure the meat is dry or it will steam rather than fry and will not brown. This will also happen if there is too large a quantity of meat in the pan. Allow a generous space between pieces of meat.

5. Fry the food initially over high heat to seal the surface of the food, then lower the temperature to complete the cooking. If the food cooks too slowly, it will become greasy. When foods are covered with bread crumbs and cooked slowly, steam forms between the food and the coating and the covering falls from the meat and burns in a dejected heap at the bottom of the pan while the meat weeps its juices into the cooking fat.

6. When beads of blood appear on the surface, the meat is ready to be turned.

7. Serve all hot food, especially fried food, on hot plates.

Pray for peace and grace and spiritual food,
For wisdom and guidance,
For all these things are good.
But don't forget the potatoes.

PAN-FRIED POTATOES

Most recipes for pan-fried potatoes suggest that previously cooked potatoes be used. However, the result will taste even better if you start off with raw potatoes. These are a crisp accompaniment to roasted or fried meats.

Serves 6

8 medium-sized all-purpose potatoes	2 tablespoons butter
	1 tablespoon oil

1. Peel the potatoes and cut each into eight pieces. Try to make all the pieces close to the same size.
2. Heat the butter and oil in a large frying pan.
3. Dry the potatoes and fry them over moderately high heat until evenly browned on all sides.
4. Reduce the heat and continue cooking, uncovered, for about 30 minutes until done. Taste one to be sure. Season with salt and pepper.

PEPPER STEAK FLAMED IN BRANDY

The cream in this recipe softens the piquancy and "pepperiness" of the steak and holds all the flavors together. This is an excellent dish for a dinner party. It is easy and quick to prepare and has ten times the flavor of a simple steak.

Serves 6

6 filet steaks	1 tablespoon oil
1 tablespoon oil	½ teaspoon salt
1½ tablespoons cracked pepper	¼ cup brandy
2 tablespoons butter	¼ cup heavy cream

1. Brush each steak with oil.

2. Press cracked pepper onto the surface of both sides of the steak, using the heel of your hand.

3. Heat the butter and oil in a skillet until it is very hot.

4. Fry steaks 4 minutes on each side. The surface should be brown and crusty while the steak remains rare in the center.

5. Season steaks with salt.

6. Add brandy.* Touch with a lighted match.

7. When the flames die down, remove steaks to a serving plate.

8. Rinse the skillet with cream and pour the "sauce" over the steaks.

* It is not necessary to preheat the brandy, because the frying pan will be so hot it will be warmed immediately and there will be no difficulty in igniting it.

FLAMING STEAK WITH MUSHROOMS

Serves 6

2 tablespoons butter
1 tablespoon oil
6 filet steaks

Topping:
1 tablespoon butter
1 tablespoon oil
1 onion, finely chopped
6 mushrooms, finely chopped

4 tablespoons finely chopped parsley
4 tablespoons finely chopped chives
2 tablespoons Worcestershire sauce
Salt and pepper to taste
¼ cup brandy

1. Heat the butter and oil in a heavy skillet.

2. Dry the steaks on paper towels and fry over high heat, allowing 4 minutes on each side.

3. To prepare the topping, heat the butter and oil in another skillet.

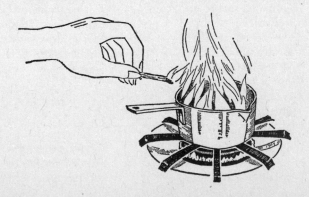

4. Add the onion and fry for 3 minutes until softened.

5. Add the mushrooms and fry for 3 more minutes.

6. Add remaining ingredients except the brandy.

7. Serve immediately, moistening each steak with the pan juices and spooning a little of the topping mixture on each steak.

8. To flame the steak at the table, heat the brandy in a small saucepan and touch it with a lighted match. Pour the flaming brandy slowly over the steaks. (Do not shake the pan or the flames will mix with the pan juices and be extinguished.) If you prefer to flame the steaks in the kitchen, pour the brandy into the hot skillet as soon as the steaks have cooked and light it with a match. The heat of the skillet will warm the brandy and it will light easily. The method of heating the brandy in a separate pan is just additional insurance that it really will flame.

BEEF STROGANOFF

It is customary to prepare Beef Stroganoff with sour cream rather than heavy cream. However, sour cream has a tendency to curdle and separate, so great care must be taken to prevent it from becoming too hot. Heavy cream will not curdle no matter how hot it gets. It enriches the sauce and gives a much better appearance to the dish. If you enjoy the slight piquancy of sour cream, add a little lemon juice to the skillet before adding the cream.

Serves 6

2 pounds filet of beef
2 tablespoons butter
1 tablespoon oil
1 small onion, finely chopped
½ pound mushrooms, thinly sliced
1 teaspoon paprika
2 tablespoons flour
½ teaspoon salt

Freshly ground black pepper to taste
1 cup beef broth
1 tablespoon brandy
2 tablespoons dry sherry
Lemon juice (optional)
¼ cup heavy cream
2 tablespoons finely chopped parsley

Parsley, parsley everywhere,
let me have my victuals bare.
OGDEN NASH

1. Trim the beef and cut it into thin strips.
2. Heat butter and oil in a skillet.
3. Fry beef over high heat until lightly browned.
4. Add onion and mushrooms. Reduce heat and fry for 2 minutes.
5. Stir in paprika and flour.
6. Season with salt and pepper.
7. Add beef broth, brandy, sherry, lemon juice (optional), and heavy cream.
8. Simmer 5 more minutes until the beef is tender.
9. Garnish with parsley and serve on a bed of rice.

LOBSTER NEWBURG AND OTHER VARIATIONS OF BEEF STROGANOFF

By substituting the following ingredients for the beef and beef broth, but keeping all the other ingredients and the method exactly the same as in the Beef Stroganoff recipe, you can also make:

Lobster Newburg—1½ pounds lobster meat and 1 cup heavy cream, plus a touch of lemon juice.

Chicken Stroganoff—8 boneless chicken breasts cut into strips and 1 cup chicken broth.

Veal Stroganoff—2 pounds veal (from the leg) cut into strips and ˈ cup chicken broth.

Ham Stroganoff—2 pounds cooked ham cut into strips and 1 cup chicken broth.

Although none of the primary ingredients in these recipes is actually browned in fat, all are sautéed quickly so that their texture becomes firm.

The following group of recipes is also based on the same principles of cooking as Beef Stroganoff. All these dishes can be used as fillings for commercially prepared and frozen individual puff-pastry shells, pies, omelettes, or crêpes.

Pork

Suckling pig was so popular at the palaces of the Caesars that in order to continue the species it became vital to restrict its appearance to special feast days.

Pigs, smiling and grunting happily, are the gentlest of animals, and any farmer will tell you that they have more sense than the silly sheep and gobbling turkeys. Nothing can compare with the aroma of bacon or sausage cooking in an early-morning kitchen. Charles Lamb has written a whole dissertation on roast pork, and we eat not only the roast but every scrap of the pork from the shoulder to the crackling fat. Yet we do not all love the generous provider of this goodness. In fact, some Muslims, Burmese, Navajo Indians, and Jews will not eat pork at all even if they are starving, proving that the pen can still prove mightier than the sword!

The many dietary taboos on eating pork not only are based on the traditional argument that the pig is unclean but can be traced even further back, to ancient mysticism and the cloven hooves of long-forgotten devils. The Carib Indians refused to eat pork because they thought that they might begin to look like the source of their strength. No record has been kept to show how they felt about the goose. On the other hand, in China, the symbol for the pig and for pork is a roof, signifying plenty; pigs are problematical only when the supply runs short.

PORK WITH NUTS AND SEASONINGS

This is a good cold-winter's-night dinner, served with puréed peas and rice.

Serves 6

2½ pounds pork tenderloin
2 tablespoons butter
1 tablespoon oil
1 yellow onion, finely chopped
1 clove garlic, finely chopped
1 green pepper, finely chopped
⅓ cup chopped walnuts, Brazil nuts, or almonds
2 teaspoons curry (or cumin) powder

2 tablespoons flour
1½ cups chicken broth
½ teaspoon salt
Freshly ground black pepper to taste
12 preserved kumquats drained
2 tablespoons finely chopped parsley

1. Cut pork into 2-inch cubes.
2. Heat butter and oil and fry pork until very lightly browned.
3. Add onion, garlic, green pepper, and nuts. Continue cooking about 3 minutes until vegetables have softened.
4. Stir in curry (or cumin) powder and flour. Add broth gradually. Season with salt and pepper.
5. Continue simmering, uncovered, about 30 minutes until pork cubes are tender.
6. Add kumquats and allow them to heat through for 5 minutes.
7. Garnish pork with chopped parsley and serve.

VEAL SCALLOPINI WITH LEMON AND BRANDY

Serves 6

2 tablespoons butter	Freshly ground black pepper to
1 tablespoon oil	taste
1½ pounds veal scallops (slices	2 tablespoons lemon juice
cut from the leg and pounded	3 tablespoons brandy
very thin)	2 tablespoons finely chopped
½ cup flour, seasoned with	parsley
½ teaspoon salt	

1. Heat butter and oil until it is very hot.
2. Dredge veal slices in seasoned flour and shake off excess flour.
3. Fry veal in butter and oil for 2 minutes on each side until tender and lightly browned.
4. Season with pepper and add lemon juice.
5. Heat the brandy and touch with a lighted match. Pour the flames over the veal.
6. When the flames die down, spoon pan juices over the veal, and serve it immediately, garnished with parsley.

Freshly cooked spaghetti is the traditional accompaniment. Veal Scallopini is ready to eat in 5 minutes, so time the spaghetti accordingly. Serve the spaghetti on very hot plates with plenty of homemade tomato sauce and some crusty Italian bread.

This recipe can also be made with chicken breasts. Add 1 teaspoon of oregano to the seasoned flour, and fry chicken for 12 minutes at step 3.

Mustard

Mustard got its name from the hot mustard seeds that were carried to England by the Romans and preserved in a "must," or young wine.

Mustard seeds were not only eaten in ancient times but used for pickling and preserving meats. What was good for meats was also good for man; eventually he thought of marinating himself and his ailments in mustard baths. The devil himself observed this ritual and proceeded to invent all those mustard-flavored, paprika-spotted eggs so dearly loved at ladies' luncheons and cocktail parties!

Mustard was used as a medicine 2,400 years ago. Greek doctors made mustard potions long before farmers started to cultivate the seeds. The Chinese ground the mustard seed to a powder and combined it with flat beer to achieve greater pungency, while the French, perhaps a shade more refined, used wine to perfect their mustard paste. Meanwhile, in England, a practical housewife discovered, in 1820, that mustard powder was at the peak of flavor immediately after it had been simply combined with water to release its oils. Riding around the country on horseback to spread the word—and distribute her product—she made a quiet fortune and laid the foundation for the Coleman Mustard Company, which, with its many subsidiaries, is today the world's largest commercial manufacturer of prepared and powdered mustard.

DEVILED VEAL KIDNEYS

Serves 4

1½ pounds veal kidneys (4 kidneys)	1½ cups chicken broth
2 tablespoons butter	2 tablespoons sherry, Madeira, or brandy
1 tablespoon oil	½ teaspoon salt
1 onion, finely chopped	Freshly ground black pepper to taste
6 mushrooms, quartered	¼ cup heavy cream (optional)
1½ tablespoons mild Dijon-type mustard	2 tablespoons finely chopped parsley
2 tablespoons flour	

1. Trim the kidneys very carefully, removing the outer membrane and the inner white core. (A pair of nail scissors will do the job.)

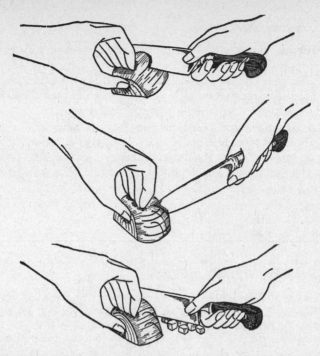

2. Cut the kidneys into ½-inch pieces or slices ¼-inch in thickness.

3. Fry kidneys in combined hot butter and oil for 3 minutes.

4. Add onion and mushrooms and fry for 5 minutes.

5. Stir in mustard and flour. Add broth gradually, and then add wine (or brandy).

6. Season with salt and pepper, add heavy cream (optional), and continue cooking for 5 minutes. The kidneys should remain pink in the center. Do not overcook or they will become tough.

7. Serve kidneys on a bed of rice, garnished with chopped parsley.

CALVES' LIVER WITH LEMON AND THYME SAUCE

Serves 4

8 thin slices calves' liver
(1½ pounds)
2 tablespoons butter
1 tablespoon oil

Sauce:
1 onion, finely chopped
2 tablespoons flour
1 cup beef broth
¼ cup lemon juice
1 teaspoon thyme
1 teaspoon tomato paste

1. Remove any veins and the surrounding membrane to prevent the liver from curling.

2. Heat the butter and oil in a large skillet. Fry the liver a few pieces at a time, for 3 minutes on each side. (Do not overcook the liver or it will become tough.) Remove the liver and keep it warm.

3. Add the onion and fry it in the same fat for 3 minutes.

4. Stir in the flour, beef broth, lemon juice, thyme, and tomato paste.

5. Return the liver to the pan and simmer it in the sauce for 5 minutes. The liver should remain pink on the inside. Serve with green noodles and cauliflower.

CRISP-FRIED TURKEY BREAST

This recipe may also be used to prepare veal cut for veal scallopini or leftover slices of rare roast beef. It is so good to eat you will wish you had doubled the recipe, and it is made in 10 minutes.

Serves 4

½ cup flour
1 teaspoon thyme
1 tablespoon paprika
1 teaspoon salt
Freshly ground black pepper to taste
8 thin slices turkey breast, leftover or uncooked

2 eggs, lightly beaten
2 tablespoons milk
1 tablespoon Dijon-type mustard
1 cup fine bread crumbs
2 tablespoons butter
1 tablespoon oil

1. Combine flour, thyme, paprika, salt, and pepper. Dredge the turkey breast in the seasoned flour. Shake off the excess flour.

2. Dip floured turkey breasts in eggs combined with milk and mustard.

3. Dredge in bread crumbs.

4. Heat the butter and oil together in a large frying pan.

5. Fry leftover cooked turkey over moderately high heat for 4 minutes on each side until the crust is crisp and golden. Allow an additional 2 minutes on each side for raw turkey slices. Serve immediately with rice and a salad.

FRIED CHICKEN WITH HERBS

Serves 4

2½-pound frying chicken, cut
  into serving pieces
½ cup flour
½ teaspoon salt
Freshly ground black pepper to
  taste
1 tablespoon rosemary

3 tablespoons finely chopped
  parsley
3 tablespoons finely chopped
  chives
2 tablespoons butter
2 tablespoons oil

1. Dry the chicken on paper towels.
2. Combine the flour with salt, pepper, and herbs and dredge the chicken pieces in the seasoned flour.
3. Heat the butter and oil in a large frying pan.
4. Brown the chicken on all sides and continue frying over moderate heat for 30 minutes, until the chicken is crisp and tender. Serve with French-fried potatoes, salad, and rolls.

CHICKEN LIVERS WITH APPLE

This combination of ingredients can be served on a bed of rice or used as an omelette filling.

Serves 4

1½ pounds chicken livers
2 tablespoons butter
1 onion, finely chopped
1 clove garlic, finely chopped
1 small apple, peeled, cored, and
  chopped
1 tablespoon paprika
3 tablespoons flour
½ cup chicken broth

½ cup apple cider
2 tablespoons apple brandy or
  Madeira (optional)
¼ cup heavy cream
½ teaspoon salt
Freshly ground black pepper to
  taste
2 tablespoons finely chopped
  parsley

1. Wash chicken livers. Cut each in half and dry on paper towels.
2. Heat the butter in a large skillet. Fry the onion, garlic, and apple for 3 minutes, until soft and tender. Add the chicken livers and fry for 3 minutes until lightly browned.

3. Stir in the paprika and flour. Add the chicken broth and apple cider gradually. Add the apple brandy (or Madeira) and cream.

4. Season with salt and pepper and simmer for 10 minutes until the livers are tender.

5. Serve, garnished with parsley, on a bed of rice.

CHICKEN AND HAM À LA KING

An à la King Sauce is a white sauce to which green pepper, pimiento, mushrooms, and sherry have been added. This sauce was created in America in the 1920s specifically to nourish audiences at political rallies. The idea was that nobody should become distracted from the speeches by showing any interest in his food. The sauce has proved to be most successful for this purpose. It is used to envelop chicken served at luncheons for gubernatorial and congressional candidates and for those seeking lesser state and local offices; it is also served with tuna fish and rice, of course. The recipe follows.

Serves 6

2 cups cooked chicken
1 cup cooked ham
2 tablespoons butter
1 onion, finely chopped
1 green pepper, seeds and membrane removed and finely chopped
6 mushrooms, thinly sliced
2 tablespoons flour
1½ cups chicken broth (or milk)

2 tomatoes, peeled, seeded, and chopped
1 cup cooked peas (or a mixture of peas and carrots)
1 2-ounce jar chopped pimientos, drained
2 tablespoons sherry
½ teaspoon salt
Freshly ground black pepper to taste
⅛ teaspoon nutmeg

1. Cut the chicken and ham into ladylike bite-sized pieces.

2. Heat the butter and fry the onion and green pepper for 3 minutes until softened. Add the mushrooms and cook for another 3 minutes.

3. Stir in the flour and add the chicken broth (or milk).

4. Stir in the chicken and ham and all the remaining ingredients and continue cooking until hot.

5. Serve on a bed of rice or use as a chicken pot-pie filling. If you elect

to serve this dish on top of a mound of steaming hot buttery noodles, you can call it Chicken Tetrazzini (with Ham).

HAM IN SHERRY SAUCE

Serves 4

2 pounds cooked ham
1½ cups chicken broth

Sherry Sauce:
1 onion, finely chopped
2 tablespoons butter
1 tablespoon oil

2 tablespoons flour
1 tablespoon tomato paste
1 tablespoon Dijon-type mustard
¼ cup heavy cream
2 tablespoons dry sherry
Freshly ground black pepper to
    taste

1. Trim ham and cut it into bite-sized cubes. Place trimmings and bone, if ham steaks are used, in a saucepan with chicken broth. Cover and simmer 15 minutes.

2. In another pan, fry onion in combined butter and oil for 3 minutes until softened.

3. Stir in flour, tomato paste, and mustard. Add strained chicken broth and stir with a wire whisk.

4. Add cream and sherry.

5. Add ham cubes and simmer about 10 minutes until ham has heated through.

6. Taste for seasoning. You may need a little pepper.

7. Serve on a bed of green or white buttered noodles and garnish with parsley.

The Kingdom of Heaven . . . is like a grain of mustard seed, which, when it is sown in the earth, is less than all the seeds that be in the earth:

But when it is sown, it groweth up and becometh greater than all herbs, and shooteth out great branches; so that the fowls of the air may lodge under the shadow of it.

MARK 4:31-32

SHRIMP WITH TOMATOES

Serves 4

2 tablespoons butter
1 tablespoon oil
1 onion, finely chopped
2 cloves garlic, finely chopped
1 green pepper, chopped
2 stalks celery, chopped
2 tablespoons flour
1 1-pound can tomatoes
1 tablespoon tomato paste
1 cup chicken broth

¼ cup white vermouth
2 pounds shrimp, cooked and
    cleaned
¼ teaspoon thyme
¼ teaspoon basil
½ teaspoon salt
Freshly ground black pepper to
    taste
2 tablespoons finely chopped
    parsley

1. Heat butter and oil in a frying pan.
2. Add onion and garlic and fry for 3 minutes.
3. Add green pepper and celery and continue cooking for about 3 minutes until softened.
4. Stir in flour and add tomatoes with their juice. Stir in tomato paste, broth, and vermouth. Add shrimp, thyme, basil, salt, and pepper. Simmer for 10 minutes.
5. Garnish with chopped parsley and serve on a bed of rice.

FLOUNDER WITH BROWN BUTTER AND ALMONDS

If you prefer not to add oil to the cooking butter, the butter can be clarified (see below). It can then be used for frying at a higher temperature with less risk of burning.

Serves 4

4 tablespoons butter
1½ pounds flounder fillets
½ teaspoon salt
Freshly ground black pepper to
    taste

⅓ cup sliced almonds
2 tablespoons finely chopped
    parsley
½ lemon, cut into wedges

1. Melt the butter and strain it through a triple layer of cheesecloth to remove the particles that cause butter to burn.
2. Fry fish fillets in this "clarified" butter for 3 minutes on each side. Season with salt and pepper and transfer to a hot serving dish.

3. Fry almonds in the same butter until both nuts and butter are lightly browned. Add parsley and spoon over the fish.

4. Garnish plate with more parsley and lemon wedges.

FROGS' LEGS

Serves 4

24 frogs' legs
½ cup milk
½ cup flour, seasoned with salt and pepper
2 tablespoons butter
1 tablespoon oil
3 cloves garlic, finely chopped

½ cup heavy cream
2 tablespoons dry vermouth
2 hard-boiled eggs, chopped
2 tablespoons finely chopped parsley
1 teaspoon capers (optional)
Juice of ½ lemon

1. Dip frogs' legs in milk and then in seasoned flour.

2. Heat the butter and oil and fry the garlic for 2 minutes. Add the frogs' legs and fry for 10 minutes until lightly browned and crisp. Transfer frogs' legs to a serving dish.

3. Add cream and vermouth to skillet and scrape up the browned pieces at the bottom of the pan.

4. Stir in eggs, parsley, capers, and lemon juice.

5. Pour over frogs' legs and serve.

Without wine we eat; with wine we dine.

9. deep-fat frying

CHICKEN KIEV · BATTER-FRIED SHRIMP WITH FRUIT SAUCE ·
FISH AND CHIPS · SOUTHERN FRIED CHICKEN · FRENCH-FRIED POTATOES
· MEAT OR CHICKEN CROQUETTES · CHICKEN BREASTS WITH HAM
AND CHEESE · FRIED FLOUNDER WITH TARTAR SAUCE · FRENCH-FRIED
ONIONS · DEEP-FRIED EGGPLANT · FRUIT FRITTERS · FRIED AND
BAKED ROCK CORNISH HENS

Deep-fat frying is one of the more difficult methods of cooking, as several conditions have to be simultaneously correct to achieve success. The correct fat must be selected, and the food must be cooked at 375° F. If too large a quantity of food is fried at one time, the food will steam as it fries, the cooking fat will become waterlogged, and the food itself will emerge greasy and distressingly unappetizing, visually and gastronomically. However, deep-fried foods can be so mouth-wateringly delicious that it is worth discovering how to make them.

The best foods for deep frying are potatoes (of course), seafood, fish, chicken, and fruits or vegetables encased in a protective batter. (Fried batter-coated fruits and vegetables are sometimes called fritters.) In addition, ground meats (insulated from the high heat by a coating of bread crumbs), filled pastries, croquettes, and chou paste can be deep-fried. Tough meats are best cooked by stewing rather than frying, which will toughen them further.

FATS FOR DEEP FRYING

The purpose of frying foods in deep fat is to produce a crisp crust to surround and envelop the food while the inside remains moist. The cooking fat must not penetrate the food but merely seal the surface. To prevent it from penetrating, the fat must be kept very hot (375° F.). The taste of the fat is a less important consideration than the temperature it is capable of reaching before it smokes, burns, or sets your house on fire.

Butter, even if it is clarified to remove all the particles, is impractical for deep frying not only because of its high cost but because it burns at too low a temperature. Vegetable oils (particularly peanut oil, which is capable of achieving the highest temperature of all vegetable oils) can be used for deep-fat frying. Solid shortenings are made from vegetable oils. They are completely tasteless and can be heated to the correct deep-frying temperature. The fat will solidify after it has cooled and can be used again. (Some people say that using deep-frying fat more than once is bad for your health, but then, so is living for a long time. If the fat becomes waterlogged or dirty, however, it cannot attain temperatures high enough to cook satisfactorily.)

Deep-fat frying involves the complete immersion of food in the fat, which means there must be at least six times as much fat as food. *It is as important to have a large quantity of fat for deep frying as it is to have a lot of water for cooking pasta.*

In estimating how much fat you will need to fill a deep fryer allowing displacement space for the food, fill the fryer with water to a depth of three inches and then measure it. One pound of solid fat is the equivalent of two cups of water.

THE DEEP-FAT FRYER

There is a utensil made especially for deep frying that is well worth owning—a "must" for a well-equipped kitchen. It has a fitted basket that can be lowered slowly into the hot fat and raised to drain the food rapidly. A deep-fat thermometer is also a necessity. When the temperature of the fat is controlled at 375° F., an impenetrable seal is formed around the food. If the temperature falls below 375° F., the fat invades the food and cannot find its way out. If the fat becomes too hot, the outside is burned before the inside is completely cooked.

HOW TO DEEP-FRY

1. Chill the food until the last possible minute so that it is shivering with cold. It will then be contracted and will not permit fat to invade it.

2. Dry it thoroughly. Wet food will splutter and waterlog the cooking fat, causing you an immense amount of extra work cleaning the stove.

3. Heat the oil to 375° F.

4. Lower the food slowly into the oil, a few pieces at a time. Too much food lowers the temperature of the oil, and the food becomes greasy. There should be as wide a disparity as possible between the temperature of the food and the temperature of the fat.

5. If the fat falls below 375° F., remove the food and reheat the fat to the correct temperature.

6. Drain the food on paper towels spread over a wire cake-cooling rack. If you put the towels directly on the counter, the surface of the food will become soggy. If you cover the food with paper towels, steam

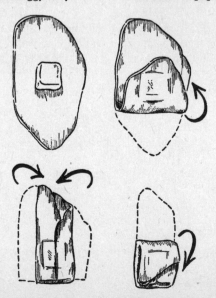

becomes trapped beneath the towels and causes the food to lose its crispness (and crispness is the whole point of deep frying).

7. Serve fried food immediately or, if there is a crisis, keep it warm on a wire rack in a preheated 225° F. oven.

CHICKEN KIEV

This is a spectacular and superb dish. If you place the butter inside the chicken breasts the night before, it will be completely ready to cook at the last minute.

Serves 6
Preheat oven to 225° F.

Filling:
12 tablespoons butter, softened (not melted)
3 cloves garlic, finely chopped
2 tablespoons finely chopped parsley
2 tablespoons chopped chives
½ teaspoon salt
Freshly ground black pepper to taste

Breasts of 6 plump chickens, boned, cut in half, and pounded thin
Oil (or solid shortening) for deep frying

Coating:
½ cup flour
2 egg yolks lightly beaten with 2 tablespoons milk
1¼ cups bread crumbs

1. Combine butter, garlic, parsley, chives, salt, and pepper. Place approximately 1 tablespoon of the butter mixture at the widest end of each breast and roll the breast, tucking in the sides to contain the flavored butter.

2. Chill rolled breasts in the refrigerator for at least 20 minutes to harden the butter.

3. Heat cooking oil to 375° F.

4. Dip each breast first in flour, shake off excess, then dip in egg mixture, and finally in bread crumbs.

5. Deep-fry breasts in oil, a few at a time, for 5 minutes until golden brown and crisp.

6. Keep cooked breasts hot in a preheated oven until all the cooking

has been completed. Serve with rice and a Boston lettuce salad with Oil and Vinegar Dressing.

SIMPLE DEEP-FRY METHOD FOR CHICKEN, SEAFOOD, VEGETABLES, OR FRUIT

Batter:
1 cup milk
2 eggs
1 tablespoon oil
1 cup flour
¼ teaspoon salt

1 tablespoon sugar (for fruit fritter batter)

½ cup flour
Oil (or solid shortening) for deep frying

1. Mix all batter ingredients in a blender until smooth.
2. Cut chicken into serving pieces, slice vegetables and fruit into ½-inch-thick slices, or separate onions into rings.
3. Dredge the ingredient in flour. Shake off the excess and dip in batter.
4. Heat the oil to 375° F. and fry chicken for 35 minutes, vegetables and fruit for 6 minutes.

Shrimp

Almost all the tons of "fresh" shrimp sold are, in fact, not fresh at all but were frozen as soon as they were netted on the high seas and are then defrosted in the fresh fish section of the supermarket. The shrimp that are served all over America in the form of "cocktails" are a special breed. Cold and stiff with disdain, they allow themselves to be dunked into countless gallons of red sauce, so staggeringly powerful that nobody notices that the poor things are completely tasteless. They are then crooked precariously over the edge of a glass dish, peering sightlessly into a sea of shredded iceberg lettuce to await their fate. Only their pink, curved contour gives any clue that these were once the noble marine crustaceans that bathed in the Gulf of Mexico.

Pink shrimp begin their lives as members of a large family. They are born from a mother who annually journeys to Tortuga for a vacation away from her home in Florida. She descends to a depth of about 120 feet, leaves half a million babies in the form of larvae, to fend for themselves, and promptly returns home. The larvae drift toward the shore, developing five legs on their heads, ten on their body, and, to balance things nicely, five sections to the tail. This symmetrical equipment enables them to make sudden dives, either backward or forward, to escape other seagoing travelers who have a fondness for baby shrimp. If they are not caught in a backward dive by an openmouthed predator, they may tremble to hear the shrimp boats coming. The result is the same in either case: They are either eaten immediately or hauled aboard, cleaned, frozen, and dropped neatly, with preservatives added, into a printed transparent bag for sale in the neighborhood market. A few are frozen in the shell for those of us who like to think that we are buying fresh shrimp, and a very small minority are really kept fresh.

Shrimp come in all sorts of colors, from the raw green variety that have a slightly green border around the edge of their tails, to gray, pink, and brown. New varieties are constantly being discovered at greater and greater depths to satisfy our insatiable appetites. They arrive on our tables in many sizes. In Denmark, their value is calculated according to how many can dance on the head of a pin, while others are so large that eight to ten weigh a pound.

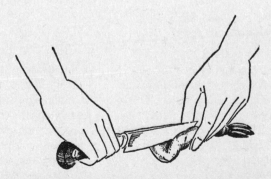

BUYING FRESH SHRIMP

Fresh shrimp, if you can find any to buy, have an exquisite flavor, but cook them immediately, for they do not last long in a temperature much above freezing. Buy the largest shrimp you can find. Twelve to eighteen shrimp generally weigh one pound. Do not buy cooked shrimp, because the cook always makes sure that there will never be a complaint about their being underdone—by overcooking them himself! Allow three pounds of uncooked, unshelled shrimp for eight people for an appetizer serving.

BATTER-FRIED SHRIMP WITH FRUIT SAUCE

Oysters, mussels, and clams are also excellent cooked in exactly the same way.

Serves 4 as an appetizer
Preheat oven to 225° F.

1½ pounds large shrimp,
  weighed raw and unshelled
Juice of ½ lemon
½ cup flour
Oil (or solid shortening)for deep
  frying
1 cup flour
1¼ cups beer
½ teaspoon salt
1 teaspoon paprika

Fruit Sauce:
½ cup orange marmalade
1 tablespoon lemon juice
2 tablespoons orange juice
1 tablespoon prepared horseradish
¼ teaspoon powdered ginger
½ teaspoon dry English mustard
  powder (or 1 teaspoon Dijon-
  type mustard)

1. Shell and devein the shrimp. Split shrimp through the back into fantails.
2. Sprinkle the shrimp with lemon juice.

3. Dip shrimp in flour, shaking off excess.

4. Heat the oil to 375° F.

5. Place all the batter ingredients in a bowl and stir with a wire whisk until well combined. Holding the floured shrimp by the tail, dip in batter.

6. Deep-fry the shrimp a few at a time, for 3 or 4 minutes, until the batter is crisp. Keep cooked shrimp in a preheated oven until all have had a preliminary cooking. Keep the shrimp in a single layer. (If you pile them on top of each other, they will steam, and the batter will lose its crispness.) Reheat the fat to 375° F. and refry for 2 minutes until they are hot and cooked to a golden crispness.

7. Place all the sauce ingredients in a blender for 10 seconds.

8. Serve the shrimp on individual plates lined with paper doilies. Garnish with lemon wedges and let each person have his own small dish of fruit sauce for dipping.

FISH AND CHIPS

Serve fish and chips wrapped in individual pages of newspaper (preferably British), lined with a piece of wax paper.

Serves 4

Batter:
¾ cup flour
½ teaspoon salt
1 teaspoon paprika
¾ cup beer

1½ pounds cod, flounder, or haddock fillets, cut into 3-inch pieces
½ lemon
½ cup flour, seasoned with ½ teaspoon salt and freshly ground black pepper to taste
Oil (or solid shortening) for deep frying

1. Place flour, salt, and paprika in a bowl. Stir in beer with a wire whisk to form a smooth batter.

2. Sprinkle fish with lemon juice. Dip in seasoned flour, shake off excess, and then dip into combined batter ingredients.

3. Heat oil to 375° F. Deep-fry fish for 8 minutes until tender and lightly browned.

4. Remove fish and drain on paper towels. Reheat oil to 375° F.

5. Lower fish into hot fat and crisp for 2 more minutes.

6. Drain fish and garnish with parsley and lemon wedges. Serve with French-fried potatoes and peas. It is traditional to sprinkle vinegar on the peas or on the fish.

Parsley

In England, when children ask where babies come from, they are always fobbed off with the answer: "From the parsley bed." This notion has survived for hundreds of years along with the stork theory. In 1748, the second son of an English noble wrote a little poem on the subject of parsley crops and their relationship to inheritance:

> This day from the parsley bed, I'm sure,
> Was dug my elder brother, Moore,
> Had Papa dug me up before him,
> So many would not now adore him.
> But, hang it, he is only one,
> If he trips off, I am Sir John.

Parsley has been known since early Greek and Roman times. Hercules was thought to have worn a garland of parsley, and Juno's horses were said to have galloped faster after they had been nipping at the parsley bed. (The same story is also attributed to Homer's heroes, and perhaps it was the parsley that made them more heroic!) Oddly enough, at Roman banquets parsley was worn by the diners like a laurel wreath to ward off the dangers of intoxication. There is obviously some sort of theory to be derived from galloping horses, overdrinking, and digging for babies in parsley beds—but it is a hard track to follow.

Parsley is one of the principal ingredients of a "bouquet garni." This group of herbs, which appears frequently in French cooking,

consists of peppercorns, thyme, parsley, and a bay leaf. In fact, only the stalks of the parsley are used in the bouquet garni, for that is where most of the flavor lies. The parsley leaves are saved by economical housewives to be used as a garnish.

Parsley is the universal garnish used in most Western European countries. It is inexpensive, long-lasting, and readily available. The best way of storing fresh parsley is to put it unwashed in a covered jar. If it is very dirty, chop it, and put the chopped parsley in the corner of a tea towel. Twist the tea towel into a knot without actually knotting it and run this little corner of the towel under cold water. All the sooty particles will run away into the sink. It is much easier to chop parsley dry than to wash it and attempt to chop it while it is still wet.

The only danger of using parsley as a garnish lies in using too much parsley too frequently.

SOUTHERN FRIED CHICKEN

Serves 6

Batter:
¾ cup flour
1 teaspoon paprika
½ teaspoon salt
Freshly ground black pepper to taste
¾ cup beer

3 1½-pound frying chickens, cut into serving pieces
½ cup flour
Oil (or solid shortening) for deep frying

1. Place flour, paprika, salt, and pepper in a bowl. Stir in beer with a wire whisk to form a smooth batter.
2. Dip chicken pieces in flour, shake off excess, and then dip in batter.
3. Heat oil to 375° F. Deep-fry chicken for 30 minutes. Remove chicken.
4. Reheat oil to 375° F. Lower chicken carefully into hot fat and fry for another 5 minutes to brown and crisp.
5. Drain well on paper towels.

If you decide to take the chicken along for a picnic, the batter stays crisp even when it is cold.

Whole trout and other fish can be cooked in exactly the same way. Reduce the cooking time to 12 to 15 minutes.

Potatoes

In Offenberg, a town in Germany, there is a statue bearing the inscription "Sir Francis Drake, introducer of the potato into Europe in the year of our Lord, 1518." Some people say that Sir Francis should not be standing so boldly in Offenberg, for it was Sir Walter Raleigh who brought the noble plant from Virginia to Ireland. Actually, it was Pedro de Cieca de Leon who, in 1538, clambered up the face of the Andes in Peru in search of gold, only to find some potatoes growing. (King Midas was a little ahead of his time in recognizing the relative importance of the humble potato compared with the luster of gold.)

The potato eventually sprouted its way all across Europe, where it fed the hungry and became a staple food. In Germany, a potato war was fought. In Ireland, priests and altar boys paraded solemnly through the potato fields, sprinkling drops of holy water on the blossoming plants and praying for Divine intervention to produce a bountiful crop to feed the hungry people.

In 1791, a group of Irish Presbyterians landed in Londonderry, New Hampshire, and planted the first potatoes on American soil—some 130 years after either Drake or Sir Walter Raleigh was supposed to have brought the potato from Virginia. Twenty-seven years later, the beetle blight attacked the Irish potatoes and caused an almost total failure of the crop. The catastrophe was devastating, and it has been estimated that close to a million Irish people died of starvation. It was a failure of the potato harvest that began the great and continuing exodus of the Irish to America.

As potatoes became increasingly popular in the British Isles, a group of Scottish fundamentalists denounced them because they had not been mentioned in the Bible. They even went so far as to say that it was the potato, not the apple, that had caused Adam's fall. (So many foods are said to have tempted Adam that, had he tried them all, he might have left us some interesting recipes instead of walking out without a word or a menu!) While the fundamentalists were being so tiresomely fundamental, the grandson of Frederick the Great in

Germany threatened to cut off the nose of any who would not plant potatoes, and Marie Antoinette danced lightheartedly through France with potato blossoms in her hair. Meanwhile, in the recesses of his kitchen, Monsieur Parmentier was tirelessly and ceaselessly cooking up new potato dishes. His writings became so important that now his name, along with the title of the unknown Duchess and the name of Anna, has become almost synonymous with the potato.

The potato has been the innocent victim of widespread rumors that it is exceptionally fattening. Weight-conscious people have come to look on it with suspicion simply because it is listed among the starchy foods. Actually, 78 percent of this sturdy tuber is water, only 11 percent to 20 percent being starch. One medium-sized potato totals 100 calories, but so does each of the following: one large apple, one large onion, one medium baking-powder biscuit, one-and-one-half tablespoons of French salad dressing—or so they say.

FRENCH-FRIED POTATOES

Serves 4
Preheat oven to 225° F.

4 large boiling potatoes (or 8 potatoes if you are serving children below the age of vanity)	Sufficient solid shortening to fill the deep fryer to a depth of at least 4 inches

1. Peel the potatoes. Slice them and cut into strips. Use potatoes directly from the refrigerator or chill them after cutting for 15 minutes in a bowl of ice water. Pat them thoroughly dry on paper towels before frying.

2. Heat the fat to 375° F. Put a few potatoes at a time into the wire basket and lower it slowly into the fat. Increase the heat under the pan until the fat regains 375° F. Fry the potatoes for about 10 minutes until they are partially cooked but not completely browned and crisp.

3. Drain the first batch of potatoes on paper towels spread over a wire cake-cooling rack. Discard the paper towels and keep the potatoes warm in a preheated oven. Continue until all the potatoes are cooked.

4. Reheat the oil to 375° F. and fry the "parfried" potatoes for another 2 or 3 minutes until crisp and well browned.

5. Drain and season with salt. Serve immediately.

MEAT OR CHICKEN CROQUETTES

The ingredients are held together with a thick, thick white sauce. This is an excellent way of using leftovers.

Serves 8

3 tablespoons butter
1 onion, finely chopped
5 tablespoons flour
1 cup beef (or chicken) broth
1½ cups firmly packed diced, cooked beef, ham, veal, lamb, or chicken
¼ teaspoon salt
Freshly ground black pepper to taste
⅛ teaspoon nutmeg
2 tablespoons finely chopped parsley

2 teaspoons Worcestershire sauce
2 egg yolks

Coating:
1 cup flour
2 egg yolks, combined with 2 tablespoons cold milk
1 cup fine bread crumbs

Oil (or solid shortening) for deep frying

1. Heat the butter in a small saucepan.
2. Fry the onion in the butter for 3 minutes until softened.
3. Stir in the flour and cook for 1 minute.

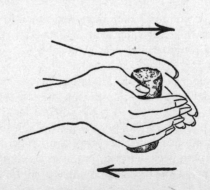

4. Add the broth gradually, stirring with a wire whisk to form a thick paste.

5. Add the meat or chicken, salt, pepper, nutmeg, parsley, Worcestershire sauce, and egg yolks.

6. Spread the mixture in a layer 2 inches thick onto a cookie sheet covered with wax paper. Chill the mixture for 2 hours until firm. Then divide it into 8 pieces and form each piece into a cylinder 3 inches long and 1 inch in diameter, rolling the mixture between your hands.

7. Roll each croquette in flour. Pat off excess flour and dip the croquette in egg yolks combined with milk. Roll it in fine bread crumbs, making sure the surface is completely coated.

8. Deep-fry the croquettes, a few at a time, in oil heated to 375° F. for 4 or 5 minutes until crisp and brown.

CHICKEN BREASTS WITH HAM AND CHEESE

Serves 6
Preheat oven to 225° F.

12 slices Prosciutto (or other thinly sliced boiled ham)
12 thin slices of mozzarella, Swiss, or Gruyère cheese
6 whole chicken breasts, boned and pounded thin
1 cup flour, seasoned with ½ teaspoon salt, freshly ground

black pepper to taste, and 1 teaspoon paprika
2 egg yolks, lightly beaten with 2 tablespoons milk
1 cup bread crumbs
Oil (or solid shortening) for deep frying

1. Place a slice of ham and a slice of cheese on each chicken breast and fold in half. Trim ham and cheese so they fit neatly into each breast without protruding from the edges.

2. Dip each breast first in seasoned flour, shake off excess, then dip in egg mixture, and finally in bread crumbs.

3. Deep-fry breasts a few at a time for 8 minutes in oil heated to 375° F. (or pan-fry for 4 minutes in a combination of 2 tablespoons butter and 1 tablespoon oil) on each side until crisp and tender.

4. Keep cooked breasts hot in a preheated oven until all the cooking has been completed. Serve with rice and string beans or peas.

This recipe can also be prepared with veal cut for veal scallopini.

FRIED FLOUNDER WITH TARTAR SAUCE

Serves 4

1½ pounds flounder fillets
½ cup flour, seasoned with
  ½ teaspoon salt and freshly
  ground black pepper to taste
2 eggs, lightly beaten
½ cup bread crumbs
Oil (or solid shortening) for
  deep frying

Tartar Sauce:
½ cup mayonnaise
1 clove garlic, finely chopped
1 teaspoon capers
1 tablespoon finely chopped
  parsley
2 sweet gherkins, finely chopped

1. Dip flounder fillets in seasoned flour, shake off excess, then dip into egg, and finally into bread crumbs.
2. Heat oil to 375° F. Deep-fry fish for 8 minutes.
3. Remove fish and drain on paper towels. Reheat oil to 375° F. and deep-fry fish a second time for 2 minutes until brown and crisp.
4. Combine ingredients for Tartar Sauce and serve separately.

FRENCH-FRIED ONIONS

Zucchini, summer squash, artichoke hearts, green-pepper strips, and parsley can all be deep-fried in batter following the directions for French-Fried Onions.

Serves 6

Batter:
¾ cup flour
¼ teaspoon salt
¾ cup milk
2 tablespoons salad oil
1 egg

4 medium- to large-sized yellow
  onions
Oil (or solid shortening) for
  deep frying
½ cup flour

1. Combine batter ingredients with a wire whisk or in a blender. Chill the batter for 2 hours.
2. Peel onions and cut into slices. Separate slices into rings.
3. Heat oil to 375° F.
4. Just before frying, dredge onion rings in flour and dip in batter. Deep-fry for about 5 minutes until crisp and golden.

DEEP-FRIED EGGPLANT

Cut the eggplant into slices ¼ inch thick. Cut slices into strips 2 inches wide. Place on a wire cake-cooling rack and sprinkle with 1 tablespoon salt. Let the eggplant strips stand for 15 minutes and then pat dry with paper towels. Dip the eggplant strips first in flour and then into the batter used for French-Fried Onions. Fry 5 minutes until crisp and golden.

FRUIT FRITTERS

Fruit Fritters, like French-fried vegetables, are made by dipping slices of fresh food into a batter and deep frying them in hot oil. The fruit remains moist and juicy inside its protective batter coat. The steam from the fruit juice causes the batter to expand into a crisp puff.

Fruit Fritters are made with a batter that is simply a combination of beer and flour in equal parts. Surprisingly, there is no lingering beer taste, and the batter is light, crisp, and delicate.

Serves 4
Preheat oven to 225° F.

1 cup flour	Juice of 1 lemon (if apples are
1 cup beer	used)
4 medium-sized firm apples	½ cup superfine sugar
(or 1 small pineapple)	Oil for deep frying

1. Measure the flour into a bowl and stir in the beer with a wire whisk until smooth. Let the batter stand for 2 hours if possible. The batter thickens as it stands. If you have to use it immediately, add another 2 tablespoons of flour.

2. Peel the fruit, remove the cores, and cut the fruit into ½-inch rings. Sprinkle apple rings with lemon juice to prevent them from darkening.

3. Dredge fruit in sugar.

4. Dip the fruit rings in the batter, holding them with tongs, and deep-fry them in oil heated to 375°. Fry the rings a few at a time for 2 or 3 minutes on each side until the batter is crisp and lightly browned. Drain on paper towels spread over wire cake-cooling racks. Keep the first fritters hot in a preheated oven.

5. Serve fritters, dusted with sifted confectioners' sugar and cinnamon, on hot plates lined with paper doilies.

FRIED AND BAKED ROCK CORNISH HENS

Rock Cornish hens always seem like such a good idea, but, unfortunately, they are frequently stringy, tough, and rather tasteless. However, if they are deep-fried first in a protective coating, they remain moist and juicy. The perfect accompaniment is a Hollandaise Sauce flavored with a tablespoon of tomato paste. Serve the hens whole, breast side up, or cut each in half and arrange, cut side down, over a bed of rice on a silver platter.

Serves 4
Preheat oven to 350° F.

4 Rock Cornish hens (1 pound, 2 ounces each), defrosted slowly in the refrigerator	3 egg yolks, lightly beaten with 3 tablespoons milk
1 cup flour	1½ cups fine bread crumbs
	Oil (or solid shortening) for deep frying

1. Dry the cavity and surface skin of the hens thoroughly with paper towels.
2. Dredge each hen in flour and shake off the excess.

3. Roll the floured hens in the egg yolks combined with milk and then press each hen firmly into the bread crumbs.

4. Deep-fry hens, one at a time, in oil heated to 375° F. until bread crumbs are lightly browned. Allow about 5 minutes on each side.

5. Drain hens on paper towels spread over wire cake-cooling racks. Transfer hens to a baking dish and bake for 20 minutes in a preheated oven until tender.

Note: A whole Rock Cornish hen may well be too large a quantity for a single serving, though half may not be quite sufficient. The problem can be solved by serving half initially and keeping the remaining half for second helpings. If you find you have made too much, the hens are delicious when cold.

10. scrambled eggs and omelettes

SCRAMBLED EGGS · PIPERADE · SPANISH OMELETTE · PLAIN AND
FANCY OMELETTES · CHEESE OMELETTE · TOMATO AND HERB
OMELETTE · MUSHROOM OMELETTE · FRIED POTATO AND BACON
OMELETTE

Eggs were the first known packaged food and are considered, by those
who consider such things, to be the most perfect of all packages. Complete, whole, and aesthetically pleasing, so perfect is the egg that the
first thing we generally do to it is break it!

Chickens came even before eggs (or was it the other way around?),
and the virtues of omelettes were known even in the deserts of ancient
Egypt. There, in the absence of two sticks to rub together, the shepherds
would break the eggs into a sling and whirl the sling around and around
at top speed until the heat that was generated by the friction caused the
eggs to set.

Since the earliest times, eggs have been considered to be symbols of
fertility. They have heralded the blossoms of springtime and the joyous
rebirth of the earth. They have, by association of ideas, also been
thought of as aphrodisiacs, and ancient German farmers smeared eggs
on plows to guarantee a bountiful harvest.

Though eggs themselves hatch only goodness and reproduce bounty,
the shells are another matter entirely. Small witches used to darken the
skies, riding in cramped wickedness in empty shells. To remove this

threat and deny the witches all means of transportation, the empty egg-shells were crushed and destroyed. It was only later that larger-sized and yet more evil witches hopped aboard their broomsticks and menaced the good world at Hallowe'en. (People who continue to break up their empty breakfast eggshells with idle spoons have not yet heard of this new development in the world of witchcraft and sorcery.)

It is said that if you really want to know whether an egg is fresh, hold the larger end tentatively against your lower lip. If it is warm, it is fresh. If not, complain to your supermarket manager with just indignation.

Most "fresh eggs" are at least a month old but seem to be all right for making soufflés, omelettes, custards, sauces, and puddings. Eggs for poaching, though, must be as fresh as a daisy or the whites will float away in the water like Ophelia's hair.

Egg whites can be frozen in a jar. If you forget how many you have put in the container, one egg white is one ounce—assuming that you have used a "Grade A" large egg weighing two ounces in the first place!

Sometimes it is more economical to buy smaller eggs than the extra-large or jumbo varieties. The savings in money may, however, lead to minor arithmetical crises if you decide to substitute them in cake recipes.

The only difference between brown eggs and white is the color of the shell and, sometimes, the price. An egg is an egg. You couldn't mistake a duck's egg for a quail's egg, because neither is likely to be available.

Eggs symbolize love eternal and should be treated accordingly; without eggs the entire culinary world would crumble.

Scrambled Eggs and Omelettes

The difference between a scrambled egg and an omelette is the difference between breakfast and brunch. One comes before the other or just flows into the other. An omelette is scrambled eggs encased in an envelope of scrambled eggs. Look!

SCRAMBLED EGGS	OMELETTE
2 eggs	2 eggs
Pinch of salt	Pinch of salt
1 tablespoon butter	1 tablespoon butter

You, of course, knew that all the time, but I can remember being quite astonished at the discovery. It is also reassuring to know that if you can make one, you can make another.

SCRAMBLED EGGS

The only secret to making fluffy scrambled eggs is to cook them slowly over low heat and eat them immediately. It may not be particularly helpful to mention this, but as there are only two ingredients needed for making scrambled eggs, the eggs and the butter, the better the butter and the fresher the eggs, the sublimer will be your breakfast. One-fourth cup grated cheese or some herbs can be added to the beaten eggs before they are cooked, or alternatively you can garnish the eggs with a little something after they have been cooked.

Serves 1

1 tablespoon butter
2 eggs
Pinch of salt
Freshly ground black pepper to taste
2 tablespoons milk or cream (optional)

Garnish:
2 anchovies, cut in half lengthwise and arranged in a crisscross pattern or
3 slices smoked salmon, shredded
1 teaspoon capers

1. Melt the butter in an 8-inch skillet.
2. Beat the eggs lightly with a fork, adding salt, pepper, and milk or cream.
3. When the butter is hot and foaming, add the eggs and stir over low heat until soft curds have formed.
4. Garnish eggs with anchovies, smoked salmon, and capers, or whatever strikes your fancy.

The hen is the egg's way of producing another egg.
SAMUEL BUTLER

PIPERADE

A Piperade is a fancy form of Scrambled Eggs.

Serves 6

2 onions, finely chopped	6 slices boiled ham, cut into
1 clove garlic, finely chopped	strips
2 green peppers, chopped	10 eggs
3 tablespoons olive oil	Salt and pepper to taste
3 mushrooms, sliced	2 tablespoons butter
2 ripe tomatoes, peeled, seeded,	2 tablespoons finely chopped
and chopped	parsley

1. Fry the onions, garlic, and peppers in oil.
2. Add mushrooms, tomatoes, and ham. Heat for 5 minutes, until tomatoes have softened slightly. (All the ingredients should retain their bright color.)
3. Season the eggs with salt and pepper and scramble in butter in another frying pan.
4. Arrange the eggs on a serving dish. Make a trough down the center of the eggs and fill with the sautéed vegetables. Garnish with parsley and serve.

SPANISH OMELETTE

A Spanish Omelette is the transition between Scrambled Eggs and an Omelette.

Serves 4

1 Spanish onion, finely chopped	1 large tomato, peeled, seeded,
2 tablespoons butter	and chopped
1 tablespoon oil	4 slices boiled ham, chopped
3 medium-sized leftover boiled	6 eggs
potatoes, grated	Salt and pepper to taste
2 cloves garlic, finely chopped	2 tablespoons finely chopped
	parsley

1. Fry onion in hot butter and oil. Add potatoes and garlic and cook until lightly browned.

2. Add tomato and ham.

3. Beat the eggs lightly, adding a little salt and pepper, and pour them into the skillet on top of the other ingredients.

4. Allow the eggs to set, lifting the edges of the "omelette" to allow uncooked part to run down the sides of the pan.

5. Serve garnished with parsley.

The Omelette Pan

Even with the best of butter, the freshest of eggs, and the greatest enthusiasm in the world, it is almost beyond the scope of human endeavor to make an omelette unless you have either your grandmother's old iron omelette pan, a seasoned aluminum version, or a Teflon skillet that has not yet been attacked with a sharp instrument.

The ideal omelette pan has rounded sides that are curved inward to prevent the eggs from spilling as they are stirred rapidly round the pan. The size is purely a matter of personal preference. Some people do not complain (audibly) at having to share a huge omelette with friends or relatives, but others prefer to have a small, plump package completely for themselves. In fact, a two-egg omelette for one person is always more moist than a six- or ten-egg omelette, which takes a long time to cook. A two-egg omelette fits exactly into an omelette pan with a 7½-inch base.

SEASONING THE PAN

Wash an iron or aluminum omelette pan, dry it, and fill it three-quarters full of cooking oil. Heat over low heat until the oil is very hot but not smoking. (You will be able to sense when it is very hot. If you add a drop of water to the oil, it will sizzle and bounce and try in vain to escape.) Remove the pan from the heat and leave it undisturbed for twelve hours. Tip out the oil and save it for another use. Wipe the pan clean with paper towels. The pan is now ready to use, and its value has quadrupled. Unless a disaster befalls, it will never need to be seasoned

An egg is always an adventure; the next one may be different.

OSCAR WILDE

again. Never wash the pan, just wipe it with paper towels and cover
with transparent wrap. Hide it under the bed to prevent anybody else
from finding it and ruining the surface by using it to fry bacon.

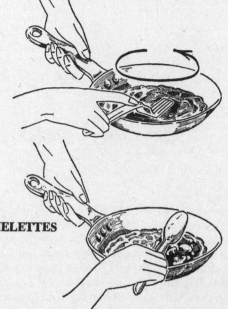

PLAIN AND FANCY OMELETTES

Serves 1

   1 tablespoon butter
   2 eggs
   Pinch of salt

   1. Place 2 eggs and a pinch of salt in a bowl and beat with a fork until they are well mixed.

   2. Heat 1 tablespoon butter in an omelette pan over moderate heat. When the butter bubbles are the size of a tiny, rising beer bubble, add the eggs.

   3. Stir the eggs immediately, holding the tines of the fork parallel with the bottom of the pan. Continue stirring as if making scrambled eggs. Stir until the eggs separate into soft curds. Spread the eggs across the bottom of the pan to make an even layer.

   4. Put the filling in a line on the side opposite the handle of the pan. (If you are making a hot filling, as opposed to a cheese filling, make sure it really is hot before tucking it inside the omelette. The cooking time inside the omelette is so brief that it will not be sufficient to heat the filling to the correct temperature.)

   5. Tip the pan away from you and slide a spatula under the unfilled half of the eggs. Lift this half and fold it over to cover the filling.

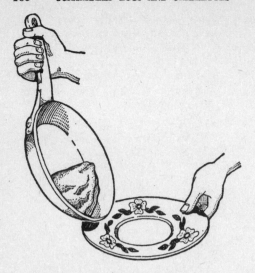

6. Slide the omelette back to the center of the pan and continue cooking for 1 minute to let the underside brown. (The side that is on the bottom will be on top when the omelette is served.)

7. Hold a warm plate in your left hand, and reverse the grip of your right hand so that your thumb is on top of the handle of the omelette pan. Tip the plate and the pan at 45° angles to each other. Invert the pan completely over the plate, and the omelette will slide out smoothly.

8. When the omelette is sitting golden and plump on the plate, brush the surface with melted butter to make it shine and add a sprig or 2 of fresh parsley for a contrast of color. Some of the omelette filling can be reserved and spooned over the completed omelette, or heat up a little of the sauce left over from last night's chicken casserole and pour it over the omelette. If you look earnestly into the back of the refrigerator, there may be all sorts of things just aching to be used.

CHEESE OMELETTE

For each omelette, add ¼ cup grated cheese to the partially cooked omelette and fold it over.

Cheese omelettes are the most difficult to make because, as the cheese melts, it tends to run beneath the eggs and stick to the surface of the pan. To prevent this from happening, avoid sprinkling the cheese too close to the edges.

TOMATO AND HERB OMELETTE

If you are in the enviable position of having access to fresh herbs and summer-ripe tomatoes, this omelette is a joy to behold and to eat. If you do not have all fresh herbs, chop fresh parsley, frozen chives, and the dried herbs together. The infinitesimal amount of moisture from the parsley helps the flavor of dried herbs considerably.

For each omelette, add ¼ cup peeled, seeded, and chopped tomato and 1 tablespoon (total) freshly chopped parsley, chives, and either tarragon or basil.

MUSHROOM OMELETTE FILLING

Serves 1

2 tablespoons butter
2 scallions, finely chopped
3 mushrooms, sliced
1 teaspoon lemon juice

¼ teaspoon salt
Freshly ground black pepper to
    taste

1. Heat the butter and fry the scallions for 3 minutes until softened.
2. Add and fry the mushrooms very briefly.
3. Season with lemon juice, salt, and pepper.
4. Fill omelette with the hot mixture and proceed with cooking.

FRIED POTATO AND BACON OMELETTE FILLING

1 tablespoon butter
1 tablespoon oil

1 small potato (or use leftover
    boiled or mashed potatoes)
3 strips bacon

1. Heat the butter and oil in a skillet.
2. Peel the potato and cut into cubes a little larger than croutons. Fry in the combined butter and oil until tender, crisp, and brown (or fry boiled or mashed potatoes until hot).
3. Fry the bacon until crisp. Drain and crumble the bacon.
4. Fill omelette with the hot mixture and proceed with cooking.

11. crêpes and their relatives

BASIC CRÊPE BATTER • MEDITERRANEAN VEGETABLE CRÊPES • SPINACH AND HAM CRÊPES • SEAFOOD CRÊPES • FRESH SALMON CRÊPES • CHICKEN AND MUSHROOM CRÊPES • BLACK CHERRY CRÊPES • STRAWBERRY CRÊPES • CRÊPES SUZETTE • PLUM CLAFOUTI • POPOVERS • YORKSHIRE PUDDING • APPLE PANCAKES • FRUIT SAUCE FOR BERRY, NUT, OR RAISIN PANCAKES • WAFFLES • CHEESE BLINTZES • SMOKED SALMON BLINTZES • CREAM PUFFS AND ÉCLAIRS • BEIGNETS SOUFFLÉS WITH APRICOT SAUCE • COCKTAIL CHEESE PUFFS • CHEESE PUFF RING • CREAM PUFF CAKE • POTATO PUFFS • GNOCCHI • FLOUNDER AND AVOCADO QUENELLES

A crêpe is a pancake with charisma. It can be served as an appetizer, a lunch dish, or even a dessert. It can cuddle a little sliced chicken, an assortment of seafoods, a combination of vegetables or fruit, or it can be served alone, folded into a triangle, bathed in fruit juice, and flamed in brandy. It can be baked into a layer cake or made into a pudding. It can become a blintz, a batter for French-fried onions, a waffle, or a popover. A crêpe can even be made (with the help of a little more flour) into a proper pancake.

All these preparations are made with almost the same ingredients, but because the proportions vary slightly and the methods of cooking are different, the results are different too!

Crêpes	Pancakes	Waffles
1¼ cups milk	1½ cups milk	1 cup milk
2 eggs	2 eggs	2 eggs
1 tablespoon butter	3 tablespoons butter	4 tablespoons butter
1 cup flour	2 cups flour	1 cup flour
¼ teaspoon salt	¼ teaspoon salt	¼ teaspoon salt
Filling	2 teaspoons baking powder	2 teaspoons baking powder

Blintzes	Batter for Frying Fritters	Beignets Soufflés, Cream Puffs, etc.
1¼ cups milk	1¼ cups milk	1 cup water
2 eggs	2 eggs	4 eggs
1 tablespoon butter	2 tablespoons butter	4 tablespoons butter
1 cup flour	1 cup flour	1 cup flour
¼ teaspoon salt	¼ teaspoon salt	¼ teaspoon salt
Filling		Filling

THE CRÊPE PAN

A crêpe pan is a very unexciting-looking utensil. It is a small, black frying pan, five to six inches across the base, with a shallow rim designed to facilitate the turning (or tossing, if you are an exhibitionist) of the crêpe. It is made of iron, and no matter how conscientiously you scrub it, the handle leaves a black smudge on your hand the first three or four times it is used. This assertion of dominance is a way for the pan to humble you into the recognition that it is the pan, not the cook, that makes the crêpe!

SEASONING THE PAN

It is easy to season a crêpe pan and, unless an accident should befall it (somebody may ruin the surface by cooking bacon and eggs in it),

it need only be seasoned once. Not only will a properly seasoned pan last for the rest of your life, but relatives may contest your will for possession of The Pan.

To season the pan, scrub it thoroughly with one of those harsh scouring powders that refrigerator manufacturers are always telling you not to use. Rinse the pan. Fill it with vegetable oil and heat it until the oil is very hot. Turn off the heat and leave the oil in the pan for twelve hours. Pour off the oil, saving it for another use. Wipe the pan with paper towels and cover it with transparent wrap. *Never* wash it or the surface will be ruined. If, by an almost inconceivable chance, you mix the crêpe batter incorrectly, it may stick to the pan. Scour the pan with salt, using a paper towel, and all will be well.

MAKING CRÊPES

1. Pour 2 tablespoons of oil into the pan and heat it over a moderate flame until it is very hot. Tip the oil into a custard cup, leaving only a thin film of oil in the pan. This will be sufficient to cook the crêpes as the batter itself contains a sufficient quantity of oil. (If the pan becomes too hot and the film of oil is lost, add a little of the reserved oil from the custard cup.)

2. Choose a kitchen spoon that holds just enough crêpe batter to cover the bottom of the pan. Pour a spoonful of batter into the hot pan and roll it around quickly until the bottom of the pan is completely covered. If there is not quite enough batter to make a completely round pancake, add a little more batter, immediately tipping out any excess. The crêpe batter will, at this point, cling to the bottom of the pan, and there is no danger of its falling out. The crêpe should be as thin as possible. (As you can readily imagine from looking at the ingredients, a

crêpe is not a mouthwateringly delicious taste treat but merely a vehicle to carry a filling.)

3. Cook the crêpe over moderate heat. After a minute or two, the batter loses its shine and becomes dull in appearance. The edges turn a delicate brown and pull away from the sides of the pan.

4. Slide a spatula under the crêpe, lift it up, and turn it onto the other side. The second side will cook more quickly than the first and will be ready in about a minute.

5. Remove the crêpe from the pan and throw it away. Now you are ready to begin. (The first crêpe simply wiped the pan for you and obligingly drank up all the excess oil, so it will not taste good at all.)

If you find when you add the crêpe batter to the pan that it shudders and pulls itself into a heap in the center of the pan, the pan itself is too hot. Wave the pan backward and forward in the air as if you were waving a flag and it will cool down very quickly. Add a little more oil to film the surface and carry on.

Crêpes have an inside and an outside. The side that is cooked first browns more evenly than the second side, which is always spotty. Stack the crêpes on a clean dishcloth, inner (spotted) side up, so that they will be ready to accept the filling.

FILLINGS AND SAUCES FOR THE CRÊPES

Crêpes are an inspired way of using up leftovers. A piece of chicken so small that it would embarrass you to put it on a plate can be cut into even smaller pieces, added to a thick cheese sauce, rolled into a crêpe, and taste as if Escoffier had autographed it.

Assuming that the batter has yielded 16 crêpes, you will need 2¼ cups of filling. The filling may consist of cooked chicken or chicken livers, meat, fish, vegetables, or fruit. Any combination of ingredients that you think will taste good together can be used to fill crêpes. In addition to the specific recipes given here, you might try a combination of crabmeat, green pepper, and tomatoes with a white sauce; diced leftover lamb and cucumbers with a curry sauce; turkey and oysters; or mushrooms with a cheese sauce.

The quantity of sauce can vary between 1 and 2 cups; this is purely a matter of personal preference. Appetizer and entrée crêpes are usually served with a plain white sauce, a cheese sauce (Mornay), Velouté, or Tomato Sauce. Part of the sauce is added to the filling ingredients to moisten them. The remaining sauce covers the filled crêpes.

The most important thing about the sauce is to make it thick enough so that the filling will retain its form when the crêpe is rolled into the

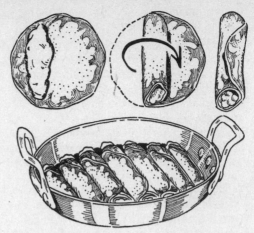

classic cigar shape. Save half the sauce, thin it slightly with whatever liquid you choose, and, when the crêpes have been reheated, spoon the hot reserved sauce over them.

Fruit crêpes can be made with any fruit, from sliced bananas to sliced fresh peaches, apples, pineapple, or blueberries. All fruit crêpes are served with a fruit sauce or whipped cream or ice cream. Fruit sauces are made by puréeing fruit in a blender or by heating the fruit juices and thickening them with cornstarch dissolved in cold juice. You can even fill crêpes with a soufflé. See page 82 (Grand Marnier Soufflé II).

If you have made mushroom or strawberry crêpes, save a few whole mushrooms or berries for garnishing the dish, or dust dessert crêpes with sifted powdered sugar. The final presentation is of the utmost importance when you are making a masterpiece.

SERVING A CROWD

The recipes for crêpes and their fillings can be doubled, quadrupled, or multiplied by any number you fancy. If you intend to make a big splash and serve strawberry crêpes and champagne to a hundred midnight revelers, it would be wise to embark on the project a day in advance and store the crêpes either filled or unfilled in the refrigerator. Should you decide that crêpes are going to become your specialty, invest in four crêpe pans. With a little practice and total concentration, you can fill one pan while emptying another while turning a third crêpe while . . . etcetera. Alternatively, you could enlist the help of a small child. Even a five-year-old can make crêpes and, given the opportunity, will leap at the chance. If there is an absence of willing help and only one crêpe pan, find a high stool, set up an assembly line, turn on the Late Late Show, and settle down in front of the stove; the crêpes will all be cooked before you realize it.

It is said that crêpes can be frozen. Indeed they can, but freezing tends to make them dry; they are infinitely more successful when they are freshly made. If you do freeze them, to reheat the crêpes, place them in a buttered baking dish, dot the surface with a tablespoon of butter, and pop them into a preheated 375° F. oven for 25 minutes; if they are at refrigerator temperature, reheat the crêpes at the same oven temperature for fifteen minutes.

BASIC CRÊPE BATTER

Yield: 16 crêpes

1¼ cups milk	2 eggs
1 tablespoon melted butter (or vegetable oil)	1 cup flour
	¼ teaspoon salt

Place all the ingredients in a blender. Turn on the motor and blend until smooth. The batter is ready for use.

Alternatively, mix the ingredients in a bowl, stirring with a wire whisk, and allow the batter to stand in the refrigerator for 30 minutes so that the milk and flour will be well combined.

If the batter is not used within a short period of time, it will become thick and will make fewer crêpes. Thin it with 2 or more tablespoons of milk.

MEDITERRANEAN VEGETABLE CRÊPES

Serves 8
Preheat oven to 375° F.

Basic Crêpe Batter	1 zucchini
1 small eggplant weighing approximately 1 pound	2 medium-sized tomatoes, peeled, seeded, and chopped
2 teaspoons salt	1 cup pitted olives, chopped
3 tablespoons oil	2 tablespoons grated Parmesan cheese
1 onion, finely chopped	2 tablespoons butter
2 cloves garlic, finely chopped	
½ green pepper	

1. Prepare 16 crêpes.

2. Cut eggplant into slices ½-inch thick. Sprinkle with salt and let stand on a wire cake-cooling rack for 15 minutes. Pat eggplant dry and cut into ½-inch cubes.

3. Heat the oil in a frying pan and fry the eggplant, onion, garlic, green pepper, and zucchini for 10 minutes over low heat, until the eggplant is soft but still retains its shape. Add the tomatoes and continue cooking for 5 minutes. Remove from the heat and add the olives.

4. Place approximately 2 tablespoons of the vegetables in a line across the nearest side of each crêpe. Roll the crêpes into a cigar shape and place, seam side down, in an oiled 10-by-14-inch baking dish. Sprinkle with Parmesan cheese and dot with butter. Heat in a preheated oven for 15 minutes.

These crêpes can also be served with a fresh Tomato Sauce.

SPINACH AND HAM CRÊPES

Serves 8
Preheat oven to 350° F.

Basic Crêpe Batter
1 10-ounce package fresh or frozen spinach
¼ cup heavy cream
2 tablespoons butter, melted
½ teaspoon salt

Freshly ground black pepper to taste
⅛ teaspoon nutmeg
1 cup chopped boiled ham (4 slices boiled ham)
1 tablespoon butter
¼ cup grated Parmesan cheese

1. Prepare 16 crêpes.

2. Fill a large saucepan with water and bring it to the boiling point. Remove the stems from the fresh spinach and wash in plenty of cold water. Add the spinach to the boiling water. Remove from the heat as soon as the water regains the boil. Drain the spinach.

3. Pour the cream and melted butter into a blender. Add a third of the spinach. Blend to form a purée. Add the remaining spinach a little at a time until it is all used.

4. Transfer the spinach to a bowl and season with salt, pepper, and nutmeg. Add the ham.

5. Place roughly ¼ cup of the mixture on the nearest side of each crêpe and roll into a cigar shape or fold the crêpes into a pocket.

6. Place the crêpes in a buttered 10-by-14-inch baking dish. Dot them with butter and sprinkle with cheese. Heat in a preheated oven for 15 minutes until very hot.

These crêpes can also be served with a Hollandaise, Velouté, Mornay, or Tomato Sauce. They are an excellent accompaniment to roast chicken and baked ham.

SEAFOOD CRÊPES

Serves 8

Preheat oven to 375° F.

Basic Crêpe Batter
1 pound shrimp, scallops, lobster meat, or a combination of firm fish. (The total quantity should measure 2¼ cups.)
2 tablespoons butter
4 scallions, finely chopped
8 small mushrooms, quartered

Sauce:
2 tablespoons butter
3 tablespoons flour
1 cup chicken broth
1 cup white wine
½ teaspoon tarragon
1 tablespoon lemon juice
¼ teaspoon salt
Freshly ground black pepper to taste
¼ cup grated Parmesan cheese

1. Prepare 16 crêpes.

2. Poach fish in simmering salted water for 5 minutes. Peel shrimp and cut fish into small pieces roughly the size of a bay scallop.

3. Heat the butter in a small frying pan. Fry the scallions for 2 minutes. Add and fry mushrooms for 2 minutes until lightly browned. Add to the fish.

4. To prepare the sauce, heat the butter in a saucepan until bubbling. Stir in the flour. Add the chicken broth and wine gradually, stirring with a wire whisk to form a thick sauce. Stir in the remaining ingredients but reserve half of the Parmesan cheese. Add half of the sauce to the fish mixture.

5. Place a portion, roughly 2 tablespoons, of the filling in a line across the nearest side of the crêpe. Roll each crêpe into a cigar shape and place it, seam side down, in a buttered 10-by-14-inch baking dish. (You will probably need two baking dishes.) Spoon the remaining sauce in a line across the center of the crêpes, sprinkle with remaining cheese, and place the dish in a preheated oven for 15 minutes, until the sauce is bubbling hot.

FRESH SALMON CRÊPES

Serves 8
Preheat oven to 375° F.

Basic Crêpe Batter	3 sprigs parsley
1 pound salmon steaks	2 tablespoons lemon juice
1 bay leaf	1 cup commercial mayonnaise
½ teaspoon thyme	2 tablespoons butter
1 teaspoon peppercorns	Hollandaise Sauce

1. Prepare 16 crêpes.

2. Place the salmon in a frying pan and cover it with water. Tie bay leaf, thyme, peppercorns, and parsley in a cheesecloth bag and immerse the bag in the water. Poach salmon, uncovered, for 8 minutes until pink and barely cooked. Drain salmon and place in a bowl. Flake the salmon and sprinkle with lemon juice. Stir in mayonnaise.

3. Place approximately 2 tablespoons of the salmon mixture in a line across the nearest side of each crêpe. Roll the crêpe into a cigar shape and place, seam side down in a buttered 10-by-15-inch baking dish. Dot the surface of the crêpes with butter and heat in a preheated oven for 15 minutes.

4. Serve with Hollandaise Sauce. Do not spoon the sauce on top of

the crêpes until they are served, as the heat of the crêpes may cause the Hollandaise to separate.

CHICKEN AND MUSHROOM CRÊPES

These crêpes are completely enveloped in a cheese sauce.

Serves 8
Preheat oven to 375° F.

Basic Crêpe Batter
2 tablespoons butter
4 scallions, finely chopped
4 mushrooms, thinly sliced
2 cups shredded cooked
  chicken
2 hard-boiled eggs, finely
  chopped
3 tablespoons finely chopped
  parsley
¼ teaspoon salt
Freshly ground black pepper to
  taste

Sauce:
3 tablespoons butter
4 tablespoons flour
2 cups milk
1 cup half-and-half
  (or heavy cream)
¼ teaspoon salt
Freshly ground black pepper to
  taste
½ cup grated Swiss cheese
¼ cup grated Parmesan cheese
½ cup freshly made bread crumbs

1. Prepare 16 crêpes.
2. To prepare the filling, heat 2 tablespoons of butter in a small frying pan. Add the scallions and mushrooms and fry them for 3 minutes. Place in a bowl and add all the remaining filling ingredients.
3. To prepare the sauce, heat 3 tablespoons of butter in a saucepan. Stir in the flour, and add the milk and cream gradually, stirring with a wire whisk to form a smooth sauce. Season with salt and pepper and stir in the cheeses. Continue cooking over low heat until the cheese has melted.
4. Add just enough sauce to the filling to moisten.
5. Place roughly 2 tablespoons of the filling in a line across the side of the crêpe nearest to you. Roll each crêpe into a cigar shape and place, seam side down, in a buttered 10-by-14-inch baking dish. Cover the crêpes with the remaining sauce and heat in a preheated oven for 15 minutes.

BLACK CHERRY CRÊPES

Serves 8
Preheat oven to 375° F.

Basic Crêpe Batter
1 2-pound can pitted Bing cherries
2 tablespoons red currant jelly
Grated rind and juice of 1 orange
1 teaspoon cinnamon
1 tablespoon cornstarch, dissolved in 2 tablespoons cherry syrup from the can
2 tablespoons butter
¼ cup sliced almonds
3 tablespoons confectioners' sugar

1. Prepare 16 crêpes.
2. Drain the cherries. Place cherries, ½ cup cherry syrup from the can, red currant jelly, grated orange rind and juice, and cinnamon in a saucepan. Cook over low heat until cherry syrup is simmering. Stir in cornstarch, dissolved in 2 tablespoons cherry juice. Stir with a wooden spoon until the sauce is thick.
3. Place roughly 2 tablespoons of the cherries with the sauce in a line across the nearest side of each crêpe. Roll crêpe into a cigar shape and place, seam side down, in a buttered 10-by-14-inch baking dish. Spoon any remaining cherries around the crêpes. Dot the surface of the crêpes with butter and sprinkle with sliced almonds. Heat in a preheated oven for 15 minutes. (Check after 10 minutes to make sure the almonds are not becoming too brown.)
4. Dust hot crêpes with sifted confectioners' sugar and serve. A heaping bowl of sweetened, vanilla-flavored whipped cream could only improve the situation.

STRAWBERRY CRÊPES

Serves 8
Preheat oven to 375° F.

Basic Crêpe Batter
½ cup red currant jelly
1 quart strawberries, sliced
Grated rind of 2 oranges (reserve fruit)
2 tablespoons Grand Marnier
1 tablespoon kirsch
2 tablespoons butter
2 tablespoons sifted confectioners' sugar
1 cup heavy cream
2 tablespoons sugar
1 teaspoon vanilla

1. Prepare 16 crêpes.

2. Spread each crêpe with red currant jelly.

3. Put the strawberries in a bowl and add the grated orange rind. Remove the white pith and cut oranges into segments, cutting between the membranes. Cut each orange section in half and add to the strawberries with the Grand Marnier and the kirsch.

4. Place about 2 tablespoons of the fruit mixture in a line across the nearest side of each crêpe. Roll the crêpes into a cigar shape and place, seam side down, in a buttered 10-by-14-inch baking dish. Add any remaining fruit and juices around the crêpes. Dot the surface of the crêpes with butter. Heat in a preheated oven for 15 minutes.

5. Whip the cream until it begins to thicken. Add the sugar and vanilla and continue beating until very thick. Dust the crêpes with sifted confectioners' sugar, and serve the whipped cream on the side.

CRÊPES SUZETTE

Serves 8

Basic Crêpe Batter
6 tablespoons butter
⅓ cup sugar

Grated rind and juice of 2
    oranges
Grated rind and juice of 1 lemon
¼ cup Grand Marnier or brandy

174 CRÊPES AND THEIR RELATIVES

1. Prepare 16 crêpes.

2. Heat the butter in the top part of a chafing dish. Add the sugar, orange and lemon rinds, and fruit juices. Heat until very hot.

3. Place the first crêpe, flat, into the sauce. Using two spatulas, fold the crêpe in half and then in half again to form a triangle. Move the crêpe to the side of the pan. Continue until all the crêpes have been immersed in the sauce and folded. The folded crêpes should cover the bottom of the chafing dish.

4. Add the Grand Marnier (or brandy). (Do not shake the pan or the brandy will become diluted with the liquid in the pan.) Ignite the brandy and flame the crêpes. Spoon the sauce over the crêpes and serve immediately.

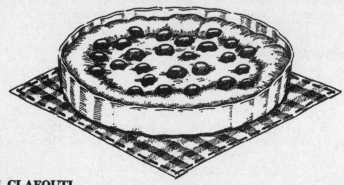

PLUM CLAFOUTI

A clafouti is a quickly made dessert using fruit suspended in a batter that is very similar to a Basic Crêpe Batter. One pound of apples, cherries, sliced peaches, berries, or any other fruit may be substituted for the plums. A bowl of whipped cream improves this and a thousand other desserts.

Serves 6
Preheat oven to 350° F.

1¼ cups milk	1 cup flour
3 eggs	1 pound firm, ripe plums
½ cup sugar	2 tablespoons confectioners'
½ teaspoon cinnamon	sugar
1 tablespoon butter, melted	

1. To prepare the batter, place the milk, eggs, sugar, cinnamon, butter, and flour in a blender and blend until smooth.

2. Pour a thin (½-inch) layer of batter into an 8-inch pie plate and place in a preheated oven for 10 minutes until it has become firm.

3. Cut the plums into small pieces, removing the pits, and place the plums on top of the baked batter.

4. Pour on the remaining batter. Return the pan to the oven and bake for another 20 minutes until firm and golden.

5. Dust with sifted confectioners' sugar and serve immediately.

POPOVERS

Popovers are made with the same ingredients as a Basic Crêpe Batter. The only difference is in the quantity of milk used.

Yield: 8 popovers
Preheat oven to 450° F.

1 cup milk	1 cup flour
2 eggs	¼ teaspoon salt
1 tablespoon vegetable oil (or melted butter)	

1. Oil eight sections of a muffin pan and place the pan in the oven for 5 minutes until it is very hot.

2. Place all the ingredients in a blender in the order listed and blend until smooth.

3. Pour the batter into the hot muffin pan, filling each section half full. Bake for 15 minutes. Reduce oven temperature to 400° F. and continue cooking for another 15 minutes.

YORKSHIRE PUDDING

Yorkshire Pudding is made from a popover batter, except that drippings are substituted for oil in the baking dish.

Serves 6
Preheat oven to 450° F.

2 tablespoons fat drippings from roast beef	1 tablespoon oil
1 cup milk	1 cup flour
2 eggs	¼ teaspoon salt

1. Remove 2 tablespoons hot fat drippings from a roasting beef and place in a 9-inch pie plate or a muffin tin. Put the plate in a preheated oven for 5 minutes until it is very hot.

2. Place all the remaining ingredients in a blender and blend until smooth.

3. Pour the batter into the hot pie plate. Bake in a preheated oven for 15 minutes. Reduce the oven temperature to 400° F. and bake another 15 minutes.

APPLE PANCAKES

Pancakes are thick crêpes.

Serves 4

Batter:
1½ cups milk
2 eggs
3 tablespoons butter, melted
2 cups flour
¼ teaspoon salt
1 tablespoon sugar
2 teaspoons double-acting
    baking powder
¼ teaspoon nutmeg

½ teaspoon cinnamon
Grated rind of 1 lemon

2 cooking apples

2 tablespoons butter
2 tablespoons oil

¼ cup confectioners' sugar
4 tablespoons butter
Maple syrup (or honey) to taste

1. Place the milk, eggs, and melted butter in a bowl and stir with a wire whisk.

2. Sift the flour and measure 2 cups into another bowl. Add the salt, sugar, baking powder, nutmeg, cinnamon, and grated lemon rind. Stir dry ingredients well with a fork.

3. Add the dry ingredients to the liquid ingredients and stir until all the ingredients are barely combined. (Don't worry about tiny lumps in the batter; they will vanish while the pancakes are cooking.)

4. Peel and core the apples and cut them into *very* thin slices. (There should be a cup or slightly more apple slices cut so thin one could almost read the newspaper through them. If you would prefer thicker slices of apple, cook them in a little butter to soften them before adding to the pancake batter.)

5. Fold the apple slices into the batter.

6. Combine the butter and oil and divide it between two large frying pans. Heat until hot. Make each pancake with ¼ cup pancake batter. When the bubbles break on the surface of the pancake, turn it onto the other side and continue cooking until the underside has browned lightly. The second side takes half as long to cook as the first side.

7. Dust pancakes with sifted confectioners' sugar and serve with butter and warm maple syrup or honey.

Note: If they are beautifully ready and somebody is still in bed, arrange the pancakes in a single layer on a cookie sheet lined with a tea towel and place it in a preheated 200° F. oven. Do *not* stack the pancakes or they will steam and become soggy.

FRUIT SAUCE FOR BERRY, NUT, OR RAISIN PANCAKES

Prepare the Apple Pancake batter, substituting 1 to 1½ cups of any other fruit, berries, nuts, or raisins for the apples. Serve the pancakes with ice cream and a Fruit Sauce.

1 10-ounce package frozen raspberries, thawed (or 1¼ cups ripe blueberries, strawberries, peaches, or other fruit)
¼ cup sugar

1 tablespoon lemon juice
2 tablespoons cornstarch, dissolved in 2 tablespoons cold water (optional)

1. Place the fruit in a blender with the sugar and lemon juice and purée.

2. Force the fruit through a strainer to remove skins and seeds. Usually the sauce is now ready to serve but sometimes the strawberries are watery, especially if it has been a rainy season or if you have given them a bath. If you would prefer a thicker sauce, heat the strained fruit in a small saucepan, and when it reaches boiling point, stir in the cornstarch, dissolved in cold water. It will thicken immediately. Continue simmering the sauce for 2 or 3 minutes to get rid of the raw cornstarch taste. (The same proportion of arrowroot makes a clearer sauce, but arrowroot is considerably more costly and often difficult to find.)

WAFFLES

Yield: 4 8-inch waffles

1 cup milk
2 eggs, separated
4 tablespoons butter, melted
1½ cups flour
¼ teaspoon salt

1 tablespoon sugar
2 teaspoons double-acting baking
powder
2 tablespoons butter, melted

1. Place the milk, egg yolks, and melted butter in a bowl and stir with wire whisk to ensure they are well mixed.
2. Sift the flour and measure 1 cup into a bowl. Add the salt, sugar, and baking powder. Stir the dry ingredients with a fork.
3. Add the dry ingredients to the liquid ingredients and stir until all the ingredients are barely combined.
4. Beat the egg whites until they stand in soft peaks. Fold into the batter.
5. Brush a preheated waffle iron with melted butter. Pour about ½ cup of the batter onto the bottom of the iron. Lower the cover but do not press it down. Bake each waffle for about 4 minutes until it has stopped steaming. Open the iron and remove the waffle with a fork. Serve with butter and warm maple syrup, ice cream, or fruit sauce.

CHEESE BLINTZES

Serves 8

Basic Crêpe Batter
2 cups cottage cheese
2 3-ounce packages
cream cheese
¼ cup sugar
2 eggs
2 tablespoons butter
2 tablespoons oil
1 cup sour cream
Cinnamon sugar
or preserves

1. Make 16 crêpes.
2. To prepare the filling, beat the cheeses in a mixer until softened. Beat in the sugar and the eggs, one at a time.

3. Brush each crêpe with cold water. Place about two tablespoons of the cheese mixture slightly off the center of each crêpe (blintz). Fold facing sides over the filling so that they almost meet in the center. Fold over the other two sides, short end first. Fold again to secure the flap.

4. Fry the blintzes in hot combined butter and oil for 3 or 4 minutes until lightly browned on both sides. Top with a spoonful of sour cream and dust with cinnamon sugar or preserves.

SMOKED SALMON BLINTZES

These are prepared in exactly the same way as Cheese Blintzes. For the filling, beat 2 3-ounce packages of cream cheese until softened. Stir in 2 tablespoons of lemon juice and ¼ pound shredded smoked salmon. After frying, top the blintzes with sour cream, finely chopped onion, capers, and freshly ground black pepper.

CREAM PUFFS AND ÉCLAIRS (CHOU PASTE)

Yield: 30 puffs or 24 éclairs
Preheat oven to 375° F.

Chou Paste:
1 cup water
4 tablespoons butter
¼ teaspoon salt
1 cup sifted all-purpose flour
4 eggs

Glaze:
1 egg yolk, combined with
  2 tablespoons milk

Filling:
1 cup heavy cream
2 tablespoons sugar
1 teaspoon vanilla

Chocolate Coating:
1 6-ounce package semisweet
  chocolate pieces
2 tablespoons water
1 tablespoon butter

1. Pour the water into a heavy saucepan. Cut the butter into small pieces and drop into the water. Add the salt. Place the pan over moderately low heat. Adjust the heat so that the butter melts completely just as the water comes to a boil.

2. Remove the pan from the heat and add the flour all at once. Beat in the flour vigorously and return the pan to a low heat. Stir the mixture for about 2 minutes, until it forms a ball. (The bottom of the pan will have a thin glaze of flour.)

3. Remove the pan from the heat again and beat in the eggs, one at a time. Beat the mixture until it is very thick before adding each egg.

4. Spoon the mixture into a large pastry bag fitted with a plain No. 6 tube. To make cream puffs, pipe small mounds (about a tablespoon each) of the mixture on buttered, floured cookie sheets, or shape the mixture between two spoons. To make éclairs, pipe the mixture into strips about 2½ inches long. Leave a space of 1 inch between the cream puffs or éclairs to allow them to expand.

5. Brush each mound with glaze.

6. Bake in a preheated oven for 35 minutes until the pastry is puffed and golden and firm to the touch. Do not take puffs out of the oven if they are soft or they will collapse. Cool on wire cake-cooling racks.

7. To prepare filling, whip the cream in a small bowl until slightly thickened. Add the sugar and continue beating until thick. Add the vanilla. Cut each puff in half and cram in as much whipped cream as possible. Cream puffs and éclairs can also be filled with ice cream, Pastry Cream (see page 215), or any of the suggestions for crêpe fillings.

8. Melt the chocolate in a small saucepan with the water and butter. Cool for 5 minutes, then dip each puff or éclair into the melted chocolate. Arrange éclairs on paper doilies and invite in a gaggle of ladies with initials on their sweaters. They will all refuse the éclairs, graciously but sorrowfully, and when they leave, there will be none left.

BEIGNETS SOUFFLÉS (DEEP-FRIED CREAM PUFFS) WITH APRICOT SAUCE

Serves 6

Chou Paste
Oil (or solid shortening) for deep frying
¼ cup confectioners' sugar

Apricot Sauce:
2 tablespoons apricot preserves
1 1-pound can apricots, drained
Rind and juice of 1 lemon
2 tablespoons dark Jamaica rum (or kirsch)

1. Prepare Chou Paste as for Cream Puffs.
2. Heat fat to 375° F.
3. Using two tablespoons, drop mounds of the mixture into the deep fat. (Do not crowd the pan or the puffs will not become crisp.) As they cook, the puffs will roll over and conveniently brown themselves on all sides.
4. Drain the puffs on paper towels and dust with sifted confectioners' sugar.
5. Heat the apricot preserves in a small saucepan and force through a strainer. Place with the remaining ingredients in a blender until a smooth sauce is formed.

COCKTAIL CHEESE PUFFS

Yield: 60 puffs
Preheat oven to 375° F.

Chou Paste
¾ cup grated Swiss cheese and ¼ cup grated Parmesan cheese (or 1 cup grated Cheddar cheese)

1 tablespoon Worcestershire sauce
1 egg yolk, combined with 2 tablespoons milk

1. Prepare the puffs in exactly the same way as the Cream Puffs on page 179, folding in the cheese and Worcestershire sauce after the eggs have been added (step 3).

2. Drop the batter by teaspoonfuls on a buttered, floured cookie sheet.

3. Glaze the puffs with egg yolk combined with milk. Bake in a preheated oven for about 25 minutes or less, depending on the size.

4. When they are baked, serve the hot puffs just as they are or fill each puff with one of the following:

- A littleneck clam or an oyster sprinkled with lemon juice or cocktail sauce
- Minced ham in a mustard-flavored mayonnaise
- Bacon wrapped around a chicken liver and broiled until crisp
- Meat, chicken, or fish in a thick, thick cream sauce
- Any of the other crêpe or omelette fillings (A sauced mixture is slightly dangerous as it tends to come as a boiling-hot surprise and does not make a welcome design as it drips down ties or onto bare flesh. For these reasons, sauce-filled puffs are best served on a plate, with a fork, on a table, with a napkin.)

CHEESE PUFF RING (GOUGÈRE)

Serves 6
Preheat oven to 375° F.

Prepare Cocktail Cheese Puff recipe. Using a pastry bag fitted with a large plain tube, make a 9-inch circle of puffs, arranged so that they

are touching each other. Glaze with an egg yolk combined with milk and bake in a preheated oven for 35 minutes until firm and golden. Slice and serve with cocktails or fill the center of the ring with chicken or shrimp salad, or chicken livers in Sauce Madeira, or Beef Stroganoff.

CREAM PUFF CAKE (GÂTEAU ST. HONORÉ)

Serves 8
Preheat oven to 375° F.

Chou Paste
1 egg yolk, combined with
  1 tablespoon milk

Whipped cream or Pastry Cream
½ cup apricot preserves
½ cup sliced almonds

1. Prepare Chou Paste. Form the mixture into a 9-inch circle using a pastry bag fitted with a plain tube, or form into a circle of separate (but touching) mounds. Brush with egg yolk combined with milk and bake in a preheated oven for 35 minutes.
2. Cool the cake and split it in half horizontally. Sandwich with whipped cream or Pastry Cream.
3. Toast the almonds in a preheated 350° F. oven for 8 minutes until lightly browned.
4. Melt the apricot preserves and force them through a strainer.
5. Brush liquid apricot glaze on the top of the cake and sprinkle almonds on top.

POTATO PUFFS

An appetizer or accompaniment to a steak or roast. If you make these once, everybody will remember and ask for them again!

Serves 8

½ recipe for Chou Paste
3 baking potatoes
½ teaspoon salt
Freshly ground black pepper to
  taste

2 tablespoons chopped chives
Oil (or solid shortening) for
  deep frying

1. Prepare Chou Paste.
2. Boil potatoes and force them through a potato ricer or grate them.

(There should be 2 cups potatoes.) Season with salt and pepper and add chives. Combine the seasoned potatoes with Chou Paste.

3. Heat the fat to 375° F. (See notes on deep-fat frying on pages 138–39.)

4. Wet two teaspoons and form the potato mixture into mounds. Slide mounds, a few at a time, into deep fat and fry for 8 minutes until puffed and golden. Serve hot.

GNOCCHI (POTATO-HERB DUMPLINGS)

Serves 6

½ recipe Chou Paste
4 baking potatoes
1 teaspoon chervil
2 tablespoons finely chopped parsley

2 tablespoons finely chopped chives
½ teaspoon salt
Freshly ground black pepper to taste

1. Boil the potatoes in their jackets until tender. Peel and force through a potato ricer, or grate the potatoes. (There should be 2 cups.) Combine potatoes with Chou Paste. Add the remaining ingredients.

2. Form the mixture into 2-inch balls.

3. Poach balls in simmering salted water or chicken broth for 15 minutes. Do not let the water boil or the dumplings will disintegrate. Serve with boiled beef or in a soup.

Avocado

Although the emperors of Rome ate avocados, this exotic fruit temporarily lost its popularity, and, until it was brought back to Europe from South America in the sixteenth century, it was virtually unknown for hundreds of years.

Several varieties of avocados were brought from Mexico to California at the turn of the century. One type survived particularly well and soon began producing a finer fruit than the original tree. In 1948, a few members of the California Avocado Association traveled back to Mexico with their improved avocados. With appropriate ceremony and a commemorative plaque, the noble avocado returned to the soil of its origin—"as the son returns to the land of its fathers to perpetuate its kind."

California avocados differ from the Florida varieties in the thickness of the skin. All avocados, however, have a very similar flavor. The thin-skinned avocados come from California and "give" slightly when they are pressed for ripeness. (The squeezing of avocados is a dangerous pastime—it turns the seller's face purple and the avocados brown.)

If you buy an avocado that is not completely ripe, leave it out at room temperature until it ripens. (It will ripen so slowly in the refrigerator that it tends to deteriorate before it softens.) Cut the avocado with a stainless-steel knife if possible and, to prevent discoloration, sprinkle it immediately with lemon or lime juice.

FLOUNDER AND AVOCADO QUENELLES

Quenelles are made basically from a foundation of Chou Paste but fewer eggs are used; the mixture is therefore very light.

Serves 4

1 cup water
4 tablespoons butter
¼ teaspoon salt
1 cup flour
2 eggs
1 pound flounder fillets, poached

1 small avocado, mashed
1 tablespoon lemon juice
1 tablespoon fresh herbs or
   1 teaspoon dried herbs (parsley, dill weed, or marjoram)

1. Pour the water into a heavy saucepan. Cut the butter into small pieces and drop into the water. Add the salt. Place the pan over mod-

erately low heat. Adjust the heat so that the butter melts completely just as the water comes to a boil.

2. Remove the pan from the heat and add the flour all at once. Beat in the flour vigorously and return the pan to a low heat. Stir the mixture for about 2 minutes until it forms a ball. (The bottom of the pan will have a thin glaze of flour.)

3. Remove the pan from the heat again and beat in the eggs, one at a time. Beat the mixture until it is very thick before adding each egg.

4. Pound the fish to a smooth paste or put it through the fine blade of a meat grinder. Combine Chou Paste, fish, avocado, lemon juice, and herbs.

5. Fill a large, deep frying pan with water and add salt. Bring to simmering point. Wet two tablespoons and form the fish mixture into ovals. Slide each oval into the simmering salted water. Continue until all of the mixture is used. Poach the quenelles for 15 minutes. Do not let the water boil or they will disintegrate.

6. Serve with Tomato Sauce or Sauce Mornay.

12. mousses

CHOCOLATE-ORANGE MOUSSE · CHOCOLATE MOUSSE · CARAMEL MOUSSE · APRICOT RUM MOUSSE · SALMON MOUSSE · EGG MOUSSE · COLD LEMON SOUFFLÉ · COLD ORANGE SOUFFLÉ · CHOCOLATE SOUFFLÉ ROLL

Mousse is an imprecise culinary term. An entrée mousse is made by suspending ground or finely chopped meat, fish, or vegetables in a flavorful broth to which gelatin has been added. Egg yolks, mayonnaise, white sauce, butter, or cream may also be added to the mixture. The mousse is chilled in the refrigerator until it has set.

Mousses in the second group are built on a foundation of beaten egg yolks and sugar, flavored with chocolate or liqueurs. Beaten egg whites, cream, and/or butter are added, and the mixture is chilled for at least four hours until it has set.

The third branch of the mousse family is a frozen dessert that is prepared by combining a fruit purée with cream.

A so-called cold soufflé is also a mousse, lightened with a large quantity of egg white and molded with gelatin so that it presents the illusion of having risen above the level of the container in which it is served. It is this illusion that gives the cold soufflé its name.

Chocolate

*The Aztecs were the first known people to unlock the secrets of
cacao beans. So sublime was the foaming drink made from the beans
that the Aztecs thought the origin of the tree must surely be divine.
The Greeks agreed and gave the cacao tree its botanical name,*
Theobroma Cacao, *or "food of the Gods."*

*Columbus carried cacao beans back to Spain after one of his
voyages of discovery. It was not until three centuries later, however,
that the Spaniards began drinking cocoa. When vanilla and sugar
were added, the popularity of cocoa spread rapidly all over Europe.
In London, chocolate shops sprang up, and when the British imposed
their infamous tea tax, hot chocolate became the most popular drink
in the Colonies. The Swiss put milk into the chocolate and changed
the form from a liquid into a solid food. In America, more chocolate
is made and eaten than any other flavoring. Chocolate and orange
have an extraordinary affinity with each other.*

Oranges

*Californians say, "If you want to eat an orange from Florida, you
have to get into the bathtub." Florida's orange-juice lovers say, "If you
roll a truck over a California orange, the pavement will not be wet."*

*An orange was the golden apple of the Hesperides, the prize sought
and stolen by Hercules. Oranges were first mentioned by Confucius
in the second of his five classics, written in 500 B.C., which suggests
that Chinese emperors were eating oranges some time before the
Florida-California dispute arose.*

CHOCOLATE-ORANGE MOUSSE

The following chocolate mousse is delicate, light, rich, and chocolaty,
with just a hint of orange. It is easy to make and can be frozen.

The eggs and sugar are beaten together to form a base. Chocolate
is added for flavoring and a secondary flavor of orange is added to make
it more interesting and to cut the richness of the chocolate. To be abso-
lutely sure the mixture does not separate, gelatin is added. (This is
strictly against the rules of the Amalgamation of Mousse Makers, Inc.,

but it works.) The whipped cream enriches the dessert and acts as a soft pedal uniting all the flavors and holding them in joyful suspension.

Although the directions suggest that there will be enough for eight guests, this recipe has been known to serve just one midnight prowler.

Serves 8

2 eggs
3 egg yolks
½ cup sugar
6 ounces semisweet chocolate pieces
¼ cup water
Rind and juice of 1 orange
2 tablespoons Grand Marnier
1 teaspoon unflavored gelatin
1 cup heavy cream

1. Beat together the eggs, egg yolks, and sugar until they are very thick.

2. Place the chocolate pieces in a saucepan, add the water, and stir over gentle heat until the chocolate has melted. Cool slightly and stir the melted chocolate into the egg mixture.

3. Grate the orange rind and stir into the chocolate-egg mixture. Add the Grand Marnier.

4. Strain the orange juice into a small saucepan. Sprinkle the gelatin *on top* of the orange juice and allow it to stand undisturbed for 5 minutes.

5. Place the gelatin and juice mixture over low heat until it has dissolved and a clear liquid has formed. Do not let it boil. Stir the hot liquid into the chocolate mixture.

6. Whip the cream until it is the same consistency as the chocolate mixture. Fold the cream into the mixture.

7. Transfer the mousse into individual serving dishes or a decorative dish. Chill for 4 hours before serving.

CHOCOLATE MOUSSE

This is a richer, denser dessert than the Chocolate-Orange Mousse. For this mousse, the eggs are separated and butter is added instead of cream. This is the traditional type of mousse served in most restaurants.

Serves 6

¼ pound bitter (or semisweet) chocolate
4 egg yolks
½ cup sugar
4 tablespoons butter, softened
2 tablespoons rum, Grand Marnier, crème de menthe, Tia Maria, or other liqueur (optional)
4 egg whites

1. Break the chocolate into small pieces and put them on a plate. Cover with another plate. Put the plates on top of a saucepan of simmering water and leave for 10 minutes, until the chocolate has melted.

2. Beat the egg yolks and sugar until the mixture is very thick.

3. Fold in the melted chocolate, butter, and liqueur.

4. In a separate bowl, beat the egg whites until they stand in soft peaks.

5. Fold the chocolate mixture gently into the egg whites.

6. Divide the mixture among individual serving dishes and chill for 4 hours before serving. Or instead of serving it in individual dishes, you can chill it in prepared chocolate cases or scooped-out orange halves.

CARAMEL MOUSSE

Serves 8

1½ cups sugar	Grated rind and juice of 1 lemon
⅔ cup water	1 tablespoon unflavored gelatin
2 eggs	1 cup heavy cream
3 egg yolks	

1. Put 1 cup sugar and ⅓ cup water in a small, heavy saucepan. Place over low heat and cook without stirring until the sugar has melted into liquid caramel. Continue cooking until it is a rich, brown color. *Very carefully* add the remaining ⅓ cup water. (The caramel is extremely hot so add the water slowly, being very careful not to burn yourself.) Set the caramel aside to cool.

2. In a mixing bowl, beat together the eggs, egg yolks, and the remaining sugar until very thick.

3. Stir the caramel into the egg mixture.

4. Add the grated lemon rind and stir.

5. Strain the lemon juice into a small saucepan. Sprinkle the gelatin *on top* of the lemon juice and allow it to stand undisturbed for 5 minutes.

6. Place the gelatin over low heat until it has dissolved and a clear liquid is formed. Do not let the gelatin boil. Stir the hot liquid into the caramel mixture.

7. Whip the cream until it is the same consistency as the caramel mixture. Fold the cream into the mixture.

8. Transfer the mousse into individual serving dishes or a decorative dish. Chill for 4 hours before serving.

APRICOT RUM MOUSSE

A fruit mousse is made in the same way as a Chocolate Mousse. The basic ingredients and the proportional relationships of the ingredients remain the same; only the flavor is changed.

Serves 8

2 eggs	Grated rind and juice of 1 lemon
3 egg yolks	2 tablespoons dark rum
½ cup sugar	1 tablespoon unflavored gelatin
1 cup canned apricots, puréed	1 cup heavy cream

1. Beat together the eggs, egg yolks, and sugar until they are very thick.

2. Stir the apricot purée, lemon rind, and rum into the egg mixture.

3. Strain the lemon juice into a saucepan. Add water, if necessary, to make ¼ cup of juice.

4. Sprinkle the gelatin *on top* of the lemon juice and allow it to stand undisturbed for 5 minutes.

5. Place the gelatin over a low heat until it has dissolved and a clear liquid is formed. Do not let the gelatin boil. Stir the hot liquid into the apricot mixture.

6. Whip the cream until it is the same consistency as the apricot mixture. Fold the cream into the mixture.

7. Transfer the mousse into individual serving dishes or a decorative dish. Chill for 4 hours before serving.

OTHER FRUIT MOUSSES

One cup of any other puréed fruit may be substituted for one cup of apricot purée in the Apricot Rum Mousse recipe, but be sure to select a very flavorful fruit and to enhance the flavor with an appropriate liqueur. Strawberries and peaches tend to become rather lost in this mixture and are more successfully made into a frozen mousse. (See Grand Marnier Soufflé IV, page 84.) Suggestions for other fruit mousses:

- 1 cup puréed raspberries and 2 tablespoons Frambiose
- 1 cup puréed blueberries and 2 tablespoons Cointreau
- 1 cup applesauce and 2 tablespoons apple brandy

See also suggestions under Other Cold Soufflés (page 198).

SALMON MOUSSE

Many entrée or appetizer mousses resemble the dessert mousses in name only. This Salmon Mousse is essentially a very thick velouté sauce flavored with salmon and sherry.

Yield: 2½ cups

½ pound poached salmon steak (or use canned salmon, drained)	¾ teaspoon salt
	Freshly ground pepper to taste
2 tablespoons butter	2 tablespoons butter, softened
2 tablespoons flour	2 tablespoons heavy cream
¾ cup light cream	2 tablespoons sherry
	1 tablespoon lemon juice

1. Mash the salmon with a pestle and mortar until it becomes a smooth paste. If you do not have a pestle and mortar, put the salmon in a small bowl and mash it with the base of a small glass jar or glass.

2. To prepare the sauce, heat 2 tablespoons of butter in a small saucepan. Stir in the flour and add the light cream gradually. Stir with a wire whisk to form a thick white sauce. Season the sauce with salt and pepper and cook over very low heat for 5 minutes. Transfer the sauce to a flat plate to allow it to cool quickly.

3. Stir 2 tablespoons softened butter into the salmon. Stir in the heavy cream, sherry, and lemon juice. Fold in the cooled white sauce.

4. Pour the Salmon Mousse into an oiled mold, cover it with transparent wrap, and chill it for 4 hours.

5. Unmold the mousse and serve on a bed of Boston lettuce garnished with lemon wedges and cucumber for an appetizer, or on freshly made toast fingers or crackers as an accompaniment for cocktails.

EGG MOUSSE

This Egg Mousse, like the Salmon Mousse, has a base of thick white sauce. Like all other mousses, it has a soft, "mosslike" texture.

Serves 6 as appetizer

2 tablespoons butter	¼ cup white wine, chicken
3 scallions, finely chopped	broth, or water
2 tablespoons flour	1 package unflavored gelatin
¾ cup milk	¼ cup heavy cream
4 hard-boiled eggs	Boston lettuce
1 teaspoon prepared mustard	1 cup tiny shrimp, cooked
2 teaspoons Worcestershire	1 tomato, sliced
sauce	½ cucumber, sliced
1 tablespoon chili sauce	Toast
½ cup mayonnaise	

1. Heat the butter in a small saucepan. Add the scallions and fry over low heat for 5 minutes until softened. Stir in the flour and add the milk gradually, stirring with a wire whisk. Leave to cool.

2. Chop the eggs finely. Place the eggs in a bowl and add mustard, Worcestershire sauce, chili sauce, and mayonnaise.

3. Measure the wine (or other liquid) into a small saucepan. Sprinkle gelatin over the wine and leave undisturbed for 5 minutes. Heat over low heat until a clear liquid has formed.

4. Stir cooled white sauce into egg mixture. Add gelatin liquid and the heavy cream, and pour into an oiled mold. Cover it with transparent wrap and chill for 4 hours.

5. Unmold the mousse and serve on a bed of Boston lettuce leaves. Garnish with tiny shrimp. Arrange sliced tomato and cucumber around mousse. Serve with freshly made hot toast triangles.

COLD SOUFFLÉS

A cold soufflé is really not a soufflé at all but a molded mousse. The capacity of the soufflé dish is temporarily increased by the use of a paper collar. When the collar is removed, the soufflé appears to have "risen" above the dish. It is the addition of gelatin to the mousse mixture that holds the soufflé in this seemingly precarious position.

A cold soufflé is a spectacular dessert. It can be prepared a day in advance and even frozen. Individual servings can be made in wine glasses with a collar tied around each glass until the soufflé has set.

A cold soufflé is made in five steps:

1. Beat the egg yolks and sugar until they are very thick. It is impossible to overbeat them. Just beat them and beat them and beat them until you cannot beat them any more, and then beat them for another 5 minutes. Add the grated rind and add the lemon juice *slowly* while

continuing to beat the mixture. (The mixture will thin slightly with the addition of the fruit juice but will become almost as thick again with persistent beating. Be patient.)

2. Whip the cream until it is the same consistency as the egg mixture.

3. Sprinkle the gelatin *on top* of the cold water. Do not add water to the gelatin or it will form a clump that is difficult to dissolve later. If there are some dry, powdery grains of gelatin on the surface, sprinkle them with cold water to make sure that every particle is softened before it is heated. Allow the gelatin to stand undisturbed. Do not stir it or it will stick to the spoon. After 5 minutes, place it over a gentle flame and, firmly resisting all temptation to stir it, let the gelatin melt until it becomes a clear liquid. Do not let it boil or it loses its setting quality.

4. Beat the egg whites until they are the same consistency as the cream.

5. Now, all you have to do is put the whole thing together. Fold the whipped cream into the egg-yolk mixture. Fold in the dissolved gelatin, and then fold in the egg whites. Transfer the mixture to the prepared soufflé dish and chill for at least 4 hours. A cold soufflé may be frozen, but allow at least 6 hours for it to defrost.

COLD LEMON SOUFFLÉ

Serves 10

5 egg yolks	⅓ cup cold water
1¼ cups sugar	2 cups heavy cream
Grated rind of 3 lemons	5 egg whites
¾ cup lemon juice	⅛ teaspoon salt
2 packages unflavored gelatin	⅛ teaspoon cream of tartar

1. Measure a piece of wax paper long enough to encircle a 1½-quart soufflé dish, allowing a 2-inch overlap. Fold paper in half lengthwise. Oil and sprinkle the top third of the folded paper with sugar. Tie the paper around the dish, sugared side inside.

2. Beat egg yolks and sugar together until very, very thick.

3. Add grated lemon rind. Add lemon juice gradually, beating constantly.

4. Sprinkle gelatin on cold water in a small saucepan. Allow to stand undisturbed for 5 minutes. Then melt gelatin over low heat.

5. In a mixing bowl, beat cream lightly.

6. In another bowl, beat egg whites with the salt and cream of tartar until they stand in soft peaks.

7. Combine egg-sugar mixture with the beaten cream.

8. Stir in gelatin liquid.

9. Fold in egg whites.

10. Pour mixture into the prepared soufflé dish and chill for 4 hours.

Gelatin

Gelatin turns water into a glistening window. Added to a clear beef consommé, it forms an aspic and holds meats and vegetables in a molded suspension, displaying each morsel like a glistening jewel. Without imparting any taste, gelatin will hold a mousse together and create the optical illusion of a cold soufflé. Gelatin is one of the most important ingredients in the kitchen, and, like all superstars, it is a little temperamental.

One envelope of unflavored gelatin measures one tablespoon and will "set" two cups of liquid. Don't feel tempted to add more gelatin, for it will produce an unpleasant rubbery texture. Gelatin will set not only water but wine and all fruit juices except pineapple. Pineapple juice must be boiled first to rearrange its chemical properties before setting with gelatin.

Before gelatin is added to cream, custards, mousses, and similar thick mixtures, it must first be dissolved in water.

Measure the water and pour into a small saucepan. Sprinkle the gelatin on the water. The gelatin powder will soften as it absorbs the liquid. Allow the gelatin to rest for five minutes. If there are any powdery grains remaining on the surface, sprinkle them with a teaspoon of cold water. Place the pan over gentle heat and stay close by. Do not stir the gelatin or answer the telephone. Remove the pan from the heat before the gelatin boils and allow it to cool slightly.

It may be incorporated into other ingredients either in a mixer at the lowest speed or by folding in gradually with a rubber spatula.

I find it best not to stand desserts prepared with gelatin directly on the shelf of the freezer. The shelf will act as a source of cold, just as an electric burner is a source of heat. The cold shelf causes the gelatin to fall in a sheet of rubber to the bottom of the bowl. Place the bowl on a double-folded layer of kitchen towel to prevent this from happening, and all will be well.

COLD ORANGE SOUFFLÉ

Serves 10

5 eggs, separated
1¼ cups sugar
Grated rind of 2 oranges
¾ cup freshly squeezed, strained orange juice
3 tablespoons Grand Marnier
2 packages unflavored gelatin

⅓ cup cold water
2 cups heavy cream
⅛ teaspoon salt
⅛ teaspoon cream of tartar
1 orange, cut into segments, for decoration

Cold Orange Soufflé is made in exactly the same way as Cold Lemon Soufflé. Add the Grand Marnier with the orange juice and decorate the top of the soufflé with orange segments after it has set.

OTHER COLD SOUFFLÉS

If your enchantment with Cold Lemon or Orange Soufflé fades, you could try some other variations. All are made in the same way. Eliminate the fruit rind and juice and in their place, stir into the egg-yolk-and-sugar mixture one of the following combinations:

- 1 cup strained blackberries and 3 tablespoons Framboise or kirsch
- 1 cup puréed fresh or canned peaches or apricots and 3 tablespoons rum or Grand Marnier
- 1 cup sweetened chestnut purée and 3 tablespoons rum
- 1 cup semisweet chocolate pieces, melted in 3 tablespoons rum, Grand Marnier, or crème de menthe (making a chocolate-peppermint cream soufflé)

See also suggestions under Other Fruit Mousses. Bear in mind, when you think of other variations, that the basic soufflé mixture is very bland, so you need a strong boost of flavor to dominate the dessert.

Raspberries

If the legend is to be believed, the red raspberry was new in the days when the gods were young. Once, all raspberries were white. Then one day, when Zeus was a baby "making the echoes of the mountains ring with his cries," the nymph Ida searched for berries with which to placate him. She scratched herself on the thorns of the bush, and since that time raspberries have been tinged with her blood! Thus the Latin or botanical name for raspberry—rubus idaeus. (Rubus means red color, and idaeus is the word from which Ida is derived.)

Fresh raspberries are always very expensive to buy, partly because they are so soft that they tend to spoil in packing and shipping. The best source is to find some raspberries growing wild or grow your own.

'Tis the dessert that graces all the feast,
For an ill end disparages the rest,
A thousand things well done, and one forgot,
Defaces obligation with a blot.
                    DR. KING, The Art of Cookery

City dwellers have an even harder time, for raspberries appear on only one rainy day a year. If this isn't your day for shopping, you have to study the stars and forecast the raspberry day next year!

Framboise, the raspberry liqueur, is made commercially in an area around Dijon, in the lovely Cote d'Or. It is drunk as an after-dinner cordial and gives a divine flavor boost to fruit desserts.

CHOCOLATE SOUFFLÉ ROLL (ROULAGE LÉONTYNE)

This memorable and extraordinary combination of ideas and techniques was popularized by the late Dione Lucas. The adaptation of her recipe seems rather wordy (and it is), but I could not find a quicker way of explaining how to unmold and roll the soufflé. The rolling technique is the same as that used for the hot rolled mushroom soufflé.

Serves 8
Preheat oven to 375° F.

5 egg yolks	¼ teaspoon salt
¾ cup sugar	⅛ teaspoon cream of tartar
6 ounces dark, sweet chocolate (or semisweet chocolate pieces)	4 ounces sweet chocolate, grated
	1 cup heavy cream
	2 tablespoons sugar
3 tablespoons cold water	1 teaspoon vanilla extract
5 egg whites	

1. Oil a 15-by-10-inch jelly-roll pan. Line the pan with wax paper, allowing 2 inches of overlap at each short end of the pan. Oil the paper lightly.

2. In a mixing bowl, beat together the egg yolks and ¾ cup sugar until very thick.

3. Break the chocolate into small pieces into a saucepan. Add the water and stir over low heat until the chocolate has melted.

4. Stir the melted chocolate into the egg-yolk-and-sugar mixture with a spatula.

5. In another mixing bowl, beat the egg whites with the salt and cream of tartar until they stand in soft peaks.

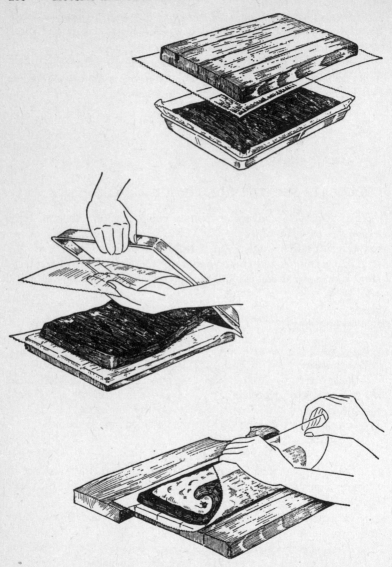

6. Fold the egg whites into the chocolate mixture, and spread the mixture evenly into the prepared pan. Bake for 10 minutes at 375° F. Without opening the oven door, reduce the heat to 325° F. and continue baking for 5 minutes.

7. Remove the pan from the oven and cover with a clean tea towel that has been wrung out in cold water. Chill in the refrigerator for 1 hour.

8. Remove the tea towel and sprinkle the surface evenly with half the grated chocolate. (This will prevent the moist mixture from sticking to the wax paper when it is inverted.)

9. Cover the back of a bread board with a piece of wax paper cut 4 inches longer than the jelly-roll pan and invert the soufflé onto it. Peel off the paper on which the soufflé was baked. Spread surface with cream, whipped until stiff with sugar and vanilla. Roll the soufflé onto a jelly-roll board from the longest side as if rolling a jelly roll. Sprinkle the roll with the remaining grated chocolate.

13. custards

CUSTARD SAUCE · SABOYAN SAUCE · CHOCOLATE CUSTARD · CARAMEL CUSTARD · CRÈME BRÛLÉE · CUSTARD PIE · PECAN PIE · QUICHE LORRAINE · SMOKED SALMON QUICHE · HAM AND ASPARAGUS QUICHE · CHOCOLATE TORTE · PÂTÉ SUCRÉE · CRÈME PATISSIÈRE · FRUIT TART · LEMON MERINGUE PIE · OEUFS À LA NEIGE · ZABAGLIONE · MOCHA ICE CREAM · STRAWBERRY OR PEACH ICE CREAM · ZUPPA INGLESE · VANILLA BAVARIAN CREAM · COFFEE PARFAIT · BREAD AND BUTTER PUDDING · RICE PUDDING WITH CHOCOLATE SAUCE · RIZ À L'IMPÉRATRICE

Custard is a combination of egg yolks, milk, and a flavoring. It can be cooked on top of the stove or baked in the oven. One of the most versatile of all culinary preparations, it can be served hot, cold, or even frozen.

A custard is used as a thin sauce for poached fruit, hot puddings, and soufflés. It can be thickened into a filling for pastries and cream puffs. It can be baked in a pie shell for dessert. With the addition of cheese and bacon, it becomes Quiche Lorraine. Pour the ingredients into a carmelized dish and it is unmolded in the form of a Caramel Custard.

When sugar is broiled on top of a baked custard, a thin surface layer of caramel is formed and it takes the name Crème Brûlée.

Sometimes the custard is combined with other ingredients, such as in the preparation of bread-and-butter or rice pudding. If puréed fruit and gelatin are added to the custard, it is transformed into a Bavarian Cream. Combine Rice Pudding and Bavarian Cream and you have Riz à l'Impératrice. From one beginning there can be many endings. . . .

CUSTARD SAUCE

Custard is a thin sauce. For a thicker sauce, reduce the quantity of milk to one cup.

Serves 4

4 egg yolks	1½ cups milk
½ cup sugar	1 teaspoon vanilla extract

1. Place the egg yolks and sugar in a bowl. Stir with a wire whisk until well combined.
2. In a saucepan, heat the milk to the simmering point.
3. Stir the hot milk into the egg-sugar mixture and return the mixture to the saucepan.
4. Heat over low heat, stirring continuously until thickened into a sauce. Add the vanilla.

SABOYAN SAUCE

To prepare this delicious sauce for puddings and soufflés, follow the directions for custard sauce, substituting 1 cup white wine for 1½ cups of milk and replacing the vanilla with 1 tablespoon kirsch.

CHOCOLATE CUSTARD

A baked custard contains more eggs than a custard sauce to ensure that the custard will set.

Serves 6
Preheat oven to 325° F.

3 eggs	6 ounces semisweet chocolate
3 egg yolks	pieces
½ cup sugar	1 teaspoon vanilla extract
2 cups milk	

1. Place the eggs, egg yolks, and sugar in a bowl and stir with a wire whisk until well combined.

2. Pour the milk into a saucepan. Add the chocolate pieces and bring to the simmering point, stirring until the chocolate has dissolved. Add the vanilla extract.

3. Pour the hot milk into the egg-sugar mixture. Pour the custard into a 1-quart soufflé dish. Place the dish in a larger container. Pour enough hot water into the outer container to come halfway up the sides of the mold.

4. Bake in a preheated oven for 50 minutes, until the custard has set.

5. Cool the custard and chill it for 4 hours in the refrigerator.

6. Loosen the sides of the custard and unmold it onto a serving dish.

CARAMEL CUSTARD

Serves 6
Preheat oven to 325° F.

½ cup granulated sugar	½ cup sugar
2 tablespoons cold water	2 cups milk
3 eggs	1 teaspoon vanilla extract (or
3 egg yolks	½ vanilla bean)

1. To prepare the caramel, cook the sugar and water in a small, heavy saucepan over low heat, without stirring, for 10 minutes, until the sugar has melted into liquid caramel. Continue cooking until it is a rich brown color.

2. Pour the caramel into a 1-quart soufflé dish. Roll the hot caramel quickly around the bottom and sides of the dish to coat them evenly.

3. To prepare the custard, place the eggs, egg yolks, and sugar in a bowl and stir with a wire whisk until well combined.

4. Pour the milk into a saucepan. Split the vanilla bean lengthwise in half and scrape the black particles into the milk. Drop the bean into the milk and bring to the simmering point, and then discard the vanilla bean. (Add vanilla extract if the bean was not used.)

5. Pour the hot milk onto the egg-sugar mixture and stir to combine the ingredients. Pour the custard into the caramelized soufflé dish. Place the dish in a larger baking dish, adding enough hot water to come halfway up the sides of the mold.

6. Bake in a preheated oven for 50 minutes, until the custard has set.

7. Cool the custard and chill it for 4 hours in the refrigerator.

8. Loosen the sides of the custard by depressing the outer edges with your finger, and unmold it onto a serving dish. It will slide out of the baking dish very easily.

The custard is baked in a water bath to prevent it from becoming too hot and thus pitted with small holes. When it is unmolded, the caramel forms a sauce around the custard.

CRÈME BRÛLÉE

Instead of making a Caramel Custard by putting the sugar around and beneath the custard, try sprinkling the sugar on top of the baked custard and then caramelizing it under the broiler. Although the ingredients for caramel custard and crème brûlée are almost identical (cream is used rather than milk in a crème brûlée), the final dishes are quite different. When the sugar is broiled, it forms a thin, brittle, crisp crust that, when tapped with a spoon, will splinter into fragments. The pieces of crunchy caramel form an excellent contrast to the soft, velvety custard.

Serves 6
Preheat oven to 300° F.

6 egg yolks
½ cup sugar
3 cups heavy cream

1 teaspoon vanilla extract (or
½ vanilla bean)
½ cup superfine sugar

Not so many years ago a bride in Hungary was not
considered ready for marriage until her husband
could read his newspaper through her strudel.

1. Beat the egg yolks and sugar in a bowl until well combined.
2. Pour the cream into a small saucepan. Split the piece of vanilla bean in half lengthwise and scrape the black sootlike particles into the cream. Drop the empty pod into the cream. Heat over a low flame until the cream reaches the simmering point. Do not let it boil. Discard the empty vanilla pod (or add vanilla extract if a bean was not used).
3. Pour the cream onto the egg yolks and sugar, stirring constantly. Return the mixture to the saucepan and stir over low heat until the custard has thickened slightly. Again, be sure not to let the custard boil or it will separate later.
4. Pour the custard into a 9-inch porcelain pie dish or an 8-inch-square glass baking dish. Place the dish in the oven for 20 minutes until a skin has formed on the surface of the custard.
5. Cool the custard and chill it in the refrigerator for 12 hours. (It continues to thicken as it stands.)
6. Preheat the broiler. Sprinkle the surface of the custard with a thin layer of sugar. Place the dish under the broiler for 5 minutes or less, until the sugar has caramelized. Chill again for 2 hours before serving. The caramel will form a crunchy, brittle layer over the creamy custard. Serve with sliced poached fruit or fresh berries.

Making Pastry

Pastry making is not at all difficult. It is just as quick to prepare your own pastry by measuring a cup of flour and a few tablespoons of water as to buy a packaged mix. Your attitude toward the pastry then becomes one of triumph rather than apology.

The choice of one pastry recipe rather than another is determined by the use to which the pastry will be put. For instance, the pastry crust that surrounds a pâté or a whole filet of beef will need to be stronger than that used for an open fruit tart.

Though the proportion of the flour to the shortening may differ from one pastry recipe to another, and egg yolks may be substituted for the water measurement, the principles of pastry making remain the same. In all cases, too much flour will cause the pastry to toughen and crumble when it is cut. Too much water will, of course, make the pastry wet, and the center of the crust will not cook through.

"Baking blind" is a term that refers to the pastry, not the cook. It simply means precooking the pastry shell before the filling is added. Generally the shell is weighted, by placing either an empty oiled pan of a slightly smaller size on top of the unbaked shell or dried beans on a sheet of foil. The weight of the pan or the beans holds the pastry in position. The purpose of weighting the shell is to prevent the pastry from shrinking and bubbling while it is baking.

The partially cooked shell is pricked with a fork before returning it to the oven to allow air bubbles to escape. This preliminary cooking ensures a crisp, well-shaped bottom crust. The shell is baked in a preheated 400° F. oven for 10 minutes. The final cooking is completed later at a lower temperature.

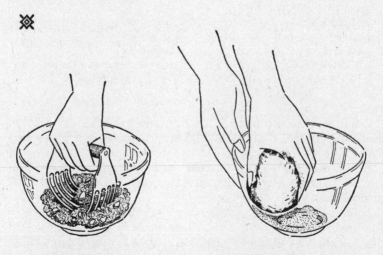

A FEW NOTES ON PASTRY MAKING

- Work in a cool kitchen.
- Use a dry measuring cup for dry ingredients; use a liquid measure for liquids.
- Flour the rolling pin and pastry board lightly.
- Roll the pastry quickly and lightly.
- Dust off any excess flour sticking to the pastry.

- Do not incorporate into the pastry any small dried pieces of dough that cling to the board. These little pieces remain as hard bullets and will not soften in baking.
- If the pastry ball is too cold when it is removed from the refrigerator, it will crack as you begin to roll it. Knead it for just a moment to soften the ingredients and then start rolling it again on a floured board.
- Fit the pastry well into the pie plate before trimming off the edges.
- Pastry can be frozen unrolled, unbaked, or baked.

CUSTARD PIE

Serves 6

Pastry:	Custard:
1¼ cups all-purpose flour	3 eggs
⅛ teaspoon salt	3 egg yolks
4 tablespoons margarine (or solid shortening)	½ cup sugar
	2 cups milk
4 tablespoons butter	1 teaspoon vanilla extract
4 or 5 tablespoons water	⅛ teaspoon nutmeg

Pastry:

1. Sift the flour and measure it into a large bowl. Add the salt and margarine, cut into small pieces. Combine margarine and flour with a pastry blender.

2. Cut the butter into small pieces and combine it with the flour mixture, using a pastry blender, until the pieces of butter are the size of small peas.

3. Stir in the water with a fork, adding only enough water to moisten the dough. (Different flours absorb different quantities of water.)

4. Gather the dough into a ball and wrap it in wax paper. Chill in the refrigerator for 20 minutes.

5. Preheat oven to 400° F.

6. Flour a rolling pin and roll the pastry on a floured board.

7. Fit the pastry into a 9-inch pie plate and cover it with oiled aluminum foil, oiled side touching the pastry. Weight the foil with a single layer of dried beans.

8. Bake the pastry shell in a preheated oven for 10 minutes.

9. Discard the foil, reserving the beans for the next batch of pastry.

Custard:

10. Preheat oven to 350° F. Stir the eggs, egg yolks, and sugar with a wire whisk until well combined.

11. Add the milk and vanilla extract.

12. Pour into the partially baked pie shell, sprinkle the surface with nutmeg, and bake in a preheated oven for about 40 minutes. (Insert the tip of a knife at the edge of the custard. If it comes out clean, the custard is done. The custard will become firmer as it cools.)

13. Cool the pie and chill it for 4 hours before serving.

Note: Pastry is easier to roll when you use butter and margarine or shortening combined rather than all butter.

COCONUT, BANANA, AND CHERRY CUSTARD PIES

Coconut Custard Pie is prepared in the same way as Custard Pie. Just add 1 cup of grated coconut to the custard mixture and bake the pie in a 9-inch pie plate. The result will serve 8.

For Banana Custard Pie, add 1 cup sliced bananas and 1 teaspoon cinnamon. Bake in a 10-inch pie plate.

For Cherry Custard Pie, add 1 cup pitted, halved, canned cherries and 1 teaspoon allspice.

PECAN PIE

Serves 8

Pie Pastry	1 teaspoon vanilla extract
3 eggs	2 tablespoons flour
3 egg yolks	2 cups dark corn syrup
½ cup sugar	1 cup pecan halves

1. Make the pastry as for Custard Pie. Fit it into a 10-inch pie plate and bake as directed for 10 minutes in a preheated 400° F. oven.

2. Place the eggs, egg yolks, sugar, vanilla, and flour in a bowl and stir with a wire whisk until well combined.

3. Stir in the corn syrup, and pour the mixture into the partially baked pie shell.

4. Top with pecan halves and bake in a preheated 350° F. oven for about 40 minutes. (Insert the tip of a knife at the edge of the custard. If it comes out clean, the custard is done.)

5. Cool and chill the pie for 4 hours before cutting. Serve with whipped cream.

QUICHE LORRAINE

Serves 6
Preheat oven to 400° F.

Pie Pastry
½ pound lean bacon
1 cup grated Swiss cheese
3 eggs
3 egg yolks

1 tablespoon flour
½ teaspoon salt
Dash of cayenne pepper
2 cups milk

1. Make the pastry as for Custard Pie. Fit it into a 9-inch pie plate or a 10-inch quiche pan with a removable base and bake as directed for 10 minutes in a preheated 400° F. oven.
2. Fry the bacon until crisp. Drain on paper towels and crumble it onto the partially baked pie shell.
3. Sprinkle grated cheese over the bacon.
4. Place the eggs, egg yolks, flour, salt, and pepper in a bowl and stir with a wire whisk until well combined.
5. Stir in the milk.
6. Pour this custard over bacon and cheese.
7. Bake in a preheated 350° F. oven for 40 minutes, until the custard is firm. Serve hot or cold.

Note: People say that you can freeze a Quiche Lorraine. You can, but it will not be nearly so good as when it is just cooked.

SMOKED SALMON QUICHE

A Smoked Salmon Quiche is one of those memorable and luxurious delights that bring joy to the heart and peace to the soul. It is made in the same way as Quiche Lorraine.

Serves 6
Preheat oven to 350° F.

Partially baked pie shell
3 eggs
3 egg yolks
1 tablespoon flour
½ teaspoon salt
Dash of cayenne pepper
2 cups heavy cream (or milk)

2 tablespoons dry vermouth
1 tablespoon lemon juice
4 scallions, finely chopped
¼ pound smoked salmon, shredded (or as much as the budget allows)

1. Place the eggs, egg yolks, flour, salt, and pepper in a bowl, and stir with a wire whisk until well combined.

2. Stir in the cream or milk, vermouth, and lemon juice.

3. Sprinkle the scallions and smoked salmon over the partially baked pie shell. Add the custard, and bake in a preheated oven for 40 minutes, until the custard is firm.

4. Serve hot or cold.

HAM AND ASPARAGUS QUICHE

Follow the directions for Quiche Lorraine, but instead of the bacon, use 1 cup of diced boiled ham plus 1 cup of cooked or canned asparagus tips.

OTHER QUICHE FILLINGS

Follow the basic recipe, omitting the bacon and substituting one of the following mixtures:

- 1 cup cooked lobster, 1 tablespoon tomato paste, and 1 tablespoon lemon juice.
- 1 cup diced, cooked Polish-type sausage and 1 tablespoon mustard.
- 6 medium-sized onions, sliced into thin rings and fried until soft in 2 tablespoons butter. This sounds bland but it is very good. Sprinkle the custard with nutmeg.
- ½ pound sliced mushrooms and ½ cup finely chopped onion, fried until soft in 2 tablespoons butter.

There is no spectacle on earth more appealing than that of a beautiful woman in the act of cooking dinner for someone she loves.

THOMAS WOLFE

CHOCOLATE TORTE

The pastry for Custard Pie and Quiche Lorraine can also be used for an entirely different preparation. In this recipe, cocoa and sugar are added to the basic pastry.

Serves 10

Pastry:
2½ cups sifted all-purpose flour
¼ teaspoon salt
6 tablespoons solid shortening
6 tablespoons butter

6 tablespoons regular (not instant) cocoa
¼ cup sugar
8 tablespoons water

1. Sift the flour into a bowl and add the salt. Add the shortening and blend with a pastry blender until small pieces are formed. Blend in the butter and stir in the cocoa and sugar.

2. Stir in the water with a fork until the pastry is sufficiently moist to form a ball. (Different flours absorb differing quantities of water so you may need a little more or less water.)

3. Wrap the dough in wax paper and chill for 20 minutes.

4. Cut the dough in half. Flour the back of an 11-by-18-inch cookie sheet and roll the pastry to cover the surface completely. Cut the pastry in half. Repeat with remaining pastry and cover a second cookie sheet. Bake in a preheated 375° F. oven for 15 minutes until crisp. Sandwich layers with Chocolate Cinnamon Cream Filling.

Chocolate Cinnamon Cream Filling:

6 ounces semisweet chocolate
pieces
2 tablespoons butter
¼ cup strong coffee
1 cup confectioners' sugar
1 teaspoon instant (not
freeze-dried) coffee
1 teaspoon cinnamon

¼ teaspoon salt
1 egg
2 tablespoons vanilla extract
1 package unflavored gelatin,
dissolved in ¼ cup cold strong
coffee
1 cup heavy cream

1. Place the chocolate pieces, butter, and coffee in a small saucepan. Stir over low heat until chocolate has dissolved.

2. Place the confectioners' sugar, instant coffee, cinnamon, salt, egg, and vanilla in a bowl. Add the melted chocolate mixture, and stir well.

3. Sprinkle gelatin on ¼ cup cold coffee in a small saucepan. Leave undisturbed for 5 minutes. Place over low heat until a clear liquid has formed.

4. Beat the cream until it is the same consistency as the chocolate mixture. Combine chocolate mixture and cream. Stir in the gelatin liquid and chill for 4 hours.

Decorating and Assembling the Torte

6 ounces sweet chocolate
2 tablespoons confectioners'
sugar

1. Break the chocolate into small pieces and put on a plate. Put the plate on top of a saucepan containing simmering water. Cover the plate with another plate. Place the saucepan over low heat for 10 minutes until the chocolate has melted.

2. Cover the back of a cookie sheet with wax paper. Spread the melted chocolate in a paper-thin layer on the wax paper, using a metal spatula. Place in the freezer to harden.

3. To assemble the torte, spread each layer of pastry with a layer of chocolate cinnamon cream, piling the layers one on top of the other. Finish with a layer of cream. Take the chocolate-layered cookie sheet from the freezer and, working with the speed of light, crumple the wax paper to form random-sized wafers of chocolate. Scatter chocolate on top of the torte and dust with sifted confectioners' sugar. Place in the refrigerator for 4 hours. Cut into squares and serve. Everybody will love you. If they ask for the recipe, tell them it takes too long to write out.

PÂTÉ SUCRÉE (FRUIT-TART PASTRY)

This pastry is quite unlike that traditionally used for pies and is just a little bit more difficult to prepare. It is made with flour, butter, egg yolks, sugar, and a pinch of salt. The shell is fully baked before being filled in order to keep its shape. To prevent shrinkage and bubbling, it is covered with a sheet of oiled aluminum foil and weighted with beans. The baked shell is filled with custard and topped with fresh or canned fruit; the fruit is then glazed.

This type of pastry is usually served freestanding by lifting it from its baking dish after it has been cooked. It can be made in a tart tin with a removable bottom. Alternatively, the pastry is sometimes formed within a flan ring and baked directly on a cookie sheet. Flan rings may be circular, square, or rectangular and are made in various sizes. These forms are all about one inch high.

Baked Pâté Sucrée freezes very well. It should not be defrosted before baking but taken directly from the freezer to the oven.

If you wish, you can make individual tart shells using this recipe. You can also glaze the surface of the crust after baking with heated and strained apricot preserves. The glazing will provide a waterproof surface so that fruit may be added directly to the shell, eliminating the custard completely. The fruit itself is then glazed to make it shine and preserve its fresh appearance.

The tart shell will remain crisp for twelve hours after it has been filled, so you can make it in the morning for serving that night. The fruits can be varied with the availability of fresh fruit. In the winter this dessert is equally good made with thinly sliced apples arranged in concentric circles or canned pears arranged with their stalks to the center like the spokes of a wheel. The tart also looks beautiful prepared with black and white grapes arranged in triangular sections, set off by rows of drained canned Mandarin oranges. Canned apricot halves and Bing cherries are also beautiful carefully arranged on the surface of the tart.

Serves 8
Preheat oven to 400° F.

1 cup all-purpose flour	4 tablespoons cold butter
Pinch of salt	1 cup dried beans (or maca-
¼ cup sugar	roni) for weighting the pastry
2 egg yolks	

1. Sift the flour onto a board and make a well in the center. Place salt, sugar, and egg yolks in the well. Cut the butter into small pieces

and add to the flour. Work these ingredients together, pinching the "liquid" ingredients—the egg yolks and butter—into the flour and sugar. Use the thumb and fingertips of one hand only to keep the mixture as cool as possible. It will seem dry and crumbly as the ingredients are combined, but do not add any water. As you keep working, it will readily become of a consistency that will enable you to form it into a ball. Wrap the ball in wax paper and place it in the refrigerator for 1 hour.

2. Remove the pastry ball from the refrigerator and knead it, squeezing it and rolling it three or four times in your hand. Roll the pastry on a floured board. When it is large enough, roll it around the rolling pin and fit it into a 9-inch tart tin or pie dish. If the pastry breaks, piece it together with the remaining pastry scraps.

3. Oil a piece of aluminum foil and place it on top of the pastry, oiled side down, touching the pastry. Fold the foil over the sides of the tart so that it conforms to the shape of the pastry. Place about a cup of dried beans or macaroni on top of the foil to keep the pastry from bubbling. Bake it in the center of a preheated oven for 8 minutes.

4. Remove the pastry from the oven and lift off the foil. (Save the beans for the next tart.) Prick the bottom of the pastry with a fork to allow the steam to escape. Lower the oven heat to 350° F. and return the pastry to the oven for another 5 minutes. It is done when a light brown rim appears around the edge of the pastry. Allow the pastry to cool in the tart tin.

CRÈME PATISSIÈRE (PASTRY CREAM)

Pastry cream is a thick custard used as an alternative to whipped cream for filling Fruit Tarts, Cream Puffs, and Éclairs.

Yield: 2 cups

5 egg yolks
½ cup sugar
4 tablespoons cornstarch

2 cups milk
2 teaspoons vanilla extract

1. Place the egg yolks, sugar, and cornstarch in a bowl. Stir with a wire whisk until well combined.

2. Heat the milk to the simmering point and add it to the egg mixture. Stir to combine, and return the mixture to the saucepan.

3. Heat over low heat, stirring continuously until thickened. Add the vanilla. Chill for 4 hours. It will continue to thicken as it cools.

FRUIT TART

Serves 8

Pâté Sucrée	1 small bunch black grapes
Crème Patissière	1 small bunch white grapes
4 tablespoons apricot preserves	1 small can Mandarin oranges,
1 tablespoon water	drained

1. Place preserves in a small saucepan with a tablespoon of water and allow them to boil, stirring once or twice with a wooden spatula. Remove from the heat and pass through a strainer. Discard the apricot skins.

2. Paint apricot glaze on the surface of the pastry with a pastry brush. Keep the tart in the tart tin even if you have the type with the removable bottom.

3. Spoon the firm, cold custard (Crème Patissière) into the shell (Pâté Sucrée), spreading it evenly with a rubber spatula.

4. Cut the grapes in half and remove the seeds. Arrange in the shell with cut sides down, starting from the center point and working to

the outer edge to form four triangles of grapes. Lay two intersecting rows of Mandarin oranges between the grapes.

5. Brush the fruit lightly with liquid apricot glaze to make it shine.

6. Remove the outer rim of the tart tin and place the freestanding tart on a serving dish.

LEMON MERINGUE PIE

The lemon custard filling, a variation of thick Pastry Cream, can also be used for filling other pastries and cakes.

Serves 8
Preheat oven to 300° F.

Pastry shell baked for 25 minutes covered with beans and foil

Lemon Custard:
5 egg yolks
½ cup sugar
Rind 1 lemon, grated
½ cup lemon juice
4 tablespoons cornstarch
2 cups boiling water
2 teaspoons butter

Meringue:
4 egg whites
⅛ teaspoon salt
⅛ teaspoon cream of tartar
1 teaspoon vanilla extract
1 cup sugar

1. To prepare the lemon custard, combine the egg yolks, sugar, grated lemon rind, and juice in a bowl. Add the cornstarch and stir with a wire whisk until smooth.

2. Add the boiling water.

3. Pour the mixture into a saucepan and stir over low heat until very thick. Stir in the butter. Cool the mixture and fill into the pastry shell.

4. To prepare the meringue, place the egg whites, salt, cream of tartar, and vanilla in a bowl. Beat until the egg whites stand in soft peaks.

5. Add the sugar a little at a time and continue beating until the egg whites are stiff and shiny.

6. Pile the meringue on top of the pie filling and bake in a preheated oven for 30 minutes, until the meringue is delicately browned. Cool before serving.

Note: Do not make meringue on wet or humid days because it absorbs the moisture from the air and becomes tough and chewy.

OEUFS À LA NEIGE ("SNOW EGGS")

"Snow Eggs" are only meringues afloat in a custard sauce. The meringue is the same recipe as is used in Lemon Meringue Pie. It can be used in a variety of other desserts as well—baked Alaska, for example. If you need a larger quantity of meringue for another purpose, add ¼ cup sugar to each egg white, keeping the remaining ingredients the same.

Serves 6

Meringue:
4 egg whites
⅛ teaspoon salt
⅛ teaspoon cream of tartar
1 teaspoon vanilla extract
1 cup sugar

Custard:
4 egg yolks
½ cup sugar
1½ cups milk
1 teaspoon vanilla extract

1. Beat the egg whites with salt, cream of tartar, and vanilla until whites stand in soft peaks. Add the sugar gradually, beating constantly until stiff.

2. Heat milk to the simmering point. Using two spoons, form the meringue into the size and shape of small eggs. Poach "eggs" in barely simmering milk for 2 minutes on each side. Remove "eggs" from the milk and drain on paper towels spread over wire cake-cooling racks. (They will shrink slightly as they cool.)

3. Place egg yolks and sugar in a bowl. Stir with a wire whisk until well combined.

4. Add hot poaching milk. Stir well and return mixture to saucepan.

5. Heat over low heat, stirring continuously until slightly thickened into a medium-thin sauce. Add the vanilla and pour the custard into a glass serving bowl. Cool the custard and float the poached "eggs" on top of the custard. Serve with fresh berries or decorate with grated chocolate.

ZABAGLIONE

A million wine-flavored air bubbles made from a simple custard.

Serves 4 to 6

4 egg yolks   ½ cup Marsala wine
⅓ cup sugar

1. Combine the egg yolks and sugar in a special zabaglione pan, an unlined copper bowl, or the top of a double boiler. Place over low heat.
2. Roll up your sleeves and beat and beat and beat and beat until you feel the egg yolks thickening and increasing in volume and doubling and tripling in bulk.
3. Start adding the Marsala a drop or two at a time, beating furiously until all the Marsala has been added. The mixture will reward your efforts by becoming more and more voluminous and lighter and lighter. Pour the Zabaglione into demitasse cups. It is incredibly rich, so a little goes a long way. Serve hot immediately.

COLD ZABAGLIONE

Cold Zabaglione has the consistency of a mousse.

Measure 3 tablespoons of Marsala into a small saucepan and sprinkle 1 teaspoon of unflavored gelatin on the surface. Leave gelatin undisturbed for 5 minutes. Then place it over a low heat until a clear liquid is formed.

Pour the gelatin into the hot completed Zabaglione mixture, stirring occasionally as the mixture cools. When it is on the point of setting,

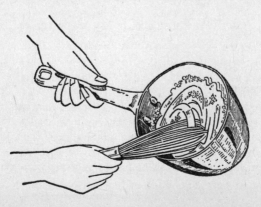

pour it into individual glass dishes. Top with whipped cream and grated chocolate.

MOCHA ICE CREAM (FROZEN CUSTARD)

Yield: 1½ quarts

4 egg yolks	6 ounces sweet chocolate
1 cup sugar	¼ teaspoon salt
1 cup milk	2 teaspoons vanilla extract
2 cups heavy cream	Ice
1 cup hot coffee	Ice cream salt

1. Place the egg yolks and sugar in a bowl. Stir until well combined.
2. In a small saucepan, heat milk and 1 cup of cream to the simmering point.
3. Pour milk and cream onto the egg yolks and sugar. Return all the ingredients to the saucepan and stir over low heat until a thin custard is formed.
4. Pour the coffee into a bowl, add the chocolate, and stir until the chocolate has dissolved. Add the salt and vanilla.
5. Combine the coffee mixture with the custard. Add remaining cup of cream and let stand to cool.
6. Pour the mixture into the freezer can. Place a layer of ice in the freezer to ⅓ the level of the ice cream in the can. Sprinkle with a thin layer of salt. Continue until three layers of salt and ice are formed.
7. Turn on the motor or crank by hand until the motor changes in sound as if it was beginning to be hard work to continue. (You will be able to feel the ice cream thickening if you are using a hand-cranked machine.)
8. Transfer the ice cream to a freezer container and freeze until hardened.

Strawberries

> Doubtless God could have made better berries,
> but doubtless God never did.
>
> IZAAK WALTON

Many dishes are named after famous people. Parmentier was the man who developed many potato recipes. Melba ate peaches; and

Veronica nibbled grapes long before Caesar thought of his famous salad. Charles V, king of France in the 1300s, should have been given another title—"King of the Strawberries." It was he who ordered his gardeners to dig up one thousand wild strawberry plants from the woods and plant them in the gardens of his palace at the Louvre. Before long, these tiny fraises des bois, or wood strawberries, were being cross-fertilized with German and, much later, Virginian varieties. Gradually, the strawberries developed into a softer fruit, five or six times their original size. Size, however, is not always a commendable quality in fruits and vegetables, for often smaller varieties are sweeter and more flavorful. Though in America we are now able to buy strawberries almost all the year long, the exquisite fraises des bois have almost disappeared. Even in France it is said that in another two generations they will be gone forever, as housing developments encroach on the lands where the fraises des bois were once found.

At one time, the ripe berries were sold at the market threaded through a piece of long straw, and maybe this is how they got their name. Straw is still used to protect the bed as the berries grow, preventing them from being splashed with mud during summer showers. The strawberries eagerly drink up the rain and become slightly waterlogged, so they are never quite so sweet as when they are gathered after a day or two of bright sunshine. For this reason, some people say that strawberries should never be washed, for much of the flavor will be washed away. Instead, they should be rinsed in wine! The wine can be strained and used in a fruit salad later.

STRAWBERRY OR PEACH ICE CREAM

Yield: 2 quarts

4 egg yolks	¼ teaspoon salt
1 cup sugar	2 teaspoons vanilla extract
2 cups milk	Ice
2 cups heavy cream	Ice cream salt
2 cups puréed sliced strawberries (or peaches)	

1. Place the egg yolks and sugar in a bowl. Stir until well combined.

2. In a small saucepan, heat the milk to the simmering point.

3. Pour the milk onto the egg yolks and sugar. Return all the ingredients to the saucepan and stir over low heat until a thin custard is formed.

4. Add the cream, fruit, salt, and vanilla.

5. Freeze the mixture, following the directions for Mocha Ice Cream.

ZUPPA INGLESE

This is an Italian name for the famous English trifle, made with medium-thick custard.

Serves 8

2 4-ounce packages ladyfingers,
    split in half
⅓ cup dark Jamaica rum
½ cup chopped candied fruit
    —cherries, citron, orange,
    and lemon peels

Custard:
3 egg yolks
3 tablespoons sugar
3 tablespoons flour
Grated rind of 1 lemon
2 cups milk
1 teaspoon vanilla extract

Cream:
1 cup heavy cream
2 tablespoons sugar
1 teaspoon vanilla extract

1. In a 1-quart soufflé dish or any attractive serving dish, arrange a single layer of ladyfingers. Sprinkle with half the rum and top with a third of the candied fruit.

2. Combine the egg yolks, sugar, and flour with a wire whisk and stir in the lemon rind.

3. In a saucepan, heat the milk to the simmering point and add it to the egg-yolk mixture. Stir to combine and return the mixture to the saucepan.

4. Heat over low heat, stirring continuously until thickened. Add the vanilla. Cool custard for 30 minutes.

5. Spoon half the custard over the ladyfingers. Arrange another layer of ladyfingers on top of the custard. Sprinkle with remaining rum and

half the remaining chopped fruit, and cover with remaining custard. Top with ladyfingers. Decorate with heavy cream, whipped with sugar and vanilla until stiff. Sprinkle with remaining candied fruit. Chill for 4 hours.

VANILLA BAVARIAN CREAM

A Bavarian Cream is a simple custard enriched with cream, flavored with fruit, chocolate, or liqueur, and molded with gelatin. It is beautiful to behold and can be made at any time of the year for any occasion or just for dinner.

Serves 6 to 8

4 egg yolks	¼ cup cold water
½ cup sugar	1 package unflavored gelatin
1½ cups milk	1 cup heavy cream
2 teaspoons vanilla extract	

1. Place the egg yolks and sugar in a bowl. Stir with a wire whisk until well combined.

2. In a saucepan, heat the milk to the simmering point and add it to the eggs and sugar. Stir to combine, and return the mixture to the saucepan.

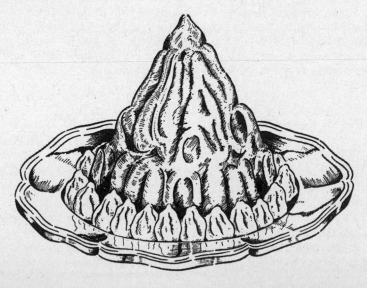

3. Heat over low heat, stirring continuously until thickened into a sauce. Add the vanilla.

4. Measure the water into a small saucepan. Sprinkle the gelatin on the surface. Leave gelatin undisturbed for 5 minutes. Place over a low heat until a clear liquid is formed.

5. Stir gelatin liquid into the custard. Cool the custard to room temperature.

6. Beat the cream until it is thick. Fold the cream into the cooled custard.

7. Oil a mold or serving dish lightly, or dip the mold in cold water and invert it for a moment before filling. Pour the Bavarian Cream into the mold and chill for 4 hours. Unmold and serve with Melba Sauce or decorate with whipped cream.

OTHER BAVARIAN CREAMS

Chocolate Bavarian Cream is made in the same way as Vanilla Bavarian Cream, except that you stir 4 ounces of sweet chocolate into the hot milk before adding it to the egg yolks and sugar.

To make Coffee Bavarian Cream, dissolve 2 teaspoons of instant coffee in the hot milk.

Grand Marnier, Benedictine, or other liqueur Bavarian Creams are made by stirring ¼ cup of liqueur into the cooled custard.

For fruit-flavored Bavarian Creams, purée fruit in the blender. (Any ripe fruit may be used, such as peaches, apricots, or berries. Berries should be strained to remove seeds.) Add 1 cup puréed fruit to the cooled custard before adding the gelatin and cream. Increase the quantity from 1 package to 1½ packages (1½ tablespoons).

COFFEE PARFAIT

A parfait is a flavored custard.

Serves 6

3 eggs	1 teaspoon vanilla extract
3 egg yolks	1 tablespoon unflavored gelatin
½ cup sugar	¼ cup cold coffee
2 cups milk	1 cup heavy cream
2 tablespoons instant coffee	½ cup grated chocolate

1. Place the eggs, egg yolks, and sugar in a bowl and stir well with a wire whisk.

2. Bring the milk to the simmering point and stir in the coffee. Pour the hot milk over the eggs and sugar, stir to combine, and return all the ingredients to the saucepan.

3. Cook, stirring with a wire whisk, until the custard has thickened. Do not let it boil or it will scorch. Cool the custard and then add the vanilla.

4. Sprinkle the gelatin over the cold coffee in a small saucepan. Allow the gelatin to stand undisturbed for 5 minutes. Place the saucepan over gentle heat for 2 or 3 minutes until a clear liquid has formed.

5. Whip the cream until it is thick but not stiff. Stir the cream into the cooled custard mixture. Add the hot liquid gelatin and stir until all the ingredients are well combined. Place in individual dishes and chill for 4 hours.

6. Decorate with grated chocolate.

BREAD AND BUTTER PUDDING

This is bread and butter baked in a custard with four and twenty flavors. For a simpler dessert, omit the candied fruit and kirsch.

Serves 6
Preheat oven to 350° F.

¼ cup raisins
¼ cup mixed glacéed fruits
¼ cup kirsch

3 tablespoons butter
8 slices bread (not the batter-whipped, vitamin- and mineral-enriched, "body-building" bread; use good firm-textured bread)

Custard:
4 egg yolks
½ cup sugar
1½ cups milk
1 teaspoon vanilla extract
1 cup heavy cream
⅛ teaspoon nutmeg

1. Cover raisins with boiling water and leave to soak for 5 minutes. Chop glacéed fruits into small pieces. Drain raisins and place in a buttered 1-quart baking dish with glacéed fruits and kirsch.

2. Butter the bread generously and cut it into fingers or triangles. Add to the baking dish.

3. Place the egg yolks and sugar in a bowl. Stir with a wire whisk until well combined.

4. In a saucepan, heat the milk to the simmering point and add it to the eggs and sugar. Stir to combine, and return the mixture to the saucepan.

5. Heat over low heat, stirring continuously until thickened into a sauce. Add the vanilla and cream.

6. Pour custard into baking dish. Sprinkle with nutmeg. Bake in a preheated oven for 30 minutes. Serve at room temperature.

RICE PUDDING WITH CHOCOLATE SAUCE

Serves 4
Preheat oven to 325° F.

½ cup rice	*Chocolate Sauce:*
2 cups cold water	1 6-ounce package semisweet
1½ cups milk	chocolate pieces
½ cup sugar	¼ cup water
4 egg yolks	1 cup heavy cream
1 teaspoon vanilla extract	1 teaspoon vanilla extract
¼ cup heavy cream	2 teaspoons butter
½ teaspoon cinnamon	

1. Measure the rice into a saucepan, cover with cold water. Bring the water to the boiling point. Remove the pan from the heat and let it stand undisturbed for 5 minutes. Drain the rice.

2. Pour the milk into another saucepan, add the sugar, and bring to the simmering point.

3. Butter a baking dish generously. Place the rice in the dish and add the milk-and-sugar mixture. Cover with aluminum foil and bake for 25 minutes until the rice has absorbed the milk.

4. Combine the egg yolks, vanilla, and cream. Add the mixture to the hot rice, stirring gently with a fork. Chill the pudding and dust the surface with cinnamon.

5. To make Chocolate Sauce, place the chocolate and water in a small saucepan. Stir constantly over very low heat until the chocolate has melted. Stir in the heavy cream and simmer over low heat for 15 minutes until a thick, rich sauce has formed.

6. Remove from heat and stir in vanilla and butter. Serve hot or cold.

Rice Pudding is a great comfort in moments of distress. It is possible, even desirable, to hide a layer of cold Rice Pudding beneath a layer of vanilla ice cream on a silver platter. Stand an array of erect poached pears in the ice cream, spoon hot chocolate sauce over the pears, and then think of a name for the whole thing.

RIZ À L'IMPÉRATRICE

This classic dessert, a very elaborate rice pudding "to the Empress' taste," shows how even the most complicated and lengthy recipe is just a series of simple steps. This is, in fact, just (just!) a rice pudding made from the ingredients for a simple custard combined with a Vanilla Bavarian Cream. Melba Sauce or Apricot Sauce provides the final touch and can be made in a blender in no time at all—which is a comfort, because the rest of it takes ages!

Serves 10
Preheat oven to 325° F.

Flavoring:
¼ cup raisins
¼ cup mixed glacéed fruits
¼ cup kirsch

Rice Pudding:
½ cup rice
2 cups cold water
1½ cups milk
½ cup sugar
4 egg yolks

1 teaspoon vanilla extract
¼ cup heavy cream

Bavarian Cream:
4 egg yolks
½ cup sugar
1½ cups milk
2 teaspoons vanilla extract
¼ cup cold water
1½ packages unflavored gelatin
1 cup heavy cream

1. Cover raisins with boiling water and leave to soak for 5 minutes. Chop glacéed fruits into small pieces. Drain raisins and place in a bowl with fruits and kirsch.

2. To make the rice pudding, measure the rice into a saucepan and cover with cold water. Bring the water to the boiling point. Remove the pan from the heat and let it stand undisturbed for 5 minutes.

3. Pour 1½ cups milk into another saucepan. Add the sugar and bring to the simmering point.

4. Butter a baking dish generously. Place the rice in the dish and add the milk. Cover with aluminum foil and bake for 25 minutes, in a pre-heated oven, until the rice has absorbed the milk.

5. Combine the egg yolks, vanilla, and cream. Add the mixture to the hot rice, stirring gently with a fork. Cool to room temperature.

6. To make the Bavarian Cream, place the egg yolks and sugar in a bowl. Stir with a wire whisk until well combined.

7. Heat the milk to the simmering point and add it to the eggs and sugar. Stir to combine, and return the mixture to the saucepan.

8. Heat over low heat, stirring continuously until thickened into a sauce. Add the vanilla. Cool the custard to room temperature.

9. Measure the water into a small saucepan. Sprinkle gelatin on the surface. Leave gelatin undisturbed for 5 minutes. Place over low heat until a clear liquid is formed. Stir gelatin liquid into the custard.

10. Beat the heavy cream until it is thick. Fold the cream into the custard. Fold the custard into the baked and cooled rice pudding.

11. Pour the mixture into a 1½-quart oiled mold or soufflé dish lined with a circle of wax paper. Chill for 4 hours.

12. Unmold and serve with Apricot or Melba Sauce.

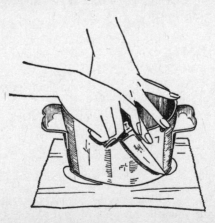

menu planning

The most important factors in planning a menu are the time you have available to prepare the dinner, your experience as a cook, and your budget.

There are several possible approaches to arranging a meal. It can be built around a favorite dish or even a particular food that is in season. If you are an experienced cook, you can safely postpone any planning until you get to the market to select the meat, chicken, or fish that will be the focus of the dinner. On the basis of that decision, you then choose all the accompaniments. By keeping an open mind you will be able to take advantage of the freshest and most appetizing ingredients. If, however, you feel insecure without a plan, read a few recipes until you find one that pleases you, then make a shopping list to be sure nothing is forgotten.

Cooking is like a word-association game in which you can make up your own rules. If you buy pork, you may think of serving it with the traditional applesauce, or perhaps you may feel that prunes or puréed chestnuts would complement the flavor of the meat. As you learn to trust your own judgment, you will find your culinary horizons broadening, and both shopping and cooking will become more interesting.

Every meal, even the simplest, could and should be an event, an important break in the day. Meal planning requires attention not only to the relationship of carbohydrates, proteins, and fats in the foods you serve but also to the harmonious blending and contrasting of taste, color, and texture.

Planning the menu for a dinner party is perhaps the most difficult part of the preparation of the dinner. Once you have decided what to cook, it is easy enough to forge ahead and cook it! When you have made up a tentative plan, try to imagine the completed main course on the table. Now imagine yourself. Are you, in your mind's eye, going to be relaxed as you take your place at the table, or will you be concerned about something that is still cooking on the stove or in the oven? Has everything become cold while an interesting but wordy guest is still toying with an artichoke leaf? Will the soufflé fall before it is served? Will you have to jump up to turn the fish or stir a sauce? If you can anticipate a potential problem, eliminate the difficulty by choosing a simpler menu and estimating how much of the dinner can be made ahead. It is also reassuring and helpful to work out a precise timetable for the final hour of preparation before the dinner is served.

As you plan the meal, don't feel that every course must be an elaborate demonstration of your virtuosity as a cook. The dinner should have a natural climax, though not necessarily at the beginning, middle, or conclusion of the meal. A complicated, rich appetizer seems even better when it is balanced with a simple entrée, such as roast chicken. The choice of dessert is dependent on all the preceding courses.

The following menus are just suggestions. To make things as easy as possible, we have suggested dishes that can be made completely in advance to flank each hot entrée. The menus and recipes specify quantities such that neither the cook nor the guests will leave the table in a state of gastronomic collapse. It should also be mentioned in passing that the food should be appropriate to the occasion; unless you are dining alone, it is not wise to follow pheasant under glass with a hot pastrami sandwich.

Let no man fancy he knows how to dine
Till he has learned how to taste and tastes combine.

                                            HORACE

MENU SUGGESTIONS*

Artichokes with *Sauce Vinaigrette*   *Veal Scallopini with Lemon and*
Stuffed Honey-glazed Duckling   *Brandy*
Peas   Spaghetti
Wild Rice   Tossed Salad
Oeufs à la Neige   *Zabaglione*

* For the recipes of menu items given in italics, see index.

Fried and Baked Rock
   Cornish Hens
Tomato Hollandaise
Peas
Carrots
Rice
Chocolate Soufflé with
   Saboyan Sauce

Tomato Soup
Belgian Carbonnade of Beef
Broccoli
Tossed Salad

Jellied Madrilène
Broiled Trout
Peas
Tossed Salad
Riz à l'Impératrice

Ham in Sherry Sauce
Spinach
Rice
Sliced Raw Mushroom Salad
Fresh Fruit and Cheese

Veal Stew with Mushrooms
   and Tomatoes
Tossed Salad
Fresh Pineapple

Claret Consommé
Roast Prime Ribs of Beef
Classic Brown Sauce
Yorkshire Pudding
Brussels Sprouts
Vanilla Bavarian Cream

Cheese Soufflé
Lobster Mayonnaise
Boiled Potatoes
Fresh Fruit and Cheese

Tomato Soup
Crisp-Fried Turkey Breast
Rice with Herbs
Peas
Fruit Tart

Broiled Chicken with Mustard
Broiled Tomato Halves
Rice
String Beans
Lemon Meringue Pie

Onion Soup
Roast Rack of Lamb
Braised Vegetable Casserole
Roast Potatoes
Cold Lemon Soufflé

Gougère (with Cocktails)
Roast Pork Loin
Braised Celery
Spinach Crêpes
Chocolate Soufflé

Tomato-Orange Soup
Poached Salmon Steaks
Mousseline Sauce
Asparagus
Boiled Potatoes
Tossed Salad
Chocolate Torte

Watercress Vichyssoise
Broiled Striped Bass
Tomato Sauce
Sliced Cucumber Salad
Boiled Potatoes
Frozen Grand Marnier Soufflé

Pear and Turnip Soup
Glazed Baked Ham
Baked Acorn Squash
Tossed Salad
Plum Clafouti

Potato Soup
Calves' Liver with Lemon and
  Thyme Sauce
Fried Avocado Slices
Peas
Rice
Fresh Fruit

Broiled Barbecued Spareribs
Rice
Tossed Salad
Ice Cream and *Chocolate Sauce*

Coquilles St. Jacques
Roast Leg of Lamb
Lima Beans
Roast Potatoes
Tossed Salad
Strawberries and Grand Marnier

Asparagus Soup
Beef Stroganoff
String Beans
Rice
Tossed Salad
Black Cherry Crêpes with
  Whipped Cream

index

VEGETABLE(S) (cont'd):
    with beer and dill, 177
    turnip soup, pear, and, 23
    vichyssoise, 22
        watercress, 23
    zabaglione, 219
    zuppa inglese, 222
Velouté sauce, 54
Vichyssoise, 22
    watercress, 23
Vinaigrette sauce, 72

Waffles, 178
Watercress vichyssoise, 23
White sauce, enriched, 54
    simple (béchamel), 54

Yorkshire pudding, 175

Zabaglione, 219
    cold, 220
Zuppa inglese, 222